Violent Entrepreneurs

Violent Entrepreneurs

The Use of Force in the Making of Russian Capitalism

VADIM VOLKOV

CORNELL UNIVERSITY PRESS   Ithaca and London

First published 2002 by Cornell University Press
First printing, Cornell Paperbacks, 2002

Printed in the United States of America

Library of Congress Cataloging-in-Publication Data

Volkov, Vadim, 1965–
   Violent entrepreneurs : the use of force in the making of Russian capitalism / Vadim Volkov.
      p.   cm.
Includes bibliographical references and index.
   ISBN-13: 978-0-8014-4016-8 (cloth : alk. paper)
   ISBN-10: 0-8014-4016-5 (cloth : alk. paper)
   ISBN-13: 978-0-8014-8778-1 (pbk. : alk. paper)
   ISBN-10: 0-8014-8778-1 (pbk. : alk. paper)
   1. Organized crime—Russia (Federation)   2. Capitalism—Russia (Federation)   3. Law enforcement—Russia (Federation)   4. Russia (Federation)—Social conditions—1991–   5. Russia (Federation)—Politics and government—1991–   I. Title.
HV6453.R8 V65 2002
364.1'06'0947—dc21

                                        2002002763

Cloth printing   10   9   8   7   6   5   4   3   2   1

Paperback printing   10   9   8   7   6   5   4   3

To my parents,
Tamara and Victor

Contents

Preface

This book was triggered by an observation. In 1995, on my way to work, I used to walk past a mansion in central Petersburg that housed the headquarters of the Northwestern Regional Anti–Organized Crime Directorate (RUBOP). Each time I would observe the same scene: people of formidable physical proportions, with very short haircuts, wearing leather jackets or long dark overcoats, walked out of the RUBOP headquarters, got into black cars with tinted windows, and departed in various directions. Others parked nearby and entered the mansion. What struck me each time was that these people looked, moved, and gesticulated very much like those whom they were supposed to be fighting—members of organized criminal groups, the so-called bandits.

Regional anti–organized crime directorates were set up throughout Russia in 1992 as an elite police force with extraordinary powers. At that time, the urban social landscape and culture were undergoing drastic changes. A new jargon corrupted everyday language, radio stations played popular songs filled with prison jargon, booksellers were switching to cheap popular fiction about the tough and fearless. It seemed that through the spoken word, gestures, and images, some new powerful subculture was beginning to dictate its values, perceptions, and attitudes. This subculture was not just a criminal underworld. The new landscape did not have a single origin; it was made up of many different cultural inputs fused together inasmuch as they all exalted violence and commerce.

Through further observation I discovered a whole set of previously unknown violent groups. Among them were criminal fraternities formed in Soviet prisons, sports teams turned racketeering gangs, organizations of Afghan war veterans, Cossack unions, and informal segments of state coercive agencies. Most of the individuals in these groups looked and spoke alike, though some occasionally wore state uniforms. The desire to explain their behavioral similarity despite stark differences in their institutional origins marked the beginning of my research. Initially I assumed they should indeed be treated as belonging to one group. To do so, however, I would have to find the attribute responsible for their likeness that justified such treatment. Preliminary research convinced me that these seemingly different groups were all engaged in the same activities: they intimidated, protected, gathered information, settled disputes, gave guarantees, enforced contracts, and imposed taxes. Their similarity, I concluded, was derived from the management of the same resource: organized violence. Hence I called them violent entrepreneurs and their activity violent entrepreneurship.

Why introduce yet another term when two labels for a similar phenomenon are already widely used? State law enforcement experts use the term "organized crime" and journalists refer to the Russian "Mafia." Generally, the invention and use of terms and concepts is part of the everyday practical activity of many social institutions. Terms reflect an external reality inasmuch as they bear the stamp of the institution that gave birth to the terms and that keeps recycling them. Defining and labeling are instrumental for any institutionalized practice. Legal terminology, for example, is part of the same tool kit as handcuffs. The word "Mafia" is instrumental in the media industry's management of public opinion; it also serves to alert society to certain dangers. For readers and viewers, most of whom have never had any experience with the underworld, the concept "Mafia" is likely to consist of a collection of movie images. Both "organized crime" and "Mafia" capture aspects of the same reality in the way relevant to the activity of respective institutions.

As a science of social institutions, sociology is bound to have its own vision of reality. It can either invent concepts of its own (for example, social mobility or gender) or redefine existing first-order concepts. Sociologists studying the Sicilian Mafia have done the latter when they argue that the "Mafia" is a "figuration of political middlemen" or a "private protection industry." Some have gone even further and have adopted a nominalist position, suggesting that the "Mafia" is nothing essential but a name for a host of methods and practices related to the use of violence. The term "organized crime" is more obliging, since it rests on the basic division of social reality into two worlds: the legitimate world and the underworld. The drawing of this division is the prerogative of the state and its core institution—law enforcement. In this case, sociology can either accept the standpoint of the state and look at the social organization of crime, or it can take a critical stance and instead study how the state draws divisions and "constructs" the underworld or Mafia. In both cases, the state is present—either in the background, as the source of definitions, or in the foreground, as the object of analysis.

Bracketing out the state as a privileged organization will give us yet another perspective, the realist, leading us back to the fundamental idea of the state of nature introduced by Thomas Hobbes in *Leviathan*. The defining feature of the state of nature is the absence of a central governing authority and, accordingly, of a law that limits the ways and means of action available to individuals. It is the realm of natural rights, where all are free to use any means, including force, to realize their interests and where everyone expects others to behave accordingly. "Where there is no common power," writes Hobbes, "there is no law; where no law, no injustice. Force and Fraud, are in war two cardinal virtues."[1] In the state of nature, property exists only as long as it can be protected by the claimant. An entirely different world is what Hobbes calls the Commonwealth, where individuals are deprived of, or willingly abdicate, their natural right to self-government in favor of a higher power that establishes protection and laws for all. Thus emerges a hierarchical and rule-governed domain, also known as the state. Furthermore, the state of nature is characterized by a plurality of force wielders constrained only by the violence potential of others but always standing in a "posture of war." Within the Commonwealth (the state), on the contrary, the use of force is monopolized by the central power. Members of the Commonwealth are disarmed in favor of one force-wielding agency and are constrained by its sovereign power to enforce the law. Since Hobbes, this basic distinction has been used to define the essence of international politics (the state of nature) and to set it apart from domestic politics (hierarchy and order). The state of nature was conceived by later theorists as the realm of international politics, and Hobbes obviously considered the state its basic unit. Nevertheless, the state of nature cannot be reduced to relations between states. In fact, any plurality of competing force wielders may form an anarchic realm isomorphic to that of international politics; and any monopoly on the enforcement of laws may constitute a kind of domestic politics.

Therefore, to make the theoretical assumption that criminal groups do something other than commit crimes, that law enforcement agencies do something other than enforce laws, and that there is no hierarchy among coercive agencies is to posit a Hobbesian state of nature rather than a Commonwealth, the state. In 1995, I was not wholly unjustified in positing the state of nature and its logic as the starting point for sociological research,

1. Thomas Hobbes, *Leviathan* (Cambridge: Cambridge University Press, 1996), 90.

even though my passport certified that I was a citizen of the Russian state. At that time, those who were supposed to enforce the law—employees of the justice and security systems—themselves acted informally as private enforcers or joined private protection companies. They were as numerous among violent entrepreneurs as their alleged adversaries from racketeering gangs. The definition of crime was subject to constant revisions, since lawmakers were preparing to adopt a new criminal code. The concept of deviant behavior withered away along with stable norms shattered by the speed of social change. Ironically, in many cases it was private entrepreneurs of violence who claimed to maintain order and exercise justice. Under the conditions in Russia in the mid-1990s, where the boundaries between public and private violence became blurred, when the de facto capacity to enforce and thereby define justice gained priority over written laws, when protection and taxation were increasingly privatized, the very existence of the "state" as a unified entity and of the public domain itself was called into question. Consequently, conventional terms that reflect the standpoint of the state, such as "organized crime" and "Mafia," otherwise very useful, became inadequate for the purposes of sociological research. Rather than redefine them, I chose to use different concepts, "violent entrepreneur" and "violent entrepreneurship," and to study "organized violence" instead of "organized crime."

In this book I consider the use of organized violence in the emerging economic market, its dynamic and its outcomes. The social reality of post-Soviet Russia in the 1990s affords an opportunity to study in real time, as it were, the processes of market building and state formation that are normally associated with a distant past. Central to my argument are various violence-managing agencies: criminal groups, private protection companies, private security services, informal protective associations of state security employees, and the like. Sometimes I also refer to them as force-wielding organizations, protection enterprises, or private enforcers. I explore their genesis, action patterns, and practices, as well as some of the basic values and norms of their members. The very fact of their plurality and relative self-sufficiency has had a structuring effect on their expectations, patterns of action, organization, and normative culture. Their relations revolve around passive deterrence, active threats, guarantees, and actual violence. At the same time, these agencies are oriented toward private profit, which they make through exchange relations with economic subjects and, at a later stage, from direct investments. The economic dimension is therefore of great importance; the economic interest creates both the basic motivation and the constraints on the use of violence. It is largely through ongoing political-economic relations among violence-managing agencies and between them and economic subjects that an initial, imperfect, and archaic institutional structure of economic exchange emerged as private ownership was being formally introduced in Russia. Initially, the system of constraints thus created was more powerful and efficient than the state's written laws. When a high violence potential and high protection costs become burdensome for most participants, the conditions for a reassertion of the state emerge. Only then do state laws and their enforcement gradually gain priority, and the central authority is able to achieve greater control over the use of force. On the basis of this assumption, I suggest that a conscious project of state building, which has become increasingly important in Russia since the end of 1998, was preceded by a consolidation of violence-managing agencies, the capitalization of their incomes, and a partial delegation of their enforcement capacity to state agencies.

I gained access to the mechanisms of private protection and enforcement, the rules and norms of criminal groups, the careers of their leaders, and the relations with police and state authorities through interviews with participants and experts. I interviewed members of criminal groups, heads of private protection companies, acting and former police employees, experts, and business people. All together I conducted twenty-six semistructured interviews (not counting conversations and observations) lasting from one to four hours, in Petersburg, Moscow, and Ekaterinburg. Throughout the book I use numbers to refer to my respondents, who are identified in the table on pages 193–94. Only in four cases was I permitted to use a tape recorder; for the others, I took notes from which I later reconstructed the interview. This method had an advantage as well: given the nature of the topics discussed, tape recording might have seriously inhibited respondents. Each respondent had a bias determined by his or her position in the system of relations in question, but by juxtaposing all the different categories of respondents, I was able to draw a more objective picture. Other primary sources included data and documents produced by RUBOP and investigative journalists in Petersburg and Ekaterinburg. Specialized press organs (for example, professional private security magazines) provided a great deal of valuable information as well.

A note of caution is in order. To focus on a particular aspect of reality implies privileging it and sometimes exaggerating its importance. When some things are foregrounded, others move to the background. I did not intend to reduce market building and state formation to the dynamic of violence-managing enterprises. But a closer look at violence-managing agencies inevitably leads us to ignore other important dimensions of state building, such as relations between the central and regional state authorities, monetary policy, ethnic issues, culture and ideology, the so-called oligarchs (though not entirely), the military, regional conflicts, and many more. My particular focus makes it possible to highlight a range of phenomena that have been largely overlooked or misunderstood. Finally, the book deals with an exclusively male world, where traditional male virtues associated with violent contests prevail. Among violent entrepreneurs, I came across only one woman, the chief of the private security company Bastion in Moscow—an exception that confirms the rule. Hence the predominance of the third-person singular masculine pronoun. This study deals with that person.

Without the assistance of many institutions and individuals I would have made little progress in producing this book. I first wrote the research proposal to study violent entrepreneurs in autumn 1997 at King's College, Cambridge. A Ford Foundation Fellowship granted me a few months of creative work. My thanks to Mary MacAuley and John Barber for providing me with this opportunity. The support of the U.S. Social Science Research Council–MacArthur Foundation Program on Peace and International Security in a Changing World was decisive. The memorable fellows' meeting in El Salvador in May 1998 was its starting point. I am grateful to David Latham, Jack Snyder, Amy Frost, and other members of the SSRC staff, and to Kennette Benedict and John Slocum of the MacArthur Foundation for their help and encouragement.

I wish to thank David Stark and the staff of the Department of Sociology who made my stay at Columbia University in fall 1999 and winter 2000 especially productive. The Harriman Institute supported my application for a visiting fellowship. Finally, St. Antony's College, Oxford, sheltered me during the writing phase. Its scholarly community provided a stimulating intellectual environment. I extend my gratitude to Archie Brown and all other members of the college staff.

The continuous intellectual inspiration and advice of many individuals guided me through this project. Charles Tilly's works on state building and his constructive suggestions shaped my vision of the subject of this book. I thank him for being both gentle and generous. I owe many insights to conversations with Diego Gambetta in St. Petersburg and Oxford, and to his writings. My indebtedness to Oleg Kharkhordin, a colleague and friend who shared all my intellectual adventures, is immeasurable. Words of appreciation are due to the poet Kirill Bykov, whose irony and wit always remind us that there is much more to life than career and comfort. I owe a great intellectual and human debt to all my colleagues and students at the Department of Political Science and Sociology at the European University at St. Petersburg. The moral support of Boris Firsov, rector of the European University, gave me a degree of freedom to work on this project. An exchange of ideas with Vadim Radaev and Vladimir Gel'man was exceptionally productive; Eduard Ponarin helped me gain access to some important respondents. David Woodruff, Bruce Grant, and two anonymous readers for Cornell University Press wrote helpful reviews of the manuscript. Jukka Gronow, Victoria Bonnell, and Venelin Ganev made constructive comments on my earlier articles. Various sections of the book were subjected to critical but friendly discussions by members of the Program on New Approaches to Russian Security at its sessions in Harvard, Washington, D.C., and Nizhnii Novgorod. Special thanks to Sergei Tikhonov, who helped me out in New York City.

I also wish to thank my supervisors, who, at various stages of my scholarly formation, taught me some valuable intellectual skills: Nikolai Raskov, Valerii Golofast, Leonid Ionin, Anthony Giddens, and Peter Burke.

Without fieldwork and the advice of experts, this project would have been impossible. I am grateful to Andrei Konstantinov (Bakonin) and Evgenii Vyshenkov for generously sharing their knowledge and experience. Collaboration with the remarkable team at the Agency for Journalistic Investigations, St. Petersburg, proved especially fruitful. I benefited greatly from the expertise of Yakov Gilinsky, Aslan Oulybaev, Kirill Metelev, Vladimir Zinenko, and Viacheslav Zhitenev. Thanks are due to many other people who agreed to spend their time talking to a sociologist about matters normally discussed only with insiders. Caroline Schwaller kindly helped me prepare the manuscript for publication. All the rest I owe to my parents, to whom this book is dedicated.

VADIM VOLKOV

St. Petersburg

Violent Entrepreneurs

I.

Veblen's Warning

Intentional projects tend to fail, but a sequence of failures can sometimes bring about the miracle of success. Although I am generally op-
timistic in this book and it has a happy ending, I have to start with some
very early signs of things going badly out of control. Russia's post-1987
economic liberalization was intended to awaken the population's entrepreneurial spirit and, by allowing greater private returns from individual economic activity, to boost economic growth. As battles for glasnost were rag-
ing in the Moscow Palace of Congresses, many would-be entrepreneurs
did receive the signal from above and plunged into private commerce.
However, they were not the only ones who got the signal. Liberalization
also awoke those who were not part of the project of reforms but who
would soon assert themselves as their beneficiaries and driving force.
Those who were dubbed "racketeers" and "bandits" and whom the authorities in the 1990s would call members of "organized crime" made
their first massive appearance in the early years of reforms, alongside the
nascent commercial class. In the midst of general optimism, a few alarming predictions about a possible undermining of reforms by the "Red
Mafia" were voiced, but even they did not give much credence to twenty-
year-olds in counterfeit Adidas sports suits who rushed to collect tribute
from traders at city markets. For a time, protection rackets would become
a daily reality for the new private businesses; the advance of bandits would
alter the urban social landscape. In less than ten years, however, many of
them would either perish in gang shootouts or become "authoritative

people" in various business communities. In the mid-1990s the world media would announce that Russian reforms were seriously threatened by organized crime.

The Mobilization of Racketeers

According to official interior ministry (MVD) data, the growth of crime in Russia was especially intense between 1989 and 1992, when most registered offenses grew at a rate of 20–25 percent each year.[1] Growth rates vary by type of crime. The dynamic of extortion deserves special attention for two reasons. In the first place, it spread particularly wide and fast compared to other forms of crime during the period in question. It had been a somewhat novel, though certainly not unknown, criminal phenomenon. In some five years, it jumped to an alarming scale. And second, it represents the main business of organized crime.[2]

Before 1988, asserts Vladimir Safonov in his comprehensive study, "extortion was not considered a widespread crime. In some regions (Altai, Vologda, Kursk, and others), it did not occur. In 1989 the number of extortion cases in the majority of Russia's regions increased by a factor of three."[3] Thus, whereas in 1986 the militia registered 1,122 cases of extortion in Russia, in 1989 the number jumped to 4,621. Then, beginning in 1990, the growth rate for extortion was approximately 15–30 percent each year, reaching a peak of 17,169 cases in 1996, which is 15.3 times greater than the number in 1986.[4] These figures reflect the trend but do not capture the scale of racketeering offenses, which was much larger than statistical accounts would indicate. According to expert estimates, only one in four victims of extortion appealed to the militia; the militia responded in only 80 percent of cases; criminal charges were pressed only against one in six racketeers; and

1. It should be remembered that the figures on registered criminal offenses are bound to reflect changes in the level and focus of activity by police organs. The statistical profile is strongly affected by accounting methods, the current political and economic interests of the ministry and its local directorates, and by changes in the criminal code that defines and classifies criminal behavior. For the best discussion of the criminal statistics, see Azalia Dolgova, ed., *Prestupnost', statistika, zakon* (Crime, statistics, and law) (Moscow: Kriminologicheskaya assotsiatsiya, 1997).

2. This proposition was advanced in Thomas Schelling, *Choice and Consequence* (Cambridge: Harvard University Press, 1984), 185.

3. Vladimir Safonov, *Organizovannoe vymogatel'stvo: Ugolovno-pravovoi i kriminologicheskii analiz* (Organized extortion: Legal and criminological analysis) (St. Petersburg: Znanie, 2000), 154.

4. Ibid., 154, 218.

only one in eleven served a prison term, and the penalty for this offense was rather lenient, a maximum of three years in prison.[5]

In part because of the complexity of this kind of crime and its relatively low incidence in Russia in the past, the strict definition of extortion was long debated. The main difficulty was to differentiate extortion from robbery and blackmail. Some stressed the postponed character of the threat as the main feature of extortion; some suggested that the object of an extortionist's demands had to be property rights rather than material goods or money, but others emphasized that the target of this offense was human freedom as such. The subsequent evolution of the legal definition of extortion led to the inclusion of these nuances in the criminal codes of 1960 and 1994 as subcategories of a single, broadly defined criminal offense.[6] Hence extortion came to be defined as activities aimed at appropriating someone's property or property rights under threat of violence or damage to that subject's property or under threat of dissemination of harmful or derogatory information. In the 1994 version of the criminal code of the Russian Federation, the maximum prison term for extortion was increased to fifteen years.[7]

In legal practice, the charge of extortion is rather difficult to prove, since threats may often be indirect or veiled. The target may not necessarily experience victimization, especially when those who practice extortion manage to present themselves in a friendly manner and refrain from any explicit hostility. It would also be difficult to call a case an episode of extortion when threats or damage come from someone who is not the direct beneficiary, that is, when the transaction is made with another, seemingly unconnected person. It is precisely because extortion, unlike robbery, involves indirect coercion and affects one's future behavior that it poses serious difficulties in terms of strict legal identification. This makes carefully staged, "soft" extortion a lucrative business carrying a high chance that the perpetrator will escape legal punishment. Safonov asserts that organized extortion is characterized by an especially high rate of latency, which reached 70 percent in some regions of Russia in the mid-1990s.[8]

What can be said of those who practiced extortion or were involved in other crimes as members of organized groups? The figure below reflects the age structure of the criminal mobilization that accompanied the post-1987 reforms. It shows the frequency of the birth years (age cohorts) of individuals whose names were entered in the standard operative database of the

5. Sergei Diakov and Azalia Dolgova, eds., *Organizovannaya prestupnost'* (Organized crime) (Moscow: Yuridicheskaya literatura, 1989), 98.

6. Safonov, *Organizovannoe vymogatel'stvo*, 10–27.

7. Valerii Verin, *Prestupleniya v sfere ekonomiki* (Economic crime) (Moscow: Delo, 1999), 47–49.

8. Safonov, *Organizovannoe vymogatel'stvo*, 157.

Northwestern Anti–Organized Crime Directorate (RUBOP), one of the twelve special police units in charge of fighting organized regional crime in Russia. Nearly twenty-seven thousand entries in the database refer primarily to individuals who have been convicted of, charged with, or suspected of criminal activities as members of organized groups and societies. In addition to the core data collected by RUBOP since the creation of the directorate in 1992, it also includes data accumulated by its predecessor organizations.[9] This particular database was transferred into private hands some time in 1996, after which it was no longer updated. The oldest individual appearing in the RUBOP database is one Efim Geller (born 23 August 1914), an antiques dealer and swindler, sentenced in 1993 for the appropriation of state property by extortion. The youngest is Yakov Tolmachev (born 4 September 1982), a schoolboy who tried to extort money from his father, a company director, by means of a staged kidnapping. The figure shows an uneven representation of age cohorts and steady growth to a peak in the proportion of younger individuals. The peak represents the largest age cohort, born in 1969 (1,518 entries) and the cohorts of 1970 (1,471), 1971 (1,441), and 1968 (1,398). The number of individuals belonging to each of the cohorts born between 1966 and 1972 exceeds 1,200; together, members of these seven cohorts, of the total sixty-eight, constitute 36 percent of all entries. In short, the individuals born between 1966 and 1972 are significantly more numerous than others in the RUBOP database. After 1972 the figure indicates a sharp decline in the numbers. This does not necessarily mean that criminal organizations reached a saturation point or that younger people were unwilling to take the path that might bring them into conflict with law enforcement agencies. The decline may be partly explained by the fact that the last update took place in early 1996; thus, the presence of post-1972 cohorts might have been more prominent had the database included more recent entries. Still, this database was accumulated at a time when organized crime was growing and reaching its peak. After 1996 crime rates stabilized and then gradually declined. The figure, therefore, can be considered a fairly accurate representation of the age structure (the proportions rather than absolute numbers) of organized crime. The predominance of one particular age group in those involved in extortion and other violent crimes committed by organized groups is also confirmed by Safonov's calculation of the age distribution of individuals convicted for extortion in three Russian regions in 1991–94: the group of eighteen- to twenty-four-year-olds outnumbers the others by a wide margin, constituting 53 percent of the total.[10]

9. On RUBOPs, see Johan Backman, *The Inflation of Crime in Russia: The Social Danger of the Emerging Markets* (Helsinki: National Research Institute of Legal Policy, 1998), 29–30.

10. Safonov, *Organizovannoe vymogatel'stvo*, 220. Safonov studied the Pskov, Belgorod, and Leningrad regions, including the city of St. Petersburg.

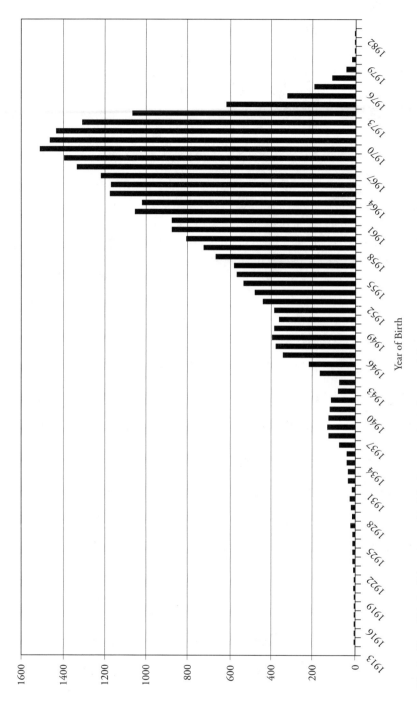

Fig 1. Year of birth of those entered in Northwestern Anti–Organized Crime Directorate records, 1990–95 (N=26,994)

What is specific about the social trajectory of the 1966–72 cohort? What external influences were likely to have affected the choice of careers by individuals born in those years? We can reasonably assume that they finished secondary school (at age seventeen or eighteen) some time between 1984 and 1990. In cases where they were drafted into the military service, which was still likely to occur for many in those years, they returned between 1986 and 1992. On their return, they were likely to face the choice of a career and a way of life, like young people elsewhere. It is well known that during those particular years the Soviet leadership introduced the first key measures to reform the system of state socialism. In 1986 the Law on Individual Labor Activity opened the possibility of private enterprise; the 1988 Law on Cooperatives further expanded the private sector, and the 1990 Law on Enterprises and Entrepreneurial Activity legalized private property and entrepreneurship. Thus, what we have so far established and what requires further explanation is this: in the period firmly associated in the country's history with the first wave of market reforms, an unusually high proportion of young men chose to become racketeers.

The Social Origins

Given the nature of racketeering activities, it would be logical to assume that these young men had the physical skills and psychological makeup that gave them a relative advantage in the use of violence. Such an advantage could have been acquired either in the specific social institutions that cultivate physical fitness and fighting skills or in particular life circumstances that produced the psychological dispositions. Furthermore, strong incentives must have existed for employing these skills in new ways and strengthening the dispositions, and there must have been economic opportunities that could be profitably exploited. Finally, there must have been specific social mechanisms that facilitated the mobilization of potential racketeers to exploit these opportunities.

Sports

Recollections and interviews allow us to reconstruct the phenomenon from within. The racketeering movement gained momentum in 1989. Groups of violent youths appeared at city markets and on street corners where private commerce flourished. Short haircuts, intimidating physical proportions, and brand-name sportswear made them look alike, as if they all belonged to one sports team. They were called *kachki* (from *nakachivat'*, to pump up one's muscles), after the regular workouts they took in gyms to build muscle power. Their activities at city markets earned them their true names: *reketiry,* racketeers, or *bandity,* bandits. These youth groups were distinguished from one another primarily by their names, which referred either to the territories where they were formed or to the surnames of their leaders.

It is by no means accidental that a huge proportion of prominent gang leaders, not to mention rank-and-file members, are former athletes. For example, Sergei Mikhailov, known as "Mikhas," the founding leader of the Solntsevskaya criminal group in the southern district of Moscow, earned the title of "master of sports" in freestyle wrestling, while his close associate Sergei Timofeev ("Sylvester"), the leader of the Orekhovskaya group, practiced karate. Sportsmen and sportsmen naturally formed the core of the emerging racketeering groups. In 1989, when the first violent conflicts between Moscow gangs broke out and the major weapons were fists and baseball bats (the age of gunfire was yet to come), sportsmen quickly proved their superiority.[11] They were a formidable force and, potentially, even a political resource. In late 1993, Otari Kvantrishvili ("Otarik"), an international-class wrestling coach, public figure, and reportedly the "godfather" of Moscow organized crime, announced his intention to create a political party: The Sportsmen of Russia. Many prominent wrestlers, weight lifters, and boxers were invited to the first congress of the athletes' party in December 1993. The plan, however, was destined to remain unrealized, as Kvantrishvili was murdered by a sniper on 5 April 1994. Also among the victims of contact killings in 1994–95 were the vice president of the World Boxing Association, world champion Oleg Karataev; the chairman of the Russian Professional League of Kickboxing, Yurii Stupen'kov; and the founder of the International Academy of Oriental Martial Arts, Vyacheslav Tsoi. All three were reportedly involved in protection rackets and managed a number of commercial companies created under the cover of the organizations they headed.[12]

In the absence of professional and commercial sports in the Soviet Union, this institution depended exclusively on state support. Fighting sports were traditionally linked to the militia and the military. The major sports clubs, such as the Dynamo and the Central Sport Club of the Army (TsSKA) and their branches throughout the country, were sponsored by the interior ministry (MVD) and the Ministry of Defense and served as their training grounds. Other major clubs, such as Spartak and the Locomotive, were

11. The careers of Mikhailov and Timofeev are well described in fiction written by the former attorney Valerii Karyshev. See Valerii Karyshev, *Solntsevskaya bratva: Istoriya gruppirovki* (Solntsevskoe brotherhood: A history of the criminal group) (Moscow: Eksim Press, 1998); idem, *Sylvester: Istoriya avtoriteta* (Sylvester: A history of the leader) (Moscow: Eksim Press, 1999).

12. Alexander Maksimov, *Rossiiskaya prestupnost': Kto est' kto* (Crime in Russia: Who's who) (Moscow: Eksim Press, 1998), 37–44.

funded by the trade unions and the Ministry of Transport. Some large state enterprises also maintained their own sports clubs and sponsored a number of teams. Because sports were prestigious in the Soviet system of values, they were one of the possible avenues for social advancement: champions were role models for the young and symbols of success. Therefore, the crisis in the state budget and in enterprise finances, combined with the corrosion of the Soviet system of values, disrupted the reproduction of the institution of sports and triggered various adaptive responses on the part of sportsmen.

Close connections—both historical and institutional—between sports and military violence make the boundary between them particularly unstable when the conditions that once created that boundary undergo a radical change. Historically, the emergence of sports as an institution and the concomitant reduction in the level of permissible violence have been an organic part of what the sociologist Norbert Elias has called the "civilizing process," a progressive transition to a more disciplined, differentiated, and less violent society.[13] From the sociological standpoint, sport is an organized group activity centered on a contest between at least two parties. A sport "requires physical exertion of some kind and is fought out according to known rules, including, where appropriate, rules which define the permitted limits of physical force," writes Elias.[14] Sports come into being when the use of violence and possible injury become significantly limited by strict rules that require a considerable degree of self-restraint from participants. By channeling the aggressive drives and physical energy of individuals into a game or a nonlethal regulated contest, the development of the institution of sport enables a society to achieve a higher degree of control over violence ("tension management"). Rather than viewing sports as an auxiliary training system for a country's armed forces, the theory suggested by Elias highlights more complex and subtle connections between the rise of sports and state building as the monopolization of violence. Let us note at this point that the historical conversion of excessive violence into rule-governed contests depends on the capacity of the state and society to maintain the institution of sport. A crisis of the state, then, may quickly unmake the results of this centuries-long conversion. As the state weakens to the point that it can no longer effectively contain violence, sports, especially fighting sports and the martial arts, can supply everything needed to create a racketeering gang: fighting skills, willpower, discipline, and team spirit. The withdrawal of state sponsorship and the relaxation of the constraints that had once turned the art of warfare into a rule-governed nonviolent (or nonlethal) competition were

---

13. Norbert Elias, *The Civilizing Process*, vols. 1 and 2 (Oxford: Basil Blackwell, 1995).
14. Norbert Elias and Eric Dunning, *Quest for Excitement: Sport and Leisure in the Civilizing Process* (Oxford: Basil Blackwell, 1986), 156.

sufficient to launch a dangerous process whereby sportsmen started to look for alternative employment.

The role of the sports milieu in criminal mobilization emerges clearly in some interviews. Denis, born in 1970, was professionally trained in an athletic school and specialized in the hammer throw.

> I went to serve in the army, then returned in 1990. But at that time, sports could no longer get you anything. I had no special education, only sports, and could hardly find a decent job. The only connections I had derived from sports, so I used them. This is when we joined this circle. First as bouncers in the bars. Two of our pals already worked with *tambovskie* [the Tambovskaya criminal group]. Seven or eight people, including myself, joined Vitalii [at that time the leader of Bortsovskaya *brigada,* the wrestlers' brigade]. (3)

Another interviewee, Vadim, born in 1969, a midranking leader *(brigadir)* of the Komarovskaya gang, attended a karate club and was drawn into the world of the protection rackets by fellow club members. "I started active participation [in protection racket activities] in 1991. I knew the founders of the karate movement in Leningrad, Illarionov and Kolia-karate, we trained at the same club, there I met other people too. I had a kind of warrior complex, wanted to test myself in action. And of course there was money" (20).

It is hardly surprising that karate clubs contributed toward breeding the future racketeers. The Japanese martial art appeared in the Soviet Union in the 1970s and was taught in an amateur if not underground manner. First semiofficial karate clubs were attached to official sports schools. But in 1981 the Central Committee of the Communist Party adopted a special resolution that banned the teaching of karate as a sport, and a special provision in the criminal code followed (an addendum to article 219). When Yuri Andropov succeeded Leonid Brezhnev in 1982 and introduced the policy of order and discipline, authorities began enforcing the ban, closing down karate clubs and threatening teachers with criminal charges. It is unclear whether the Party was suspicious of the ideologically alien philosophy attached to karate or whether it was asserting the priority of state organs in the martial arts, but, as a result of this policy, some karate specialists were charged and imprisoned. Consequently, Vladimir Illarionov (whom Vadim mentions), one of the founders of the karate movement in Leningrad, was sentenced to eight years in prison. After his release, he resumed teaching karate, which had been unofficially accepted after 1985.[15]

The lifting of the ban on karate drew a fresh wave of young people to the

15. Vladimir Illarionov, "I porazhenie ot pobedy ty sam ne dolzhen otlichat' ..." (And you yourself should not tell defeat from victory ...), interview with Vladimir Illarionov, *Chernyi poyas* 1 (1999), http://www.koshiki-karate.com.

martial art. Imported films about the Hong Kong Mafia suggested a possible practical application, while the rising private businesses became a logical target. The first regular racketeering organization to emerge in Leningrad in 1985 was known as the Gang of Kolia-karate or as the Sediuk Brothers' Gang. Nikolai Sediuk ("Kolia-karate"), who practiced with Illarionov, was an experienced karate master and a coach at the Ring sports club. The club became the resource center for the racketeering gang of up to a hundred members. An extremely dangerous and skillful fighter, Kolia-karate was also distinguished for his entrepreneurial mind and his greed. The gang of fighting specialists also featured a theater and film actor, Arkadii Shalolashvili, whose talents no doubt served to dupe numerous victims. For two years the gang enjoyed a monopoly on the regular collection of tribute from shadow and legal businesses in the city. In 1987 the leadership of the gang, including the Sediuk brothers, Shalolashvili, Goga Gevorkian (nicknamed "Maxi-Schwarzenegger"), and a number of others were convicted. After that, the gang never reassembled in its original form: the karate master was shot dead promptly after his release in July 1993; the actor died of cirrhosis; and other former members were recruited by new gangs.[16]

The shared experience of being one sport team, which involves regular training and competition as well as shared victories and defeats, is likely to create strong trust and group coherence. Combined with professional fighting skills, this provides a potential social basis for the conversion of teammates into members of a racketeering gang. A vital source of cadres for racketeering groups in Leningrad, for example, were three specialized sports institutes that provided professional education in physical culture and sports coaching: the Institute of Physical Culture, named after Lezghaft, the Military Institute of Physical Culture (VIFK), and the High School of Sports Mastery (ShVSM). VIFK and ShVSM specialized exclusively in fighting sports and martial arts such as boxing, wrestling, and judo. For instance, one of the founding leaders of the Tambovskaya criminal group, the head of the group's enforcement branch, Valerii Ledovskikh, is known to be a former boxing coach and a graduate of the Lezghaft institute. ShVSM and VIFK each spawned a racketeering group consisting of former sportsmen, the Wrestlers' Brigade and the so-called Shvonder's Brigade, respectively. The latter was named after the brigade leader Alexander Koupriashev, nicknamed "Shvonder," and consisted solely of VIFK cadets (normally, VIFK graduates received officer's epaulettes). The brigade taxed retail trade and small businesses in the district around the Finland railway station near the institute. It

16. Andrei Konstantinov, *Banditskii Peterburg* (Petersburg bandits) (Petersburg: Folio-press, 1997), 140–46.

dissolved after Shvonder (not himself a VIFK member) was shot dead by one of the brigade members, nicknamed "Babiokha," in February 1993 (5). The former freestyle wrestling coach of VIFK, Georgii Pozdniakov, was, until his murder in April 2000, the right-hand man of the leader of the Tambovskaya criminal group, Vladimir Kumarin.[17]

The Afghan War

Directly connected to the spread of private violence was the end of the war in Afghanistan in 1989, which brought home nineteen- and twenty-year-old recruits with combat experience and a postwar syndrome similar to the well-known posttraumatic stress disorder caused by the Vietnam war.[18] Psychologists have established that the extraordinary experience of the Afghan war was responsible for profound changes in the psychic and social dispositions of participants. In particular, permanent exposure to the risk of being killed had reduced the sense of danger and created a specific readiness to die. These, in turn, produced a combination of increased self-reliance in the face of death and a heightened appreciation for the combat brotherhood that emerged from shared experience and combat interaction.[19] Since it was a means of total resocialization, the war also transformed the normative system of young soldiers and created a particular "Afghan culture."[20] This culture subsequently gave rise to a multitude of veterans organizations, some of which were named after Afghan provinces, such as Panjer and Herat (see below), reminding their members of the place and time when they lived a "true" life.

But what had facilitated the psychological accommodation of recruits to extreme conditions of warfare became a factor of conflict and alienation when the war veterans returned home. It was not only that "authentic" relations characteristic of the combat brotherhood were incompatible with "tedious" social conventions and bureaucratic routines prevalent in a peaceful society. The increasingly negative public attitude toward the Afghan war as useless and unjust rendered meaningless the sacrifice made by the entire generation, causing bitter responses and a withdrawal into the closed circles of

17. Department of Investigations, "Chernaya metka" (The black mark), *Smena,* 27 April 2000, 3.

18. Stephen Sonenberg et al., eds., *The Trauma of War: Stress and Recovery in Vietnam Veterans* (Washington, D.C.: American Psychiatric Association Press, 1985).

19. D. Ol'shansky, "Smyslovye struktury lichnosti uchastnikov Afganskoi voiny" (Meaningful personality structures of participants in the Afghan war), *Psikhologicheskii zhurnal* 12, 5 (1991): 120–31.

20. R. Abdurakhmanov, "Psikhologicheskie problemy poslevoennoi adaptatsii veteranov Afganistana" (Psychological problems of postwar adaptation among Afghan veterans), *Psikhologicheskii zhurnal* 13, 1 (1992): 131–34.

brothers in arms.[21] The decaying welfare state was ill prepared for the systematic social rehabilitation of war veterans, leaving them alone to cope with the postwar stress and to search for a place in the rapidly changing society. Similar experiences awaited participants in the first Chechen war and in numerous other conflicts across the post-Soviet space. According to a sociological survey, 75 percent of those who fought in Chechnya in 1994–96 wished to return to war; and over 50 percent expressed readiness to work in state or private security and enforcement.[22]

The largest protection agency set up by Afghan war veterans is the eight thousand–strong Herat Association, which has over fifty subsidiary companies in Russia and countries of the former Soviet Union. Initially set up as a military sports club in 1991, Herat expanded and by 1995 had become a network of licensed security companies that provide a wide range of protective services (on the legal security sector, see chapter 5).[23] Interviews and other sources indicate that Afghan war veterans have also contributed to the growth of protection rackets. In Ekaterinburg, for example, the participants in the Afghan war and other local conflicts formed a criminal group known as Afgantsy (the Afghans). The group specialized in protection services, the insurance business, wholesale trade, and swindling. It dissolved after its leader, Vladimir Lebedev, was murdered in August 1998.[24] There are cases where those who have combat experience in local conflicts participate in protection rackets under the cover of officially registered war veterans associations, such as Afganvet in Petersburg. "Actually, Afganvet had a tough reputation in these circles. [They were] even more tough than ordinary bandits, and everyone knew that. My brother took an active part in all that, I was involved only occasionally. The Afghans built and protected a number of parking lots in the city, small shops, and so on, like everyone else. Bandits did not bother the Afghans much. There were of course cases where they had to pull out Kalashnikovs when bandits tried to take over one of the parking lots. And people knew we had to support the disabled. . . . Later many went to [work in] private protection companies" (11).

Combat experience gives one vital physical and psychological advantages

21. A. Kinsburgsky and M. Topalov, "Reabilitatsiya uchastnikov Afganskoi voiny v obshchestvennom mnenii" (The rehabilitation of participants in the Afghan war in public consciousness), *Sotsiologicheskie issledovaniya* 1 (1992): 104–8.

22. D. Pozhidaev, "Ot boevykh deistvii–k grazhdanskoi zhizni" (From warfare to peaceful life), *Sotsiologicheskie issledovaniya* 2 (1999): 74.

23. Mikhail Sergeev, "Chtob ne propast' poodinochke, ikh ob'edinil 'Gerat'" (They were united by "Herat"), *Chastnyi sysk, okhrana i bezopasnost'* 3 (1995): 16–18.

24. *Obzor struktury organizovannykh prestupnykh formirovanii Sverdlovskoi oblasti* (Review of organized criminal organizations in Sverdlovskaya oblast'), report by Sverdlovsk RUBOP (Ekaterinburg, 1999), 1.

in a business where violent conflicts are routine, and former comrades in arms provide indispensable connections for postwar employment. Roman, born in 1969, grew up in a suburban Moscow neighborhood. At the age of seventeen he received the highest title in boxing, master of sports. After completing his schooling, he was drafted into the army and sent to fight in Afghanistan. On his return in 1989, Roman began to cooperate with various groups of swindlers and shadow businessmen, providing them physical protection and participating in violent disputes. At the same time, he never missed an opportunity to take part in local wars as a mercenary and fought in Abkhasia, the Transdniester Republic, and even Bosnia. His current major business is managing the illegal production of vodka from cheap ethyl alcohol imported from Belorussia. "These were wholly Afghan channels. You see, it is very easy for me to work in the country, because as a result of my war trips I have acquired a wide circle of acquaintances in different places, including even here in the tax police. They recommended to me the right people for the business"(13).

Many former militia and special paramilitary employees were also active members of racketeering organizations. There is no reliable data on the number of participants or the rate of their participation in organized crime, but some rough estimates of the level of corruption and crime in state law enforcement organs are available. Throughout the 1990s some 25,000 law enforcement employees (approximately one quarter of all discharged) were expelled for unlawful activities each year, and up to 15,000 each year (62,844 in 1986–90 and 75,168 in 1991–95) were charged with criminal offenses.[25] Low morale, combined with declining salaries, compelled members of this professional group to search for another, more profitable way of using their skills. Subsequently, retired or dismissed state employees continued their careers in the legal private security sector (see chapter 5); many of them had temporary employment either as informal enforcers or as full-time members of racketeering groups.

The Market

Valerii Karyshev, known as the attorney for a number of notorious gang leaders, cites the recollections of a well-to-do banker who began his career as a leader of the Liuberetskaya gang, named after the Moscow suburban district of Liubertsy. "It all started when I became a racketeer. Remember the law on cooperation?" recounts Leonid K.

---

25. Dolgova, *Prestupnost', statistika, zakon,* 46–48.

The Rizhsky market [the largest Moscow city market at the time—V. V.] was the place where the first "cooperators" offered shish kebabs, jeans, exotic company labels, shopping maps of Moscow, and so forth. On weekends the market was very busy. Gradually we got there too—the guys who had gone through gyms, sports schools, or just street gangs. The first racketeers who practiced a rough *naezd* [assault] were just simple guys. Our major manuals were videos about the American and Hong Kong Mafia; we watched them in video salons to get some experience. . . . So do you know that the Rizhsky market can be considered the birthplace of the Moscow racket? That's where the first *brigady* [brigades], which turned into well-known *gruppirovki* [gangs], made their appearance. But at that time we consisted of small brigades, five to ten guys each. We visited the market and looted cooperators, petty traders, kiosks.[26]

The Soviet authorities hardly anticipated such a development when they began to admit elements of private commerce. The goal of the liberal policies was to spur people's economic initiative and entrepreneurial spirit in order to improve the country's economic performance. The economically active part of the population responded by setting up small enterprises, the *kooperativy*, which produced and traded consumer goods. Although the name referred to a kind of collective ownership, in practice these organizations became virtually indistinguishable from small capitalist enterprises. Growing at a rate of 450 percent in 1988 and 150 percent in 1989, they reached 193,000 at the beginning of 1990, providing jobs for nearly 5 million people.[27] Visible signs of the new movement were the booming city markets where privately produced or imported goods were sold, as well as private cafés and shops.

The number of cooperative shops and cafés in Moscow, Leningrad, and other large cities grew, as did the number of racketeering brigades that visited them to collect protection money. In the city of Sverdlovsk (now Ekaterinburg) the two would-be powerful gangs Tsentral'naya and Uralmashevskaya first emerged as racketeering brigades at Tsentral'nyi (central) and Uralmashevskii (located next to the Ural Machine Building Plant Uralmash) markets, respectively. A large number of brigades from Kazan', the Siberian industrial towns of Kourgan and Novokuznetsk, as well as the far eastern region migrated to Moscow and Leningrad, where opportunities for commercial activities were growing so fast that local racketeers were unable to fill the niche.

26. Valery Karyshev, *Zapiski banditskogo advokata* (Notes of a bandit's attorney) (Moscow: Tsentrpoligraph, 1998), 30–31.

27. Anthony Jones and William Moskoff, *Ko-ops: The Rebirth of Entrepreneurship in the Soviet Union* (Bloomington: Indiana University Press, 1992), 16–33.

My Petersburg respondents recall a large market in the suburban Leningrad area of Deviatkino where the first racketeering brigades arrived to collect tribute from the cooperative trade:

> In 1989 in Deviatkino all brigades stood side by side; initially, there were no clear divisions between *tambovskie, malyshevskie, kazanskie,* [gang names] and so forth, as happened later. Each brigade *poluchala* [received tribute] from *kommersanty* [businessmen, traders] who were not involved with other brigades. There was plenty of room for everyone. We also set up our own *kommersanty,* provided them with trading spots, and then protected them for a fee. The only rule was that we not assault or rob each other's *kommersanty* (23).

Thus the same pattern emerged in many places throughout the Soviet Union. City markets and other sites for the free economic exchange of privately produced goods began to attract those who were able and willing to display and use force. Former sportsmen were the pioneers of this movement—gyms and sports clubs were the initial breeding grounds for the fresh wave of organized crime. Sports, though the core of the new criminal phenomenon, were certainly not its only source. Former participants in local wars, ex-convicts, former employees of state security and police organizations, and even members of the revived Cossack movement also filled the ranks of racketeering groups. What made all those disparate groups similar was their capacity to use and manage physical force and to organize this key resource for a particular kind of entrepreneurial activity. But little would have happened had this kind of force become available in a different economic context. Most likely, violent groups would have caused a minor disruption of the public order, as happened in Moscow and Kazan' in the mid-1980s, when youth gangs simply raided the cities in search of adventure and random trophies. The emergence of the private economy made a huge difference, providing the resource base and structuring the management of force to enable regular extraction. By the time political debates about the desirability of private property and capitalism reached their peak, the transitional economic model was already in place. In a sense, the gym and the street market were at the origin of a peculiar local capitalism: the small business provided the economic base for the new gangs and the latter supplied "protection." We may also read this pattern in a general form: the gym as a symbol of organized force and the street market as an elementary form of free economic exchange. The socioeconomic relations between the two realms and their evolution throughout the 1990s are my subject.

Members of the Malyshevskaya criminal group in 1990. *Far left*, former militiamen Sergei "Broiler" Miskarev; *far right*, Yurii Alymov "Slon" (assassinated in 1996). By permission of the Agency for Journalistic Investigations, St. Petersburg.

The Problem

Now we are in the position to make an important distinction. Not least, this book is about organized crime, one of the most sensational and, consequently, most poorly understood phenomena of post-Soviet Russia. Mainstream accounts of organized crime lump together all kinds of illegal or deviant behavior, such as theft, smuggling, swindling, extortion, robbery, bribery, illicit trade, money laundering, murder, and so on, conducted by members of organized groups. The growing snowball of alarming data on these forms of crime does create an image of pervasive deviance and chaos. As one specialist has put it, "Russian organized crime is both a symptom and a cause of the country's chaotic transition to a post-Soviet era."[28] Accordingly, some researchers have chosen the sociological theory of deviance as the general explanatory framework.[29] With social norms and their legal expression as the implicit frame of reference, this approach seeks to explain crime as a result of the failure of different social institutions to ensure the proper social integration of individuals and groups. Admittedly, the explanatory capacity of the concept of deviant (criminal) behavior is limited by the cultural and historical relativity of norms.[30] It becomes less relevant in the case of a transitional society when social and legal norms are in flux and cannot serve either as the authoritative frame of reference for members of society or as the point of departure for the sociological analysis of human behavior. The recognition of this fact has led some to turn to the theory of anomie ("normlessness"), which accounts for the conditions of a rapidly changing society suffering from the disruption of its normative order, and to explain the proliferation of crime in Russia in terms of this theory.[31] Although no one would dispute the relevance of the concept of anomie for the post-Soviet condition, this theory implies, mistakenly in my view, that all forms of organized crime are equally dysfunctional and disruptive. It also fails to explain the paradox highlighted by the following telling joke: if everything is so chaotic in post-Soviet Russia, why is crime so organized?

The "Communist" Legacy Approach

Other explanations stress the political and cultural specificity of Russia and place the main emphasis on the legacy of state socialism. Stemming from the alarming publications of the late Soviet period on the "Red Mafia," which condemn the criminal alliance between corrupt Communist Party officials and underground dealers in the Brezhnev period, the legacy-centered approach has become the most convenient explanation of Russian organized crime.[32] Stephen Handelman's ethnographically rich book has given this approach wide popularity in the West.[33] "The fierce and often violent compe-

28. Mark Galeotti, "Mafiya: Organized Crime in Russia," *Jane's Intelligence Review,* special report 10 (June 1996): 3.

29. Yakov Gilinskiy, *Crime and Deviance: Stare from Russia* (St. Petersburg: Russian Academy of Sciences, 2000).

30. Frances Heidensohn, *Crime and Society* (London: Macmillan, 1989), 1–15.

31. Tanya Frisby, "The Rise of Organized Crime in Russia: Its Roots and Social Significance," *Europe-Asia Studies* 50, 1 (1998): 27–49.

32. Arkadii Vaksberg, *The Soviet Mafia* (New York: St. Martin's Press, 1991); Alexander Gurov, *Krasnaya Mafia* (The Red Mafia) (Moscow: Mico, 1995).

33. Stephen Handelman, *Comrade Criminal: Russia's New Mafiya* (New Haven: Yale University Press, 1995).

tition for the spoils of Communism has forged a special kind of frontier character, a unique post-Communist variety of felon," writes Handelman. "He . . . is a curious blend of the Soviet establishment and the classic Russian underworld."[34] The alliance between the corrupt excommunist *nomenklatura* and the Soviet criminal underworld, concluded for the purpose of appropriating former state property, has since been coined the "Russian *mafiya*," and has been discussed in connection with the allegedly traditional Russian culture of lawlessness and informal relations.[35] It is not difficult to see that the overdetermination of the Russian transition by various aspects of the legacy of "communism" conveniently rescues the policy of "shock therapy" and the underlying idea of liberal capitalism from responsibility for some major failures in the reforms. It also caters to the post–Cold War mentality and its inherent search for enemies and threats by constructing a "new threat," which, on closer look, is simply the old one, since, as Handelman asserts, the *mafiya* is communism unwilling to die.[36]

The Economic-Institutional Approach

In fact, an alternative explanation for Russia's organized crime has already emerged through the application of economic sociology to the studies of the Sicilian Mafia and the projection of these findings on Russian realities. Diego Gambetta, who offered a rational explanation of the Sicilian Mafia as the industry of private protection, was also one of the first to highlight a genetic similarity between Sicilian and post-Soviet criminal phenomena.[37] The business of private protection that proliferated shortly after the establishment of formal property rights regimes in Sicily and Russia consists of producing a substitute for trust in a market economy where business culture does not encourage honest cooperation and where the state justice system is ignored. Russian organized crime, therefore, may be seen as a response to a certain institutional demand by the nascent market economy, namely, the need to protect property rights, a need not satisfied by public protection and enforcement agencies. Drawing on the work of Gambetta, Federico Varese has further highlighted similar formative and institutional conditions in

34. Ibid., 10.
35. Annelise Anderson, "The Red Mafia: A Legacy of Communism," in *Economic Transition in Eastern Europe and Russia: Realities of Reform,* ed. Edward Lazear (Stanford: Hoover Institute Press, 1995); Mark Galeotti, "The *Mafiya* and the New Russia," *Australian Journal of Politics and History* 44, 3 (1998): 415–29.
36. Paul Williams, ed., *Russian Organized Crime: A New Threat* (London: Frank Cass, 1997).
37. Diego Gambetta, *The Sicilian Mafia: The Business of Private Protection* (Cambridge: Harvard University Press, 1993), 252–55.

early capitalist Sicily and in Russia's transitional economy and has thus grounded the use of the term "Russian Mafia" in more rigorous comparative research.[38]

The neoinstitutional framework, increasingly relied on by Russian and Western scholars, requires one look at the market of services related to the institutional environment, such as information, security, enforcement, and dispute settlement. This approach explains the proliferation of private enforcers in terms of a market model.[39] Accordingly, Russian criminal groups represent one of the possible institutional arrangements for the protection of property rights and form a shadow system of arbitration. Faced with mounting transactional difficulties and several available options for coping with them, economic agents compare protection costs incurred by different enforcers and "buy" those institutional services that are cost-efficient. Since the actions of the state bureaucracy and of law enforcement remain arbitrary and the services provided by the state tend to have higher costs, private enforcers (read: the Mafia) outcompete the state and firmly establish themselves in its stead.

But who are private enforcers? What exactly do they do and how they do it in post-Soviet Russia? What are the mechanisms of enforcement? These questions have rarely been asked. In the neoinstitutional studies, "private enforcers" tend to appear as abstractions and are seen as sharing the same set of attributed behavioral assumptions as economic subjects. An insufficient empirical knowledge of the concrete mechanisms and activities of private enforcers, especially those in the criminal sector, often leads economists to unjustifiably privilege the role of economic subjects, as if private enforcers were merely passive providers of a commodity the selling of which wholly depends on the level of demand and available choices. In a recent book on institution building in Russia, the author, for example, assumes that "in many instances economic subjects can choose to 'hire' a state, an SGO [self-governing organization], or a private protection organization to insure contract

38. Federico Varese, "Is Sicily the Future of Russia? Private Protection and the Rise of the Russian Mafia," *Archives Européennes de Sociologie* 35, 1 (1994): 224–58.

39. Vladimir Tambovtsev, *Gosudarstvo i perekhodnaya ekonomika: Predely upravliaemosti* (The state and transitional economy: The limits to manageability) (Moscow: Teis, 1997); Vadim Radaev, *Formirovanie novykh rossiiskikh rynkov: Transaktsionnye izderzhki, formy kontrolia i delovaya etika* (The formation of new markets in Russia: Transaction costs, forms of control, and business ethic) (Moscow: Tsentr politicheskikh tekhnologii, 1998); Vladimir Tambovtsev, "Ekonomicheskie instituty rossiiskogo kapitalizma," in *Kuda idet Rossiya? Krizis institutsional'nykh sistem* (Whither Russia? The crisis of institutional systems), ed. Tatyana Zaslavskaya (Moscow: Intertsetr, 1999), 193–201; Svetozar Pejovic, "The Transition Process in an Arbitrary State: The Case for the Mafia," *IB Review* 1, 1 (1997): 18–23; Jeffrey Sachs and Katharina Pistor, eds., *The Rule of Law and Economic Reform in Russia* (Boulder: Westview Press, 1997).

compliance."[40] While plausible theoretically, such assumptions tend to un-
derestimate the actual capacity of force-wielding organizations to determine
choices available to economic subjects. The marketing strategy of private enforcers, once called "the offer one cannot refuse," implies that the initiative
all too often belongs to force-wielding organizations rather than economic
subjects. The strategy of such organizations, however, may not and often
does not consist of open coercion but rather of the creation of a field of possibilities with pre-given choices. It is true that under conditions where enforcement options are multiple, customers are likely to have some degree of
choice. Still, the selection of more efficient protection and enforcement options, especially in a transitional period, may be much less the result of
choices made by economic subjects than the outcome of competitive relations between different wielders of force with regard to the efficiency of the
use of force, level of taxation, form of organization, and even normative culture. A purely economic reading of institution building that implicitly
adopts the point of view of the economic subject leaves out a whole set of
political relations between the owners of the means of violence which produce and change the set of constraints within which economic subjects have
to operate.

On the other hand, the institutional-economic approach has a number of
important advantages. First, it contains—explicitly, in Gambetta, and implicitly, in neoinstitutional analyses—a methodologically important distinction, which I will adopt in a modified form. Instead of dividing groups and
their activities into legal and illegal, this approach first distinguishes between
those who provide institutional services, such as protection and dispute settlement, and those who have to buy these services, regardless of whether they
are involved in a legal or an illegal economy. In other words, the market of
protection, legal or otherwise, should be distinguished from the markets for
other conventional goods, be it cars or heroin. This helps to explain the centrality of violence and coercive capacity in the business of Mafia-style groups
and conceive of their functional integration into economic structures. This
distinction allows us to redefine the nature and role of organized crime in
post-Soviet Russia.

Second, the neoinstitutional reading of post-Soviet organized crime enables us to connect it to market building, that is, to the creation of new
structures rather than the persistence of the old. Facing an entirely different
system of constraints and opportunities, even the criminal organizations inherited from the past tend to alter their forms of activity, not to mention the
new ones that emerged to exploit the opportunities. The behavior of a single

40. Timothy Frye, *Brokers and Bureaucrats: Building Market Institutions in Russia* (Ann
Arbor: University of Michigan Press, 2000), 143.

criminal group, especially in the early phase of economic liberalization, is violent and predatory. The interaction of many groups brings about a system that limits and governs their activities, creating relative order. In comparison to later and more complex institutions, and even more to ideal models, the early capitalist set of economic institutions appears imperfect and inefficient, far inferior to those provided by the ideal state. In the absence of a shortcut to institutional perfection, cruel and ugly social forms are bound to endure for a period of time. It is more productive, I argue, to trace the evolution of actual market institutions than to evaluate the success or failure of market reforms in Russia by comparisons to abstract models.

Third, while not compromising the principal role of the economy, the institutional approach allows us to bring the state back in as a key player. This has been productive in past studies of European market building and proves increasingly relevant in the present. Moreover, if institutional sociology is combined with the analysis of social practices, it becomes possible to conceive of the state not as an entity "out there" or as an essential source of power, but as a particular mode of the use of force, as itself an effect of a certain dynamic relationship of forces that have reached a temporary equilibrium. In adopting this position, we will be able to study state formation while looking at "organized crime" or the "Russian *mafiya*."

The "Predatory Man"

The analytical distinction between the market of institutional services (the market of protection) and the market of other goods and services corresponds to an empirical division in the underworld. The genetic core of organized crime is the group that has an advantage in the use of force and provides protection and enforcement to all other criminal businesses. Thomas Schelling has argued to the effect that organized crime is to the underworld what the government is to legitimate business.[41] That is why the activities of the underworld require a monopoly of force within its domain of operation. Those who rely on organized force to protect, settle disputes, and enforce, in exchange for a share of permanent income are themselves rarely engaged in the criminal activities they supervise. Although smugglers, thieves, swindlers, and other types can appear as part of the same network as those who protect and govern them, it is vital not to overlook crucial empirical and analytical distinctions between the two. In fact, they are engaged in fundamentally different kinds of activities, rely on different skills and resources, live off different forms of income, observe different normative codes, and so on—all these distinctions will be substantiated by the Russian material in

41. Schelling, *Choice and Consequence*, 182.

the following chapters. Other groups, those engaged in conventional criminal (or legal) activities, germinate "under" the core group, which ensures a secure environment for conducting their business. Henceforth I will refer to this core group when using the terms "organized crime" or "criminal groups" and will argue that other types of criminal businesses and know-how would not have spread on such a scale without the core groups specializing in the use of force and government. In a sense, this book accounts for the conditions of possibility of organized crime.

From the sociological perspective, the type of social action is more significant than the legal status of the group or organization that provides protection and enforcement. Even when "organized crime" is understood in the manner suggested by Schelling, that is, as involving a monopoly of force in order to extort and govern, the legal definition conveyed by the term unjustifiably narrows its sociological application. Organized crime can be imagined only when the state and the system of justice it effectively enforces are in place. Otherwise, there is little more than a number of competing protection agencies with weak legitimacy. In this case, they should be treated as one category and distinguished from those who buy protection rather than differentiated among themselves. In current Russian business parlance, for example, the term *krysha*, "roof," is used to refer to agencies that provide institutional services to economic agents irrespective of the legal status of providers and clients. Such agencies are not necessarily criminal groups but are composed of a variety of criminal, semilegal (informal), legal, and state organizations. In the definition of *krysha*, legal status is secondary to type of action and function in the economic realm. On the one hand, *krysha* may be placed alongside *mafia, yakudza, triads, cosa nostra,* and other similar names, since it shares with them some major features inherent in private protection agencies. On the other hand, *krysha* is not necessarily a secret underground organization—in fact, it rarely is. It is the name for a whole range of different transitional forms of protection and enforcement, including those provided by the state.

Furthermore, the division between agencies that use force to protect and govern and those that produce conventional goods and have to buy protection is characteristic of many societies throughout history. The use of force (or coercion) constitutes a specific type of social action distinct from the economic action characteristic of the realm of exchange. According to Gianfranco Poggi, the division thus emerges between political and economic power and, accordingly, between wielders of force and owners of capital.[42] As exemplified in the works of Max Weber, Norbert Elias, Karl Polanyi,

---

42. Gianfranco Poggi, *The State: Its Nature, Development, and Prospects* (Stanford: Stanford University Press, 1990), 3–33.

Frederic Lane, Charles Tilly, Douglass North, and others, one of the most challenging tasks for historically oriented sociology and economics has been to explore the historical patterns of relations between these two forms of power and between states and markets as their respective forms of institutionalization. In addition to looking at how state policies launched markets and how the locus of economic development shifted from the state, as a military-political organization, to civil society, as the realm of peaceful economic competition, most of these authors have also accounted, if only indirectly, for the historical victory of the "economic man" (the bourgeois) over the "predatory man" (the chevalier). According to Karl Marx's critique, this victory also affected the ontological presuppositions of the modern ("bourgeois") social sciences, as it shifted its focus toward rational economic behavior and cast it as a human universal.

The economic framework alone is insufficient for coming to terms with the proliferation of organized violence in the context of market reforms in Russia. A vision that rests on the idea of "economic man" and uses the metaphor of supply and demand to account for the "market" of protection has to be modified to account for the reappearance of the supposedly extinct "predatory man" and the social milieu he forms. What happened to Russian society after 1989 looks like the actualization of the grim prediction once made by the early founder of institutional economics, Thorstein Veblen, when he wrote of the habits of the predatory class and its modern successors:

> The traits of the predatory man are by no means obsolete in the common run of modern populations. They are present and can be called out in bold relief at any time. . . . With varying degrees of potency in different individuals, they remain available for the aggressive shaping of men's actions and sentiments whenever a stimulus of more than everyday intensity comes in to call them forth. And they assert themselves forcibly in any case where no occupation alien to the predatory culture has usurped the individual's everyday range of interests and sentiment.[43]

Veblen's warning contains some key concerns that moved the present book. The decade of violence—Russia's "roaring nineties"—offers an opportunity to explore the world of the "predatory man" who asserted himself forcibly and, for a moment, overshadowed the "economic man" whom the masterminds of reforms had authorized to bring about the miracle of the market. The years when the "predatory man," the so-called bandit, came forward and made himself into a regular participant in business life, were also a time when a new economic order was in the making. Was this a coincidence? A pathology? Or perhaps a temporal overlap hints at some positive interrela-

43. Thorstein Veblen, *The Theory of the Leisure Class* (New York: Penguin, 1994), 264.

tionship between the proliferation of various force-wielding organizations and the birth of a new economic order? The 1990s were also the period when the state withered away and when a new round of state formation began in Russia. How, then, does the dynamic of the nonstate use of force relate to the cycle of state formation?

In an attempt to answer these questions, this book combines two narratives. One reconstructs the evolution of forms of violent entrepreneurship in the context of a brief but eventful history of Russian reforms; the other explores relations between violent entrepreneurs and economic subjects and explicates mechanisms of protection and enforcement. Any evolutionary narrative contains a chronology of changes; the structural narrative explains them. What follows is a brief account of the two narratives.

The story presented in this book starts in about the year 1987 (some time between the 1986 Law on Individual Labor Activity and the 1988 Law on Cooperatives), when private entrepreneurship began to emerge and extortion clothed as protection followed. The period between 1987 and 1992 entailed a rapid proliferation of racketeering gangs and informal protective associations of various kinds, which discovered and perfected methods for exploiting new opportunities in emerging markets. To be sure, many criminal groups formed much earlier, but it was only in the late 1980s that protection rackets became the dominant business of organized crime. The year 1992 was significant in many ways. Sweeping economic liberalization and the beginning of massive privatization are well-known facts. Less well known is the pivotal Law on Private Protection and Detective Activity, which legalized private protection agencies and for several years formally sanctioned many of the activities already pursued by racketeering gangs and other agencies. It turned many informal protective associations into legal companies and security services, and their members into licensed personnel. Tens of thousands of former state security and enforcement employees transferred to the private security industry after 1992. The years between 1992 and 1997 saw ferocious competition between violence-managing agencies for the expanding commercial opportunities. The peak of violence was passed in 1995. During this period, private protection and enforcement became institutionalized and a market of protection emerged. At the same time, the state lost its priority in the realm of protection, taxation, and adjudication. By 1997 the elimination contest had brought about a consolidation of larger protection agencies with greater financial resources and sustained relations with regional authorities. Large criminal groups turned to longer-term investments and transformed themselves into financial-industrial holding companies. At the end of 1998 the first signs of a new policy to strengthen the state became visible. The consolidation of the state was pursued with varying degrees of success after 1998, culminating in a radical turn to the politics of state formation at the end of 1999. The presence of nonstate force-wielding organizations was increasingly called into question. Finally, in 2000 the state leadership named the rule of law its top priority, implying a unified set of rules and a monopoly over their enforcement.

I also focus on two interdependent sets of relations affecting the behavior of participants. The first involves relations of exchange between violence-managing agencies (wielders of force) and economic subjects. The second entails relations of competition and cooperation between violence-managing agencies themselves. When every wielder of force is related to at least one economic subject (or to any actor lacking its own protective capacity) and to another wielder of force (a "threat"), a relation of exchange called "protection" emerges. The wielder of force supplies protection and receives in return other benefits (pecuniary or otherwise) in a given proportion. But protection is as much a relation with the "client" as between competing protection agencies when it comes to defining and redefining by means of force the size of an agency's domain or the number of its "clients" The proliferation of racketeering gangs that preyed on the emerging private business was nothing other than the rise of a system of interdependence enabling a redistribution of resources. Once this system was discovered by sportsmen and criminal elements, other groups and organizations joined in, each simultaneously a "threat" and a source of "protection."

What of relations between economic subjects? Their relations were mediated (enforced) by their protection agencies through a system of guarantees backed by force. Pure economic relations existed only on paper; in reality, they were closely intertwined with relations of force, as economic enterprises coordinated their activities with their protective agencies, while the latter established safe avenues for future economic relations between their clients. Understandably, this occurred in the realm of new entrepreneurs in trade and in a few thriving sectors of production rather than in stagnant former socialist enterprises. Virtually any organization with a force-wielding capacity and the appropriate skills could act as a private enforcer and earn substantial income. I call the art of extracting such income "violent entrepreneurship." The ongoing interaction involving private enforcers and economic subjects produced stable patterns and a system of constraints accounted for by each participant and a set of institutions governing economic exchange emerged. Other kinds of economic institutions existed as well, but I have chosen to focus exclusively on violent entrepreneurship.

The "iron cage" created by private protection and enforcement agencies contained the source of its own decline. First, as economic relations stabilized, the use of force was recognized to be increasingly costly. As the violence potential of economic enterprises increasingly became a source of deterrence and thus altered the expectations of the participants in economic exchange, violence was employed less frequently in daily business and began to lose its supreme value. The hundreds of thugs making up each criminal group became obsolete. Second, the leaders of criminal groups and other enforcement agencies began capitalizing their incomes and accumulated substantial economic assets. This altered their interests and their role in the sphere of economic exchange: having become capitalists, they preferred to hire security specialists and lawyers rather than rely on their original enforcement teams of former sportsmen. This, however, did not exclude the pointed use of strong-arm tactics against competitors.

The narrative sketched above is plausible only insofar as it assumes that no central authority, that is, no state, exists. One of my basic premises is that the Russia of the 1990s was close to the state of nature, where anarchy rather than hierarchy prevails. Such a diagnosis, even though it is contradicted by the existence of all the attributes of a Russian state, is empirically correct, I argue, at least until the very end of the 1990s. The image of the state as one private protection company among others does more justice to the reality in question than a view of the state as the source of public power. On the theoretical level, it was necessary to bracket out the state in order to highlight the dynamic of unconstrained competition among violence-managing agencies and its outcomes. This enabled me to show how such competition first corroded the foundations of the state in everyday economic activity and later created the momentum for forming a larger monopoly in place of a heterogeneous realm of private protection agencies. The rebuilding of the state from above followed.

2.

Violent Entrepreneurship

The term "violent entrepreneurship" refers to the economic dimension of the activities of wielders of force. Simply speaking, violent entrepreneurship is the way in which groups and organizations that specialize in the use of force make money. The term was previously mentioned by authors studying the Sicilian Mafia.[1] I suggest using it in a broader and more systematic way; that is, the concept of violent entrepreneurship is applicable not only to certain outlaw groups but also to legitimate agencies and even states.[2] In this chapter I will elaborate the concept with reference to the criminal sector. In chapters 5 and 6 I will extend its application to legitimate agencies.

Violent entrepreneurship can be defined as a set of organizational solutions and action strategies enabling organized force (or organized violence) to be converted into money or other valuable assets on a permanent basis. If consumer goods, for example, constitute the major resource for trade entrepreneurship, money for financial entrepreneurship, information and knowledge for informational entrepreneurship, and so forth, violent entrepreneur-

---

1. Anton Blok, *The Mafia of a Sicilian Village: A Study of Violent Peasant Entrepreneurs* (Oxford: Basil Blackwell, 1974); Diego Gambetta, *The Sicilian Mafia: The Business of Private Protection* (Cambridge: Harvard University Press, 1993), 77.

2. For decades, the policy of the military in El Salvador, for example, involved escalating threats and the excessive use of violence to increase extraction from the landowning class. See William Stanley, *Protection Racket State: Elite Politics, Military Extortion, and Civil War in El Salvador* (Philadelphia: Temple University Press, 1996).

ship is constituted by socially organized violence, actual or potential (coercion). Violent entrepreneurship is a means of increasing the private income of wielders of force through ongoing relations of exchange with other groups that own other resources. The main unit of violent entrepreneurship can be called a "violence-managing agency."

A robber does not qualify as a violent entrepreneur but a stationary bandit does, since the latter strives to establish permanent tributary relations with inhabitants of his domain and provides certain services that justify his demand for tribute. Although superiority in the use of physical force is the general condition for violent entrepreneurship, that is not its substance. The conversion of organized force into permanent revenue involves a variety of methods that appear as the exchange of certain services (or of claims to provide them) for money or other valuable assets. Such services or claims normally include "protection," "justice," "government," "enforcement," and a number of competitive advantages for economic subjects. The revenues of violent entrepreneurs take the form of tribute or (income) tax collected in a regular manner at a relatively fixed rate—as if in payment for the benefits that wielders of force deliver to the subjects in their domain. From this it becomes evident that violent entrepreneurship can be successfully conducted only after a monopoly on the use of force and, accordingly, on taxation, has been effectively established over a particular domain, however small. The interference of rival governing and taxing authorities suspends the business until a firm division is reestablished—normally with recourse to violence or threats. That is why wielders of force always tend to think in terms of "territories" or "spheres of interest" (not necessarily in the geographical sense), and why boundary maintenance is crucial. Outside the monopolized domain, naturally, lies the realm of rivals and threats. A monopoly of force within and unconstrained competition without are logical necessities for violent entrepreneurship.

Finally, we should emphasize that violent entrepreneurship is a private affair. That is to say, it involves a relative freedom in the strategic and tactical decision making regarding the use of violence or threats, autonomy from other authorities, and the possibility of earning private income, which depends on the efficiency of entrepreneurship. Thus, if a violence-managing agency (ultimately, the state) is subordinated to a higher authority or subjected to harsh public control, then its entrepreneurial capacity is considerably limited (but is much less so in the sphere of international politics). And, conversely, salaried state security employees become violent entrepreneurs when they secure an additional income by trading their services as private individuals. Once agents who have the needed resource capacity acquire relative autonomy from the principal, they gain a potential opportunity to conduct violent entrepreneurship.

Extortion and Protection

Extortion is a particular act, a criminal offense, whereas a protection racket is an institutionalized relationship. In Russian legal practice, criminal charges would normally be pressed only after an enduring relationship between a racketeer and the alleged victims has been broken down into concrete episodes of extortion, each of which can be reliably proved. In cases where these relations are so "smooth" that they involve virtually no violence or threats and are so carefully maintained that they reveal no signs of monetary transactions, extortion is almost impossible to prove, even when a protection racket has existed for years. The sociological task, then, is almost the reverse of the juridical: to trace how separate episodes of extortion are transformed into a durable institutionalized, businesslike relationship. First I will deal with only one elementary form of violent entrepreneurship: relations associated with physical protection. Then I will account for a more sophisticated form of this activity: enforcement partnership.

Extortion

Extortion is at the center of the plot in the famous early Soviet novel *The Golden Calf* (1931), written by satirists Iliya Ilf and Evgenii Petrov. In an attempt to get rich, the con man Ostap Bender seeks and finds an underground millionaire, a "golden calf," whom he pursues and threatens to get him to part with his money. Fearing repression from the socialist state, and unable to ward off the extortionists, the millionaire can do nothing but hand over his money to Bender. Throughout the Soviet period, "golden calves" looked mostly gray from the outside; they did their best to disguise themselves as ordinary Soviet citizens. Hence the major action in the novel is to identify such a golden calf and then subject him to refined (and hilarious) methods of psychological pressure.

The Soviet shadow economy greatly expanded in the 1970s. It comprised a variety of businesses that grew sporadically to exploit gaps and loopholes in the state economy: the illegal production of consumer goods and alcohol, the concealment of legally produced goods from state accounting offices, various ventures for appropriating state property, antiques businesses, swindling, underground gambling facilities, and so forth.[3] The breed of "golden calves" expanded accordingly, but Bender's successors lagged behind, since identifying potential victims was still a problem. What made things worse

---

3. See Gregory Grossman, "The Second Economy in the USSR," *Problems of Communism* 26, 5 (1977): 25–40.

was that some serious underground dealers even managed to secure informal patronage of corrupt high-ranking Party authorities who could provide them with some protection. The few racketeering groups were composed mainly of ex-convicts *(ugolovniki)*, like the notorious Gang of the Mongol, which terrorized the Moscow underworld in 1969–72. The gang was created by Gennadii Kar'kov ("Mongol") when he came to Moscow in 1969 after three years in prison for theft of state property. Another member of the gang was Viacheslav Ivan'kov ("Yaponchik"), the future leading criminal figure of the 1990s, who was convicted of extortion in the United States in 1996. The gang pursued underground dealers allegedly hiding enormous riches, which they could not put to any productive use under state socialism, and staged brutal assaults to force the victims to give up their property. Unlike refined fictional extortionists, the real ones kidnapped victims, put them in coffins, and placed the coffins on trucks for the "last journey" to the cemetery. The gang was arrested in 1972 and its leader sentenced to fifteen years in prison.[4] For underground "millionaires," riches were a dangerous stigma. Were they to be identified by state bodies or extortionists, trouble was imminent. Unlike the state, extortionists would take away only property, not one's freedom.

A substantial part of the assets of new entrepreneurs in the post-1987 boom originated in the shadow economy of the late Soviet period, but those who responded to the new economic policies and who had no connections to the underworld were also regarded suspiciously by the public. After all, what the "cooperators" and private traders were now doing openly had only yesterday been a criminal offense, speculation or illicit trade. From the very beginning, the new private sector emerged in an institutional environment distinguished by its lower levels of security and protection, despite the unchanged police capacity, at least in the first two or three years of perestroika. One of the effects of the residual Soviet moral attitude toward private entrepreneurs undoubtedly shared by law enforcement employees was the stigmatization of the whole group. *Kooperator* and, especially, *chastnik* (privateer, private businessman) for some time carried connotations of marginality, and the words were often used in a disparaging manner, despite efforts on the part of official propaganda to ennoble them. Public opinion surveys revealed mixed and increasingly negative attitudes toward private businessmen.[5] The

---

4. Alexei Trabarin, *Vory v zakone i avtoritety* (Thieves-in-law and *avtoritets*) (Moscow: EKSIMO-Press, 2000), 20–40.

5. In 1989 45 percent of the nationwide sample felt positive and 30 percent negative about cooperative activities; a year later, this had changed to 30 and 42 percent, respectively. Cited in Vadim Radaev, "Practicing and Potential Entrepreneurs in Russia," *International Journal of Sociology* 27, 3 (fall 1997): 25–29.

first entrepreneurs were viewed as industrious but dishonest and often criminal.[6] A former militia officer expressed this attitude as follows: "Why should we care about these cooperators if they only care about their own pockets?" (4).

The peculiarity of late Soviet business conditions was that the victims of protection rackets were legitimate businessmen theoretically entitled to state protection but rarely provided with it in practice. The first years of economic reforms saw the spread of direct and brutal extortion from private businessmen. Statistics on these offenses are either absent, because victims rarely reported them to the police; if they did, the offense disappeared in the columns of numbers, classified under existing official subcategories such as "grievous bodily harm," "hooliganism," or "kidnapping."[7] But the gruesome experience is certainly recorded in the memories of participants (from both sides) and abundantly reproduced in popular literature. The simplest method was to kidnap a cooperative director and, using an electric iron (or a soldering iron—the two are equally prominent in racketeering folklore), threaten the person until a sum of money was paid. From the recollections of a racketeer:

> Of course sometimes we had recourse to brutal forms of assault. [We would] pull up and say to him: "Now, come on, scum, you pay." And he paid. Those who did not agree were subjected to our pressure. After all, we had good manuals, those Mafia movies. The soldering iron was pretty popular and so were handcuffs with which we attached the client to the radiator. Sometimes we took him out to a forest or locked him in a cellar.[8]

Even after the demands of extortionists were satisfied, the latter were unlikely to leave the victim and would continue exploiting his fear to exact regular payments. A common rule of racketeers is that once someone has yielded to intimidation and paid even ten rubles, he or she is "naturally" obliged to pay until the end of life. A previous payment normally serves as a weighty argument in a gang dispute over the right to collect tribute from a given businessman or company.

Another popular method was to take a businessman into a forest and make him dig his own grave. Once the victim was broken down and ready to accept all conditions, he would be "asked" to write out an IOU or to sign a

6. Ibid., 27.

7. According to law enforcement experts, car theft is reported in 80 percent of cases; other property theft in 40 percent; bodily harm in 25 percent; while extortion is reported in only 10 percent of cases. Cited in Azalia Dolgova, ed., *Organizovannaya prestupnost'-4* (Organized crime-4) (Moscow: Kriminologicheskaya assotsiatsiya, 1998), 36.

8. Cited in Valery Karyshev, *Zapiski banditskogo advokata* (Notes of a bandits' attorney) (Moscow: Tsentrpoligraph, 1998), 34.

document transferring property rights. The only real concern of extortionists was not to exceed the proper level of intimidation, since this could lead
either to the victim's death or to an appeal to the police, who would then in-
tervene. One such case led to the arrest in 1990 of Nikolai Suleimanov, the
godfather of the five hundred–strong Chechen crime group in Moscow. One
of the companies Suleimanov and his group controlled was the Car Maintenance Station No. 7, a prestigious garage tailored to maintain foreign-made
cars. Among the clients, many of whom were the first nouveaux riches,
Suleimanov identified potential targets of extortion and acquired information about their property. One of the victims, the director of a joint venture,
Soiyz International, one Balakirev, reported the racketeering assault to the
police after being continually brutalized. The police set up a video camera to
record the episode of extortion involving 2.5 million rubles (unprecedented
for 1990). The following fragment of a conversation between Suleimanov,
his associate Akhmadov, and Balakirev was recorded in a café after Balakirev
had been taken to a suburban forest to dig his own grave.

> Suleimanov: Imagine the Chechens and a man with lots of money. I tell my
> men: go talk to him. The guys bring him out [of town, to a forest]—give us
> the money. They clogged his mouth, but his nose was congested, you know.
> He had a cold, and the nose did not breathe, you know.
> Akhmadov: And the man died, you understand? In principle, they did not
> want it, but the man died. Of course now it doesn't matter whether they
> wanted or not . . .
> Suleimanov: So it's just two million and a half. How much did Brezhnev have?
> Balakirev: No one needed this money.
> Suleimanov: Right! Shrouds do not have pockets.[9]

Consequently, Suleimanov was sentenced to four years in prison, but was released and transferred to Chechnya two years later. He was murdered on his
return to Moscow in 1995.

When a business involves physical risk, an offer of protection sounds
more than appropriate. One businessman recalled how he and his partner
started their first private enterprise: "Every day we expected the bandits to
turn up. You know, this anticipation was the worst thing. So when they indeed came, it was kind of a relief. We were lucky the problem was resolved in
a civilized way" (14). The first racketeering brigades were quick to discover
the effectiveness of framing an assault as a protection offer. Their tactics were
flexible enough to accommodate both outright brutal extortion and firm

9. Cited in Nikolai Modestov, *Moskva banditskaya* (Moscow bandits) (Moscow: Tsentrpoligraph, 1996), 48–49.

protection clothed as partnership or even friendship. It has been reported that "Mikhas'," the leader of the Solntsevskaya crime group in the southern districts of Moscow, instructed his associates to be friendly and helpful to people, like a real "Mafia."[10]

Protection Rackets

We need to distinguish analytically between a protection racket and extortion: extortion does not occur on a regular basis or within the context of a broader organization in whose name the money is collected, and it does not offer regular or imaginary services in return. How were acts of extortion transformed into protection rackets? Initially, protection meant primarily physical protection from other such gangs. Its most elementary form was the protection arrangement at city markets, where the density of trade was high. If the market was not monopolized by one racket, it was divided into segments by several groups, who protected their clients from one another. Each racketeer was a visible threat and a protector at the same time. Each group had its representatives at the market who supervised traders, collected fees, and offered real protection if the situation required. "The only rule was not to assault or rob each other's *kommersanty,*" summed up one of the leaders whose group operated at the Deviatkino market in Leningrad (23).

In big cities, any newly opened commercial enterprise, a shop or a café, would be visited occasionally by various mobile brigades searching for "free objects." All the different scenarios of such a visit can be reduced to the inquiry: "Whom does this business pay?" meaning, "Does it have protection?" The owner's inability to answer the question, that is, to name a group or its leader who collects a protection fee, determined the outcome of the visit: "From now on you will pay us." Then the director was given the name of the group or its leader and a telephone number that he or she would provide when another brigade arrived with the same question. Any other brigade had the right to verify the truthfulness of the answer by inquiring whether such and such group really protected that particular client. In cases where the answer was no, the other group not only imposed its protection but often punished the owner—physically or with a fine—for cheating. The protection fee would start at between three hundred and four hundred U.S. dollars per month and tended to increase over time until it reached 20–30 percent of the revenue of the client's business.

Not all businesses were equally attractive and vulnerable to the racketeering takeover. Small enterprises with fast cash turnover, low investment re-

10. Valery Karyshev, *Solntsevskaya bratva: Istoriya gruppirovki* (Solntsevskoe brotherhood: A history of the criminal group) (Moscow: Eksim Press, 1998), 65–67.

quirements, and relatively simple technology were the most lucrative. Thus, the wholesale and retail trade as well as businesses specializing in the import of consumer goods and providing services were the first to become private and, accordingly, to fall under private protection. A survey of the retail sector in three Russian cities conducted in 1996 showed that private protection had become routine. Over 40 percent of retail trade shop owners in Moscow, Smolensk, and Ulyanovsk admitted frequent "contact with racket" but also considered it a relatively minor problem (an average 3.13 on scale of 1 to 10) compared to state taxes and capital shortfalls. The study also revealed that shopkeepers believed that private protection served as a substitute for state-provided police protection, and, to a lesser extent, for state-provided courts.[11] Small entrepreneurs gradually established working relations with racketeers and, as interview sources indicate, viewed these relations as beneficial, given the existing business environment. They saw racketeers as providers of real services and demanded them when circumstances required. The following fragment of an interview with a Moscow businessman illustrates such an attitude:

Q: Did you experience assaults or protection offers from racketeers?
A: Yes, such cases occurred. Like this happened to one of our directors-general. Business was up, and he bought a new apartment and a new car, and instantly these guys came to demand money. By coincidence, just shortly before that, one of our new Kamaz trucks had been stolen. And we said to them, Okay, you will be our roof if you help to find the stolen car. Obviously, they did not manage to find it, they came again, we repeated our condition, and that was it, they left.
Q: Do you think protection is beneficial for businessmen?
A: I think that, in principle, this is a suitable option *(normal'yi variant)*. Like in that case, if the guys helped to find the car, it was worth working with them, maybe even signing a kind of agreement. But when all they can do is demand money. . . . This is not serious. . . . A serious racket will not engage in petty extortion, it can cost them a lot. It's no use driving people to utter despair, because anyone can go to RUBOP, and an official investigation will begin. (14)

Few racketeers have an initial intention to protect someone, but they are led to do so in practice. In other words, protection is a structural outcome of interaction that has priority over the intentions of individual participants. All the racketeer intends to do is to collect money, the more the better. In their language, this is conveyed by the word *poluchat'* (to get, to collect), which also stands for the protection racket as a whole. Each of them taken in isola-

---

11. Timothy Frye and Ekaterina Zhuravskaya, "Rackets, Regulation, and the Rule of Law," *Journal of Law, Economics, and Organization* 16 (October 2000): 478–502.

tion would prefer easy extortion, but as part of a system of many interrelated racketeers, he is compelled to protect. The nature of protective relations is difficult to grasp when a protector and his victim are taken in isolation: the relation will always look like extortion. But the concept of protection in fact implies a multiplicity of interacting wielders of force, each of whom can simultaneously act as a threat and as protection. To rephrase Kenneth Waltz's presentation of this relationship with regard to states, the means by which other states are threatened are, in their very existence, the means of security for each given state.[12] Hence, an isolated instance will always appear as extortion (i.e., when threat and protection coincide but get divorced for a fee), but if time and other wielders of force are added to the picture, protection does become a "real" service provided to the client—in the sense that there is no possibility that any of the participants will reasonably doubt the fact of genuine protection. In this case, the wielder of force has something to offer, imposing a relationship of exchange rather than bluntly demanding a ransom. Discussing the "extortion-protection" dilemma, Charles Tilly admits, albeit indirectly, that it also involves a strong element of subjective interpretation:

> Which image the word *protection* brings to mind depends mainly on our assessment of the reality and externality of the threat. Someone who produces both the danger and, at a price, the shield against it is a racketeer. Someone who provides a needed shield but has little control over the danger's appearance qualifies as a legitimate protector, especially if his price is no higher than of his competitors'.[13]

In fact, this uncomfortable moral dilemma does not bear on two different situations, but rather emerges within the single field created by many wielders of force through their interaction. Each wielder of force can be the protector of those who are his clients and a threat, anonymous and potential or quite concrete, to those who are not. As a class, they are both at the same time. The trick of protection, then, lies in the internal—and inevitable—division of wielders of force into rival parties, so that each of them is a genuine and concrete protector against an abstract threat in which this protector also takes part. The institution of the protection racket springs from the absence of a monopoly of force.

12. The original phrase is: "The means of security for one state are, in their very existence, the means by which other states are threatened." Kenneth Waltz, *Theory of International Politics* (Reading, Mass.: Addison-Wesley, 1979), 64.

13. Charles Tilly, "War Making and State Making as Organized Crime," in *Bringing the State Back In,* ed. Peter Evans, Dietrich Rueschemeyer, and Theda Skocpol (Cambridge: Cambridge University Press, 1986), 173.

To return to the late Soviet period, private businessmen who paid protection fees were not shielded from unexpected events. Even though a businessman who paid protection fees no longer had to fear a soldering iron or a grave-digging experience—this would now be considered an assault on the protection agency—it was not uncommon at that time for criminal groups themselves to strip their clients of their assets, drive them out of business, or even kill them. This was a matter of course because racketeering groups considered the clients whom they protected to be their property. The claim to protect implicitly contained the claim to ownership. They usually referred to the businessmen as "our *kommersant*" or "our *baryga*," signifying both their responsibility for the businessman's activities and their right to own him, which was normally expressed in the right to collect regular fees but could also lead to a carefully staged gradual confiscation of assets.

The essence of these elementary informal property relations, however, lies not in the relations of racketeers to their businessman but in the relations among racketeering groups themselves. Owning a businessman meant having the ability to secure the right to collect a protection fee from him vis-à-vis other potential claimants. Occasionally, therefore, racketeers really had to protect their clients willy-nilly in order to enforce their right of ownership. This clarifies why property rights are sometimes defined as relations of exclusion.[14] Subsequently, criminal groups differentiated themselves according to their policy toward the businesses they protected: some aimed at maximal gains and thus undermined the businesses, some were more future-oriented and redistributed property rights to account for the interests of their clients and thereby achieve sustained long-term profit. The function of violence-managing agencies in the latter case shifted toward providing competitive advantages to their clients. Later, as the institutions of property rights developed throughout the 1990s, criminal groups and other violence-managing agencies became legitimate shareholders in some of the businesses they had once protected.

The Economy of Protection

The use of force is not a subject that readily lends itself to economic analysis. One way to introduce the economic dimension is to take into account the central claim the wielders of force make and the relations of exchange implied in this claim: protection. Protection requires (organized)

14. "The essence of property rights is the right to exclude, and an organization which has a comparative advantage in violence is in the position to specify and enforce property rights." Douglass North, *Structure and Change in Economic History* (New York: Norton, 1981), 21.

force and its strategic use. A protective capacity involves the use of force to control other competing or potential forces within a certain domain.

Tribute and Protection Rent

In his pioneering studies, the economic historian Frederic Lane has demonstrated how a political economy of protection can be developed. Lane considers protection a genuine service and the demand for such a service an objective necessity. In the first place, he distinguishes between enterprises called "governments," which manage organized violence to produce protection, and those that produce other goods and services and pay governments for protection. Protection costs may take the form not only of direct payments for a concrete "amount" of protection, but also of taxes, bribes, gifts, trade tariffs, and the like, forms that obscure their true nature. Whatever the form, argues Lane, they constituted an important parameter of the political economy of early capitalism by altering the structure of production costs and creating new commercial opportunities.[15] Then, by shifting the emphasis from the "racket" to the "protection" element and by presenting this relationship as a contract between the "provider" and the "customer," Lane opened the possibility of analyzing protection in economic terms.[16]

Profits from the management of violence take two forms. The surplus that the government (or prince) receives above the cost of production of protection services, that is, above the cost required to maintain the military capacity or undertake a military action, constitutes tribute. Because protection tends to be a natural monopoly whatever the size of the territory and the number of enterprises under protection, the government is able to raise the price of protection above its own costs and receive a monopoly profit. What gives Lane grounds to argue the case for some degree of productivity in the protection business is, first, the ability of the stronger power to extract wealth from the weaker and thus to increase the general amount of national wealth and, second, the possibility of accumulating and investing tribute into economic development. Even if the military elite spends the surplus on conspicuous consumption or wants previously unsatisfied, it stimulates new forms of production, he insists.

In particular circumstances, customers not only carry the burden of protection costs but are also able to earn profits as a result of being better pro-

15. Frederic Lane, *Profits from Power: Readings in Protection Rent and Violence-Controlling Enterprises* (Albany: State University of New York Press, 1963), 2.
16. Frederic Lane, *Venice and History: The Collected Papers of Frederic C. Lane* (Baltimore: Johns Hopkins University Press, 1966), 383.

tected than others. Such profits emerge from trade competition and resemble differential rent, since they are derived from differences in the protection costs paid by competing parties for access to markets. Lane calls them "protection rents." Merchants would receive a protection rent in cases where their governments provided them with a comparative advantage either through special trading conditions or lower protection costs, compared to others in the same market. All merchants engaged in long-distance trade had to pay for protection to avoid damage, but those who paid less for solid protection in a dangerous business environment earned protection rent as a result of more competitive prices reflecting lower costs. At the end of the eleventh century, for example, the Venetians obtained a charter exempting them from all tariffs in the Byzantine Empire and thus secured a differential in their favor. The privileges for Venetian merchants were secured by placing the Venetian navy at the service of the Byzantine emperor in his war against the Norman king of Sicily and were then continuously renewed through various naval operations. Consequently, the Venetians were able to sell their wares at prices that must often have been higher because of the higher protection costs of less privileged traders. Their government's use of its naval power earned them huge protection rents.[17] Lane explains the rise of Venice as an example of the clever management of organized force that allowed a reduction of costs for the "customers" and higher protection costs for their competitors, imposed by all available means, including violence. The result may be a general increase in the power and wealth of a given nation. "During the Middle Ages and early modern times protection rents were a major source of the fortunes made in trade," writes Lane. "They were a more important source of profits than superiority in industrial techniques or industrial organization."[18]

Transaction Costs

The argument regarding the productivity of governments or other suppliers of protection, in the form set forth by Lane, is valid only if one admits that the redistribution of resources from the weak to the strong is a basic and inevitable process, so that productivity can, in principle, be measured only by the gains of particular parties within the framework of an essentially zero-sum game. Lane's analysis is vulnerable to a Smithonian objection that the creation of commercial monopolies or the forging of trade routes and trade agreements through the use of force is unproductive in the long run, since it may divert resources from their most efficient allocation. Lane's model of

17. Ibid., 387.
18. Ibid., 421–22.

the interaction between violence-managing and conventional commercial enterprises is not the only way to grasp the conditions under which the use of organized force can be productive. Another reading of the role of coercion in economic history has been suggested by Douglass North. This approach accounts for the capacity of wielders of force, the modern state in particular, to create and enforce certain rules that make up the institutional environment of economic activity; it also makes it possible to compare the effects of different institutional arrangements.

What does the neoinstitutional analysis tell us about the role of protection agencies? Asymmetries of information possessed by participants and agents about the essential attributes of what is being exchanged and the need to enforce compliance with the terms of the contract gives rise to transaction costs. In other words, significant resources are invested in a system of measurements, rules, and their enforcement to make the orderly exchange of goods possible. The rules that govern exchange behavior make up social institutions, which, throughout history, have created order and reduced uncertainty in exchange. Any system of exchange, from local barter to global long-distance trade, presupposes certain mechanisms of enforcement. In small face-to-face communities, enforcement comes about through shared norms and the direct monitoring of compliance. Within such dense local networks, transaction costs are low (if individuals respect customs), but so is the scale of trade. With the growth of specialization and the development of long-distance trade, exchange relations have tended to extend beyond proximity in time and space and to involve impersonal relations. Here the importance of information and the difficulty of enforcing contracts grow substantially. Transaction costs begin to affect production costs. Agents respond to the growing uncertainty by expanding clientelist networks, exchanging hostages, establishing organizations that can effectively ostracize merchants who cheat, and by appealing to governments to use force or relying on private enforcers. The creation of these more complex institutions incurs mounting costs, and trade will develop, North argues, only to the extent that the gains that merchants make exceed the transaction costs of trade.

Enforcement arrangements differ in cost and efficiency, that is, they require different levels of resources for their maintenance and vary in their geographical reach. In some cases, economic agents will devise a system of protection and enforcement whose costs are not prohibitive for the expansion of their trade. Informal business associations and private enforcers do enable trade to expand but their potential is nonetheless limited. The most efficient solution, argues North, is an impersonal third-party enforcer that introduces a universal system of measurement, monitors compliance with formal contracts, and punishes failure to comply according to a set of standardized procedures. Due to the economy of scale, neutral third-party enforcement will tend to be less expensive, and due to the universality of the rules it enforces it will further expand the realm of predictable and rule-governed behavior. This third party, then, is the modern state, which uses its coercive power in an impersonal manner, providing protection and enforcement to all those formally entitled to it by citizenship. "The state trades a group of services, which we shall call protection and justice, for revenue. Since there are economies of scale in providing these services, total income in the society is higher as a result of an organizational specializing in these services than it would be if each individual in society protected his own property."[19] Thus, more efficient protection and enforcement create the potential for economic growth.

In many cases, however, agencies that have an advantage in the use of force and therefore the capacity to define and enforce property rights fail to create efficient institutions. Their predatory behavior impedes economic growth, unless the force of competition or the organized interest of the economic society places constraints on their pursuit of short-term gains and compels them to adopt a more balanced economic policy. The neoinstitutional theory, however, has relatively little to say about how and under what conditions this happens. In chapter 4 I will return to the problem of why some protection agencies are led to act to keep protection costs within economically acceptable limits. At this stage, it is important to highlight the useful insight contained in the writings of Lane and North. In both models, interrelations between force-wielding organizations and their policy toward the economic subjects for whom they stand as protectors and enforcers critically affect the economic performance of the domain in which each force-wielding organization maintains its monopoly, be it a state or a private protection agency enjoying a fair degree of autonomy.

Enforcement Partnership

"Enforcement partnership" is a translation of the Russian *silovoe partnerstvo*, a phrase used by an *avtoritet*, a crime group leader, when he tried to explain to me the role of his group in relation to business enterprises. The respondent described how they searched for business opportunities for their clients, backed formal contracts with their guarantees, concluded informal settlement agreements, recovered debts, and provided physical protection. "We are enforcement partners of sorts," noted the *avtoritet* (23). In an attempt to settle the intellectual property issue I thanked the respondent for

19. North, *Structure and Change in Economic History,* 23.

what I considered a precious analytical insight (to which he did not pay much attention) and said that I intended to use the term as an analytical category. He did not object.

Now I turn to a more complex set of activities performed by violent entrepreneurs that are related to enforcement partnership. By "enforcement partnership" I mean the function of a violence-managing agency (a criminal group, a private protection company, or a similar organization) devolving from the skillful use of force and information on a commercial basis that allows an institutional environment of business activities to be maintained for its client enterprises. The institutional environment involves security, contract enforcement, dispute settlement, informational support, and relations with higher agencies (e.g., the state bureaucracy) if these obtain.

Violent entrepreneurship denotes the profit-oriented social action of wielders of force; enforcement partnership is the function that allows them to be profitably integrated into the field of market exchange; a durable set of constraints is one outcome of the activities relating to that function. There is another, very important element that holds the system together and gives it its operational capacity—a set of values and patterns of normative culture.

The spread of protection rackets in the cooperative sector in 1988–90 was still an economically peripheral phenomenon. The major economic assets were still in the hands of the state, the administrative system was in place, and the fiscal crisis was a few years ahead. The transition from protection rackets to full-fledged enforcement partnership occurred some time after 1992, with the massive expansion of the private sector. By then, criminal groups had accumulated sufficient power resources, finances, and experience to participate in the economic transition. On the one hand, violent entrepreneurs forced their services on customers, and, when the latter had no other options, they had to begin "working with" criminal groups. My observations also convinced me that violent entrepreneurs were very successful in generating demand for their services. Yet, on the other hand, the demand for enforcement partnership was objectively high, and crime groups were frequently called on by businessmen to resolve their problems. It was not uncommon for a single incident of a business company "hiring" a criminal group to result in permanent "cooperation," which the customer was unable to terminate. Hence the initiative did belong to violent entrepreneurs, yet their rise would not have been so significant without the presence of independent demand-generating factors. First I will account for the demand artificially created by violent entrepreneurs, then for the independent institutional demand and, finally, for the function of enforcement partnership itself.

The Artificial Demand

The tactic of physical threats and the resulting social atmosphere of insecurity, galvanized by daily media reports of crime, earned criminal groups many permanent clients. But it was the deliberately created transactional problems that significantly expanded the demand for enforcement partners. The following typical example illustrates the demand-generating mechanism. The Petrenko family (the name has been changed) came to St. Petersburg from Ukraine in search of business opportunities. After a time, in cooperation with the Komarovskaya criminal group, they established a trade company that advertised wholesale delivery of goods in high demand at low prices. The company requested from its customers a prepayment of not less than half the value of the contract. Once it had accumulated many prepaid orders, mainly from retailers in provincial cities, the company would simply disappear, only to reappear later under a different name. This simple trick is known as *kidok* (from *kinut'*, to abandon, to cheat). When cheated clients who came to Petersburg to recover their money managed to find the company's director, thugs from the Komarovskaya group persuaded them to withdraw their claim and return home. However, when, instead of a cheated client, two criminal authorities *(vory v zakone)* from Siberia came to reclaim goods or money, *komarovskie* bandits readily returned what was owed. In their turn, the Siberian enforcement partners no doubt received their 30 to 50 percent commission (16).

It is not only that enforcement partners gain in both cases—when they organize scams and when they help to return money—they also stimulate the general demand for enforcement partners by increasing the risks of doing business on one's own. Virtually every criminal group at the beginning of the 1990s practiced both the enforcement of scams by "its" businessmen and the recovery of "its" businessmen's assets embezzled by others. Gradually, this activity was rationalized in the direction of preventive insurance against scams: the enforcement partner sought to acquire information about the prospective contractor and demanded guarantees from the latter's enforcement partner. While it was considered legitimate for crime groups to cheat businessmen, their norms discouraged such behavior toward one another and required major retaliation in cases when it occurred. A tactic similar to the "fly-by-night operator" described above was also applied by criminal groups to credit relations; that is, a criminal group sometimes got a businessman a loan or credit with the aim of subsequently embezzling it. In the absence of reliable information about the prospective client, the only way for the credit institution to reduce its loss would be to appeal to an enforcement partner to resolve the problem on its behalf through interaction with that criminal group. It is thus not difficult to see how this system of interdependence tended to drive out of business those who did not pay to and who, accordingly, did not have an enforcement partner. After a certain point, the demand for enforcement partnerships was likely to become self-perpetuating.

In the language of violent entrepreneurs, the stimulation of demand for an enforcement partnership is called "to create a problem" *(sozdat' problemu)*, which also implies a follow-up offer for its resolution or an opportunity for another enforcement partner to resolve the problem—for a fee. It is true that relations between criminal groups were tense and often slid into open warfare, preventing long-term cooperation. It would therefore be incorrect to suggest that enforcement partners deliberately provided profitable job opportunities for one another, though there were many cases of short-term cooperation. Rather, the system of interdependence worked so that conflicts between enforcement partners, which inevitably caused some losses, nonetheless helped to keep tensions and risks at a level that provided sustained gains for wielders of force as a class at the expense of the economic class—despite certain gains that some of its representatives were allowed to achieve.

Transactional Problems

However much violent entrepreneurs strove to "create problems," the number of real problems created by ill-conceived transition policies and the consequences of the rapid privatization of the Russian economy was incomparably higher. Major policy measures included the removal of price controls, the liberalization of trade, and the privatization of economic assets. The speed of change was a key issue. "To the reform team, the speed at which ownership was transferred was of primary importance," write the authors of a study on privatization. "The managerial elite and criminals would increase their advantage with each month that passed, and the methods traditionally used to sell a company in a market economy were viewed as too time-consuming."[20] This miscalculation turned out to be a real gift to the criminal elements.

Hundreds of thousands of existing enterprises were privatized between 1992 and 1996 and many more were created. The majority of large and medium-sized enterprises came to belong to their employees, including the management, while the share of external owners was relatively low. There is no evidence that during the first phase of privatization criminal groups man-

20. Joseph Blasi, Maya Kroumova, and Douglas Kruse, *Kremlin Capitalism: The Privatization of the Russian Economy* (Ithaca: Cornell University Press, 1997), 39.

aged to acquire any significant part of that property; moreover, there is little proof that they actually tried very hard. But there is ample evidence that criminal groups and other violence-managing agencies were subsequently drawn to govern property transactions, for which their major resources and skills proved indispensable. The origins of this development lay in a combination of mounting transactional problems, the inefficiency of existing legal institutions at resolving these problems, and the high costs of access to legal institutions (the high costs of legal economic activity).

Transactional problems included the failure to observe contracts (to deliver goods or pay for goods delivered), nonpayment of debts, shortages of the cash needed for transactions, and problems of the secure delivery of goods. Constraints and incentives that make parties observe a contract are regarded by neoinstitutional theorists as effects of a certain institutional environment made up of a set of norms and the methods for their enforcement.[21] Premeditated cheating aside, it was insufficient business experience, opportunism, and a low level of responsibility that led to multiple transaction failures. Successive surveys of Russian entrepreneurs indicate that, throughout the 1990s, low contractual discipline and a low reliability of business partners remained the most acute problem.[22] In commodity exchanges, opportunism was not uncommon: clients or brokers could list their goods on several different exchanges simultaneously, accept the highest bid, then renege on contracts concluded on other exchanges.[23] Business failures and shortage of cash led to a proliferation of mutual debts between enterprises. Central government policies only deepened the nonpayment crisis.[24] A manager whose company in August 1994 owed 7 billion rubles and was owed 8 billion, described the overall situation this way: "All enterprises now have their debts, we owe our suppliers and our customers are owed. Everybody owes each other and nobody pays, and we are all looking for God-knows-what guarantees."[25]

21. See Douglass North, *Institutions, Institutional Change, and Economic Performance* (Cambridge: Cambridge University Press, 1990), 27–60.

22. Businessmen surveyed at the First and the Second Congress of Entrepreneurs named the low reliability of business partners as the most serious problem. *Informatsionnyi biuleten' KCBR* 5 (December 1995): 32–35. Other surveys confirmed this evaluation. See, for example, Vadim Radaev, *Formirovanie novykh rossiiskikh rynkov: Transaktsionnye izderzhki, formy kontrolia i delovaya etika* (Moscow: Tsentr politicheskikh tekhnologii, 1998), 116–27.

23. Timothy Frye, "Caveat Emptor: Institutions, Credible Commitment, and Commodity Exchanges in Russia," in *Institutional Design*, ed. Dave Weimer (Boston: Kluwer Academic Publishers, 1995).

24. See David Woodruff, *Money Unmade: Barter and the Fate of Russian Capitalism* (Ithaca: Cornell University Press, 1999).

25. Cited in Noreena Hertz, *Russian Business Relationships in the Wake of Reform* (Oxford: Macmillan, 1996), 101.

The emergence of thousands of new financial institutions in the early 1990s was accompanied by the progressive growth of unpaid debt. According to available rough estimates, the total value equaled 3 trillion 609 billion rubles (1.64 billion U.S. dollars) in the beginning of 1994, 8 trillion (1.75 billion U.S. dollars) in 1995,[26] and reached 44 trillion rubles (7.9 billion U.S. dollars) in 1996.[27] Many banks operated at high risk, with their own reserves much lower than required by existing norms. The situation was further complicated by the hyperinflation in 1992–94, which devalued outstanding debts not tied to stable currencies and increased losses caused by failure to repay them in time.[28]

Existing studies of entrepreneurial behavior in Russia have identified several possible ways of dealing with transactional problems. These include relational contracting, informal settlement, and the use of state arbitration, private arbitration commissions, or private enforcers. The studies have generally established a high reliance on relational and informal methods, a low but increasing use of state arbitration, and a substantial reliance on private enforcers.[29] At the same time, the findings tend to vary, because the probability of recourse to each of the above methods depends significantly on the nature of the business, its size, the time it was started, the previous occupation of the executive manager, and other variables. Those entrepreneurs who admit high expenditures on business protection are also less inclined to appeal to an arbitration court to resolve conflicts. They also display a higher readiness to resort to violence when confronted with cheating.[30] There are a number of factors beyond the

---

26. Estimates presented at the seminar of the chiefs of security services of Russian banks in Moscow in January 1995. Mikhail Pavlov, "Za kreditom v karmane" (For the credit in the pocket), *BDI* 2 (1995): 15.

27. Svetlana Glinkina, "Osobennosti tenevoi ekonomiki v Rossii" (Distinguishing features of Russia's shadow economy), *Nezavisimaia Gazeta,* 18 March 1998.

28. Annual inflation rates for 1992, 1993, and 1994 were 2,510, 840, and 220 percent respectively.

29. According to data collected in 1994, 20 percent of sampled entrepreneurs preferred to appeal to the state justice and enforcement system, 15 percent to "bandits" and private protection companies, 11 percent relied on themselves, 14 percent used other (unspecified) means for resolving disputes, and 40 percent did not respond. Cited in Vladimir Tambovtsev, *Gosudarstvo i perekhodnaya ekonomika: predely upravliaemosti* (Moscow: Teis, 1997), 76. A survey conducted in 1996–97 showed that 11 percent of sampled entrepreneurs were inclined to use violence to solve business problems, 42 percent have experienced the use of such a method, and 53 percent admitted regular payments for protection services. More than a third in this last category described the payments as substantial. Radaev, *Formirovanie novykh rossiiskikh rynkov,* 129, 174, 185.

30. Vadim Radaev, "Corruption and Violence in Russian Business in the Late 1990s," in *Economic Crime in Russia,* ed. Alena Ledeneva and Marina Kurkchiyan (London: Kluwer, 2000), 79–81. Radaev groups enterprises by the frequency of confronting violence and the expenditures they make on business protection. In the group with high expenditures for protection, 23 percent admit to the use of force and 14 percent appeal to courts; among those whose

control of researchers that affect the accuracy of the results of such surveys. First, in my experience, businessmen who work with enforcement partners from criminal groups are even more reluctant to reveal details of their business practices than the enforcement partners themselves. They would tend to be underrepresented in the samples. Second, while it is possible to distinguish analytically between the different means of resolving transactional problems, it is much harder to do so on the empirical level, since they are often combined in practice. According to my observations, informal meetings and settlements, which businessmen readily name as the method of dispute resolution, may actually involve the physical or symbolic—background—presence of enforcement partners. Even a verbal mention of them (e.g., "Let's not involve bandits, let us settle this peacefully") can sometimes function as an implicit appeal to private enforcers in the course of what counts as an informal settlement. Finally, there is evidence that, in some cases, businessmen first appeal to arbitration courts for a formal decision and then hand this decision to criminal elements for enforcement. This method, which businessmen could rightfully call the "use of state arbitration," is increasingly valued by criminal groups, because it protects them from allegations of extortion.[31]

The Low Reliance on State Justice

For a long time, the low level of reliance on the state's legal institutions remained one of the major preconditions for the spread of alternative methods of adjudication and enforcement. One cause of low reliance was the intricacy of existing laws, the low efficiency of the courts in handling matters, and weak enforcement. The privatization campaign was conducted in the context of poorly defined property rights, piecemeal and incomplete company laws, and lack of enforcement.[32] The creation of an efficient legal framework proceeded in a follow-up manner; the enactment of legislation lagged even further behind.[33] Since 1992, state arbitration courts (*arbitrazh*)

---

protection expenditures are at a moderate level, the figures are 10 and 22 percent, and among those with no private protection, 3.5 and 29 percent, respectively.

31. This was revealed by respondents 5 and 23 in the course of interviews. The practice is also mentioned in the study of criminal debt recovery by Piotr Skoblikov, *Vzyskanie dolgov i kriminal* (The collection of debts and crime) (Moscow: Yurist, 1999), 23.

32. Cheryl W. Gray and Kathryn Hendley, "Developing Commercial Law in Transition Economies: Examples from Hungary and Russia," in *The Rule of Law and Economic Reform in Russia,* ed. Jeffrey Sachs and Katharina Pistor (Boulder: Westview Press, 1997), 152.

33. Gordon Smith has termed the disjuncture between legal reform and law enforcement an "enforcement gap." See Gordon Smith, "The Disjuncture between Legal Reform and Law Enforcement: The Challenge Facing the Post-Yeltsin Leadership," in *State-Building in Russia: The Yeltsin Legacy and the Challenge of the Future,* ed. Gordon Smith (New York: M. E. Sharpe, 1999), 102.

have been responsible for handling commercial disputes.[34] According to the law, arbitration courts are to hear cases no later than two months after the appeal. In practice, however, the majority of cases in 1993–97 were processed much more slowly than prescribed, three to four months on average, with thousands of cases stalled for over a year.[35] This was an especially sensitive issue in default cases during periods of high inflation of the ruble, since courts could not grant judgments in foreign currencies.

A court verdict also did not lead to an immediate triumph of justice, because enforcement remained even more problematic. Formally, courts had bailiffs *(sudebnye ispolniteli)* for that purpose, but in practice they could do little in the face of widespread sabotage. To begin with, the state organs of justice have no responsibility for finding the debtor or property in cases where they cannot be found at their official address. The plaintiff is left to pursue the matter at his or her own cost. Furthermore, it is still common for companies to siphon off their assets to a different, specially established company in anticipation of juridical complications. A similar tactic is available to private individuals—they register their property in the names of their relatives, friends, mistresses, etc. This, for instance, explains an unexpectedly high proportion (over 35 percent) of women among the nominal owners of one of the most prestigious and expensive executive cars, the Mercedes 600, in St. Petersburg.[36] When it is acknowledged that valuable assets are not in the debtor's possession, the only thing court officials are required to do is to oblige the debtor to dedicate half his or her monthly salary to payment of the debt—which in reality amounts to no compensation at all. According to the claims made by the minister of justice in April 1995, only 50 percent of all court decisions involving property disputes were enforced. The minister also underscored an alarming tendency to reduce the number of appeals to arbitration courts in property disputes and explained it as the litigants' preference for out-of-court settlements.[37] Other sources place the enforcement rate for 1997 even lower, at 32 percent.[38]

---

34. There is also *Treteiskii sud,* the "third-party court" (mediation), which can be set up by the parties on the basis of certain formal rules prescribed by the law to resolve economic disputes, but its rate of use so far remains low. Economic cases in which one of the parties is not an entrepreneur can be heard by courts of general jurisdiction.

35. In 1993 the number of cases processed after the two-month deadline was over 236,000 (of 275,000); in 1994, 254,000 (of 285,000) of which more than 16,000 were kept in courts for over a year. The same tendency continued in 1997, with 539,000 delayed cases. Cited in Skoblikov, *Vzyskanie dolgov,* 45.

36. Data were collected and processed by the author together with the Agency for Journalistic Investigations, St. Petersburg.

37. "Esli diktatura, to tol'ko zakona" (If there is dictatorship, then it is only dictatorship of law), interview with the minister of justice of the Russian Federation, Valentin Kovalev, *Pravda,* 19 July 1995.

38. Cited in Skoblikov, *Vzyskanie dolgov,* 30.

Low efficiency and weak enforcement were not the only reasons for ig-
noring the official justice system. Unjustifiably high costs of legal economic activity, which can also be viewed as the cost of access to the state
system of justice, have pushed a great many active economic subjects into
using alternative justice mechanisms.[39] According to different estimates,
the shadow economy in the mid-1990s constituted between 20 and 45
percent of the GDP.[40] Among the major causes of growth in the shadow
economy, scholars most frequently name predatory and complicated taxation, the intricate and unstable character of bureaucratic norms, corruption, and the arbitrariness of executive powers.[41] It is important to note,
however, that only a small proportion of the shadow economy is constituted by illicit business and trade. The nature of business in large segments
of what is usually called the "shadow," "gray," or "informal" economy is
consistent with the law. Rather, it is because businessmen avoid formal relations with the state registration and taxation authorities and circumvent
the rules set by the latter that they do not make use of the state system of
justice inaccessible to businessmen due to the risks of punishment.[42] Until
the very end of the 1990s, formal taxes could reach up to 80 percent of
revenue, to which the indefinite and unpredictable costs informally
claimed by state bureaucracy should be added. The following statement
from a businessman from Omsk echoes the widespread justification for the
use of criminal protection: "We are prepared to work with the racket be-

39. On the costs of legal economic activity, see Ella Paneyakh, "Izderzhki legal'noi ekonomicheskoi deyatel'nosti i nalogovoe povedenie rossiiskikh predprinimatelei" (Costs of legal
economic activity and the tax behavior of Russian entrepreneurs), in *Konkurentsiya za nalogoplatel'shchika: Issledovaniya po fiskal'noi sotsiologii* (Competition for the taxpayer: Studies in fiscal sociology), ed. Vadim Volkov (Moscow: Moscow Social Science Foundation, 2000), 26–48.

40. The MVD assessment of the share of the shadow economy in the GDP is the following: 1991—10–11 percent; 1993—27 percent; 1994—39 percent; 1995—45 percent;
1996—46 percent. The State Committee for Statistics arrived at lower figures: 1992–94—
9–10 percent; 1995—20 percent; 1996—23 percent. Cited in Leonid Kosals, "Tenevaia
ekonomika kak osobennost' rossiiskogo kapitalisma" (The shadow economy as a feature of
Russian capitalism), *Voprosy ekonomiki* 10 (1998): 59.

41. V. Ispravnikov and V. Kupriyanov, *Tenevaia ekonomika v Rossii: Inoi put' i treiya sila*
(The shadow economy in Russia: Another way and a third power) (Moscow: n.p., 1997);
Tenevaia ekonomika v Rossii (The shadow economy in Russia) (Moscow: Fond Perspektivnye
tekhnologii, 1997); Tatiana Dolgopiatova, ed., *Neformal'yi sektor v rossiiskoi ekonomike* (The
informal sector in the Russian economy) (Moscow: Institut strategicheskogo razvitiya pred-
prinimatel'stva [Institute for the Strategic Development of Entrepreneurship], 1998).

42. For a study of tax evasion, see Eva Busse, "The Embededdness of Tax Evasion in Russia," in *Economic Crime in Russia*, ed. Alena Ledeneva and Marina Kurkchiyan (London:
Kluwer, 2000), 129–44.

cause it charges 10 percent [actually more—V. V.]. The state takes 90 percent in taxes, and even more in fines."[43]

Apart from the low efficiency and prohibitive costs of access to the state system of justice, there are more subtle reasons for entrepreneurs' and managers' low reliance on the law. As a study of Russian business relationships has revealed, "courts are not used partly because they are seen as destroyers of relationships."[44] Managers, especially those whose careers became intertwined in Soviet times, regard their networks as a valuable asset. In a similar vein, it has been argued that the low reliance on the law can be attributed more to residual traditional behavior with its inherent personalistic features than to formal cost-efficiency considerations. "The shift to relying on private contract enforcers," writes Kathryn Hendley, "is a more logical progression than a shift to relying on law, since it does not force the general director to cede power to impersonal forces."[45]

The Function of Enforcement Partnership

In contemporary business parlance, activities related to enforcement partnership are captured in a modest phrase, "to solve questions" *(reshat' voprosy)*. What does this involve? The early racketeering groups were mainly engaged in physical protection from other such groups and from outright swindling *(smotreli chtoby ne naezzhali i ne kidali)*. Part of this activity also entailed providing armed convoys to protect goods being transported. The leader of a criminal group testifies: "Early on we had a businessman who conducted charter trips to Sweden to import goods. We met him at the border and convoyed to Leningrad. But these were low profits, mainly in kind" (23).

As private business developed and the volume of transactions increased, enforcement partnership became more diverse and complex. The most mundane form was the monitoring of transactions *(soprovozhdenie sdelok)*, which consisted of collecting information about prospective contractors, meeting their enforcement partners, exchanging guarantees, and supervising the fulfillment of obligations. If complications arose, enforcement partners would agree on a form of compensation and then ensure that "their" busi-

---

43. Cited in Alla Chirikova, *Zhenshchina vo glave firmy* (Women as heads of the company) (Moscow: Institute of Sociology, 1998), 179–80.

44. Hertz, *Russian Business Relationships,* 111.

45. Kathryn Hendley, "Legal Development in Post-Soviet Russia," *Post-Soviet Affairs* 13, 3 (1997): 242.

nessmen follow the agreed-on scheme. From the interview with a *brigadir* of a Petersburg criminal group:

> Q: What did you do actually?
> A: Well, we had a large warehouse, for example, and we checked potential customers [i.e., those who loaned goods for retail trade], collected information about them, went to see their offices, found ways to arrange the whole thing so that they could not cheat. On the whole, we worked as an ordinary security service. Or when those businessmen could not pay back on time we met other businessmen's partners, so to speak. We asked them [the "partners"]: do you vouch for him? And they did, or conversely, if our businessman could not repay, we worked out a payment schedule, calculated when he could repay and gave our guarantees.
> Q: Was it not easier to cheat?
> A: What for? Then there will be a conflict, we'll have to hide. Who will run the business while we live on the mattresses? They cheat when the money is really big. (3)

Expert and interview sources indicate that the majority of high-value business agreements could only be concluded on the condition that enforcement partners, be they criminal groups or legal security services, participate and provide mutual guarantees. The mere absence of a recognized enforcement partner on one side could spoil the prospective deal. Consider the following case:

> A Moscow company negotiated a prospective contract with a Polish company to purchase twenty-five thousand U.S. dollars' worth of chocolate, for which the company hoped to receive fifty thousand U.S. dollars after selling it in Russia. The Moscow company applied to a bank to finance the lucrative deal but the bank demanded that its "roof" should first meet the "roof" of the trade company. The company did not have a "roof," and its director had to urgently find an old "friend" who dealt in private enforcement and ask him to join negotiations with the bank as his "roof." The loan was issued under the guarantees of the "friend."[46]

The "solving of questions" also involves obtaining licenses, registrations, permits, and so on for client enterprises from state authorities. Informal settlements with the state tax police are the most difficult task, requiring strong connections with local authorities. State authorities, such as fire or sanitation services, can also be employed to put pressure on competitors or debtors. "In the past, if someone refused to pay they could damage the shop

---

46. Cited in Skoblikov, *Vzyskanie dolgov,* 73.

or just burn it. Now they've understood that it is cheaper and safer to get fire inspection to close it down for a week or two. And the effect is the same" (4).

How do economic subjects pay for enforcement partnership and in what form? The evolution of enforcement partnership is described by the participants using three terms: "to collect" *(poluchat')*, "to control" *(kontrolirovat')*, and "to hold a share" *(byt' v dole)*. A brigade of racketeers "collects" (the tribute in cash) from a business in return for protection from other such brigades. A criminal group "controls" a business enterprise when, in addition to physical protection, it introduces into the enterprise its own bookkeeper or regular auditor who supplies information about business transactions and their value, while the group supervises and secures major contacts and transactions for a fixed share of profits. At this stage, the group can be said to have shifted from racketeering to enforcement partnership. When a group of violent entrepreneurs that "solves questions" for a given business enterprise invests its money into this enterprise and introduces its representative onto the board of directors, it becomes a shareholder and increases its share of the income. Most estimates made by experts and participants assess the cost of permanent enforcement partnerships with crime groups at 25–30 percent of the revenue of the client enterprise. Apart from cash, protection payments can take virtually any form that the parties find convenient, including insurance, rent for a trading spot, charity, particular services, and many more.

Piotr Skoblikov, the author of a comprehensive study on debt recovery in post-Soviet Russia, names three major ways of illegally settling a debt. The first involves a meeting between the enforcement partner of the creditor and that of the debtor, and, if the side of the creditor manages to produce documentary proof of the debt, the enforcement partner of the creditor takes responsibility for its repayment—normally by putting pressure on the indebted businessman to make him or her pay. In practice, debt recovery involves a lengthy investigations to locate the debtor and his or her assets, to establish their value, to collect information about the debtor's enforcement partners, and so on. If the enforcement partner is unknown or absent, the debtor, his family, or his property may be subjected to threats to compel him to either repay the debt or to come forth with an enforcement partner. It is not uncommon in a situation like this for businessmen to have to urgently find an enforcement partner. Once the meeting has been arranged, some sort of resolution, not necessarily a peaceful one, will follow.

The second option is purely criminal. It consists either of intimidating the creditor to make him forget the debt or of physically eliminating him—if the debt is markedly higher than the cost of contract killing. This solution, however, also depends on the creditor's level of protection and the probability of retaliation. According to a survey of entrepreneurs whose lives were seriously threatened, in 40 percent of cases they were required to forgive a large debt.[47]

The third possible option emerges when the two sides are unable to settle the dispute but are either not inclined to use strong-arm tactics or have used them but have reached a stalemate. In this case, an arbiter, normally a highly respected criminal authority, a *vor v zakone,* is invited to resolve the problem by the norms of criminal justice. In this case, by deciding to invite a *vor v zakone,* the conflicting sides recognize him as the highest authority and agree to be bound by his decision. In most cases, the price of debt recovery by criminal groups or of a third-party settlement is 50 percent of the debt.[48]

When analyzing enforcement partnerships, we should distinguish between the restitution of damage or the recovery of debts and preventive measures aimed at risk control. The first addresses past behavior (which has caused damage) and often involves a reference to future behavior (threats). The second presupposes a certain degree of control over other people's future behavior (fulfillment of contracts) and rests on the past record (reputation) of an enforcement partner rather than on the open threat of violence. It involves a mechanism of deterrence, which shapes the expectations of participants and involves, in the words of Schelling, the skillful nonuse of military forces.[49] Preventive risk control, relatively exempt from any formal criminal allegations, constituted an increasingly large share of the mundane activities of private enforcers throughout the 1990s.

When the crisis of nonpayment was most acute, it was also common for criminal groups to set up special subdivisions whose business it was to invent and enforce complex schemes for resolving the problem of nonpayment between enterprises. In his study, Skoblikov gives the following example. Machine-building enterprise X owes a large debt to electric power plant Y for electricity supplies but is short of cash to pay the debt. A direct barter exchange is impossible because Y does not need the products of X. Then, an intermediary (backed by criminal group N) finds oil-processing plant Z, located in a far-off region, which requires the machinery produced by X but is also short of cash. The intermediary compels plant X to supply Z with the necessary equipment, whose value is higher than the monetary equivalent of the debt of X to Y. In payment for the equipment, Z in turn supplies, at the wholesale price, gasoline to a company set up by N, which the latter then sells for cash through a chain of gas stations it controls. Then the intermedi-

47. V. Mazein, "Taktika vyzhivaniya biznessmena, kommersanta" (Survival tactics of businessmen, commercial employees), *Mir bezopasnosti* 5 (1998): 25. Cited in Skoblikov, *Vzyskanie dolgov,* 78.

48. Skoblikov, *Vzyskanie dolgov,* 76–81.

49. Thomas Schelling, *The Strategy of Conflict* (Cambridge: Harvard University Press, 1997), 9.

ary finds a crisis-hit coal-mining enterprise and compels it to supply to a certain quantity of coal to electric power plant Y at a discount rate, in payment for the debt of enterprise X, for which the intermediary pays cash to the mine. This chain, assembled and bound by the guarantees of private enforcers, can get them as much as 50 percent of the cash value of the debt of X to Y. The profit of criminal group N is derived from the discount received in each deal and from the difference between the wholesale and retail price of gasoline, which serves to convert the barter deals into cash.[50]

Since the late 1980s, by means of spontaneous invention, imitation, and trial and error, various individuals and groups discovered certain methods that allowed them to earn incomes by using force and to increase them by reducing their own costs. We have called these methods violent entrepreneurship and accounted for its major forms: physical protection and enforcement partnership. Physical protection, which consists in the use of force to deter threats and which at the origin was little more than protection racket, is the first elementary form of violent entrepreneurship. Enforcement partnership is a more sophisticated relationship that involves risk control, supervision of contracts as well as creation of competitive advantages by violent entrepreneurs for the client enterprises. Both forms contain a key element: the capacity to determine or limit the course of action of other participants in the economic market, either by means of direct physical coercion or by affecting their expectations. It is this very capacity that constitutes the utility or the "service" that violent entrepreneurs provide and that allows economic subjects to continue or expand their business activities. The purchase of this service is compulsory, although in the condition of multiplicity of violence-managing agencies its provider can be a matter of choice and its price—of negotiation.

We should also mention the structural outcome of the activities of violent entrepreneurs that differs from their intended goals, such as income, survival, or expansion. The set of activities related to enforcement partnership, whether performed by criminal groups, private protection companies, formal and informal security services, or other violence-managing agencies, creates a certain structured environment that provides at least some degree of predictability and order in the otherwise chaotic markets during the period of their formation. This becomes possible once different violence-managing agencies, through conflicts, agreements, and daily practice, work out a set of common rules for governing the field of economic exchange. However primitive, until the end of the 1990s this set of rules remained simpler, more convenient, and, most importantly, much better enforced than the incipient system of state justice.

50. Skoblikov, *Vzyskanie dolgov,* 84–85.

Thieves and Bandits

Before we address the problem of how the system of rules governing the behavior of violent entrepreneurs and their relations with economic agents emerged and evolved, let us introduce another agent that participated in this process. In our analysis of violent entrepreneurship and its function, we have so far confined ourselves to the new criminal groups created and led primarily by former athletes, former members of the military, or other specialists in violence, who had few previous connections to the traditional criminal culture. They brought the organizational skills and norms of their previous professions into the new one. Alongside the new groups that responded to the crisis of state socialism and the advance of capitalist relations and ideology, there remained a powerful legacy of the traditional Soviet underworld that was affected by, and itself exerted an influence on, the changing social-economic realities. Inasmuch as the transformation undermined the socialist state and society, it divided and hollowed out the traditional underworld. In just a few years, the challenge posed by the advance of the new criminal groups oriented purely toward racketeering and the quick capitalization of criminal finances have changed almost all aspects of the old criminal fraternity except its facade. The basic concepts that the waning criminal tradition managed to transmit to its successor were further redefined by changing practices. My general understanding, which emerged from numerous conversations with people from both sides of the legal divide, is that despite a certain continuity on the level of personalities, the underlying rift between the traditional Soviet underworld and the new world of violent entrepreneurs is much stronger than is often assumed.

The World of Thieves

The criminal fraternity, known as *vorovskoi mir,* the world of thieves, crystallized in Soviet prisons and labor camps in the 1930s. Since the pathbreaking structuralist analysis of the thieves' oral culture, published in 1935 by the future leading specialist in medieval Slavonic literature, Dmitrii Likhachev, after his release from a camp, the world of thieves has received a fair amount of scholarly attention.[51] The world of thieves is an informal so-

---

51. Dmitrii Likhachev, "Cherty pervobytnogo primitivizma vorovskoi rechi" (Primitive features in the speech of thieves), in *Yazyk i myshlenie,* proceedings of the USSR Academy of Science, vols. 3 and 4 (Moscow: Akademiya nauk, 1935), 3:47–100; Valerii Chalidze, *Criminal Russia: Essays on Crime in the Soviet Union* (New York: Random House, 1977); Alexander Gurov, *Professional'naya prestupnost'* (Professional crime) (Moscow: Yuridicheskaya literatura, 1990); Alexander Gurov and Ivan Ryabinin, *Ispoved' vora v zakone* (The confession of a thief-in-law) (Moscow: Rosagropromizdat, 1991); Viacheslav Razinkin, *Vory v zakone i prestupnye*

ciety and a subculture that united "professional" thieves of various kinds and regulated their relations with one another and with the outside world. A particular jargon, an ideology, initiation and exclusion rituals, a strict code of norms, a hierarchical organization, and communal funds are its distinguishing features. The leadership of the world of thieves consists of the so-called *vory v zakone,* which is normally translated either in a straightforward manner as "thieves-in-law" or, more loosely, as "thieves professing the code."[52] Henceforth, following current usage, I will also call them simply *vory,* or "thieves," but will imply the closed elite fraternity insofar as it personifies and propagates the norms of a broader criminal society.

The world of thieves had several predecessors but no clear beginning. It turned into a powerful countrywide organization only with the rise of the system of labor camps which, as Federico Varese puts it, "supplied a source of contacts for criminals and an opportunity to share their experiences and devise ways of promoting their common interests."[53] Internal migrations in the Gulag archipelago and the high turnover rate of inmates spread the culture and organization of the *vory* within and outside the realm where it had been conceived. Since the raison d'être of the society of the *vory v zakone* was first of all the organization and governance of inmates to enable them to survive the harsh camp regime and even to exploit it, prison life was its ultimate system of reference. The society also extended into civic life to govern and exploit active thieves who were, understandably, either former or future inmates. Camp authorities, though declared the major enemy by the *vory,* also had an interest in them as agents of order and it was not unusual for these authorities to use the *vory* to manage inmates. Generally, the more strong and oppressive the state regime became, the more organized and powerful the underworld was.

The best way to understand the society of *vory v zakone,* the governing elite in the world of thieves, is to describe the system of norms that its representatives observed. The first rule prohibited cooperation with any state authorities. Anyone who had ever served in the army or worked for or been a member of a state organization could never aspire to receive the title of thief-in-law. "The major collective representation of thieves that determined their relations with external reality is their idea of a struggle between the two

klany (Thieves-in-law and criminal clans) (Moscow: Kriminologicheskaya assotsiatsiya, 1995); Joseph Serio and Viacheslav Razinkin, "Thieves Professing the Code: The Traditional Role of *Vory v Zakone* in Russia's Criminal World and Adaptations to a New Social Reality," *Low-Intensity Conflict and Law Enforcement* 4, 1 (summer 1995): 72–88; Federico Varese, "The Society of the *Vory-v-zakone,* 1930s–1950s," *Cahiers du Monde Russe* 39, 4 (October–December 1999): 515–38.

52. This translation is preferred by Serio and Razinkin.
53. Varese, "The Society of the *Vory-v-zakone,*" 525.

worlds," writes Likhachev. "The thief, like a primitive man, divides the whole world into two parts, 'its own'—the 'good one'—and 'the alien'—the 'bad one'."[54] A consistent and conspicuous rejection of any order from state authorities, whatever it may cost the thief, constituted a major element of his behavioral idiom. Some fundamental norms of thieves (and their prison records) were tattooed on their bodies. Thus, a typical tattoo reads: "The authoritative thief is an uncompromising rejecter" *(avtoritetnyi vor—neprimirimyi otritsala)*.[55] Rejection often led to severe punishments by prison authorities, such as solitary confinement in an especially rough cell *(kartser)*. But after the punishment had been taken, the standing of the "martyr" improved and a tattoo signifying this event in the thief's career would appear on his body. The body thus became a kind of book where other inmates could read the thief's personal history, provided they knew the code. This practice earned *vory* the name *sinie,* "the blue ones," a reference to the color of tattoos. The complex of norms that prohibited any relation with state authorities was tied to the function of boundary maintenance performed by thieves-in-law, that is, to the reproduction of the underworld as a separate system pure of representatives of the "alien" system and secure from its interventions.

The more consistently the true *vory* rejected the formal system, the more ardently they embraced their own. Another set of norms promoted the thieves' devotion to their fraternity and their profession. It performed an integrating function. It was forbidden for a thief to have a wife and family. He also had to turn his back on his kin—mother, father, brothers, etc. Another prominent tattoo says: "I won't forget my own mother." "Mother" refers here to the thieves' family, which gave the bearer of the tattoo a second birth, rather than the biological mother. In fact, a large number of early Soviet thieves began their careers after escaping from an orphanage. The oath not to forget, then, implied permanent support of the crime family, mutual help, and allegiance to the code. The code also prohibited work, since the true thief can live only on what has been stolen. Any physical labor would undermine his honor and status.

The third set of norms regulated relations among members of the world of thieves, including those among *vory v zakone* themselves. It has to do with the function of mediation and tension management in the criminal commu-

---

54. Dmitrii Likhachev, "Cherty pervobytnogo primitivizma vorovskoi rechi" (Primitive features in the speech of thieves), published as an appendix to *Slovar tiuremno-lagerno-blatnogo zhargona,* ed. Danzik Baldaev (Moscow: Kraia Moskvy, 1992), 366.

55. Danzik Baldaev, ed., *Slovar tiuremno-lagerno-blatnogo zhargona* (A dictionary of prison camp slang) (Moscow: Kraia Moskvy, 1992), 462.

The leader of the Akulovskaya criminal group, Alexander "Sasha-Akula" Anisimov (left), with his buddy, "the Chinese." Heavy tattoos testify to long prison experience and allegiance to the traditional criminal culture. By permission of the Agency for Journalistic Investigations, St. Petersburg.

nity. Strict norms regulated the use of violence and generally tended to prohibit it unless it was sanctioned by a collective decision of *vory,* normally against those who betrayed the fraternity or insulted a *vor v zakone.* In general, however, thieves were supposed to steal, swindle, or rob without bloodshed, but in particular circumstances, such as the defense of thieves' honor, killing was endorsed. The world of thieves lived by its own system of unwritten laws. Thieves-in-law, then, were the bearers of the knowledge of such laws and, accordingly, of their application to the practice of criminal justice. According to the *vor v zakone* Evgenii Vasin ("Dzhem"), the leading criminal authority in Russia's Far East until his death in custody in November 2001, "A thief-in-law they call a person, who can pass the just judgment, who can achieve a resolution without bloodshed. This is what I used to do in prison."[56] Another word for *vor v zakone* is *zakonnik,* which literally means "lawyer." One of my respondents defined this category as follows: "*Vor v zakone* is like a doctor of informal law" (1). All important decisions were to be taken and grave disputes settled according to the "justice" *(po spravedlivosi)*

56. *Kommersant,* 5 October 2001, 12.

at a *skhodka,* a thieves' gathering. No killing of a *vor,* for instance, could be carried out without the prior approval of a *skhodka. Vory* were responsible for organizing *skhodkas* (normally disguised as weddings or birthday celebrations) and for enforcing their decisions.

Finally, in addition to the norms related to boundary maintenance, integration, and tension management were those that address the economic reproduction of the world of thieves. The economic base was the so-called *obshchak,* the communal fund (actually consisting of several independent funds) to which all *vory* had to donate all their income and from which they received material support, especially when serving their prison terms. The "classic" *obshchak* was used first and foremost to provide supplies of money, goods, food, tobacco, and drugs to prisons and labor camps; its purpose was to "warm up the zone" *(gret' zonu).* The resources of the *obshchak* were used to provide start-up money for those just released and, later, to bribe officials to waive imprisonment or reduce its duration. Thus, the prospect of getting guaranteed support from the *obshchak* mitigated possible deprivations caused by the "zone," reduced the fear of imprisonment, and thereby encouraged thieves to remain faithful to the profession once chosen. As a widespread tattoo says: "Prison is my native home" *(tiur'ma-dom rodnoi).*

Accordingly, *vory v zakone* were entrusted to manage the *obshchak.* Those elements of their code of behavior that prescribed an ascetic lifestyle, forbade luxury, and permitted only a minimum of necessary property followed from the responsibility for the common fund. Excessive consumption might cause suspicions about misappropriation of the common money—a sin punishable by death. Also, it was the image of the *vor* as a personification of faith and faithfulness in the underworld brotherhood that turned many old-style *vory* into zealous ascetics. After all, their power over criminals rested neither on violence nor on wealth but on a kind of moral authority backed by tradition.

How did someone become a *vor v zakone?* To achieve this status, an individual had to have an "ideal" criminal biography beginning at an early age, containing no association with the state, and revealing an impressive prison record and episodes of the "right" behavior vis-à-vis state authorities and his own fraternity. The authoritative *vor* Vasia Buzulutskii, for instance, served his first term at the age of fourteen, spending, with a few short breaks, almost forty years in various prisons and camps. Another legendary *vor* of the old persuasion, Vladimir Baboushkin ("Vas'ka Brilliant") served ten prison terms, almost his entire life.[57] A candidate for the title *vor v zakone* had to earn respect through his character, intellect, and faithfulness to traditions—

57. Modestov, *Moskva banditskaya,* 79–80.

as evaluated from the perspective of the criminal profession. The initiation ritual of "coronation" could be conducted only on receipt of recommendations from three or more *vory*. Its central element was an oath of allegiance.

There were of course many more rules and features pertaining to the society of the thieves-in-law. Some changed but the chief ones survived until the 1980s, as did the criminal society itself. My analysis is confined to those properties that make up the ideal type, since a systematic comparison between the *vory* and the new *bandity*, to which I now turn, is possible only by constructing the respective ideal types.

Ideal Types Compared

The term *bandit*, as it is currently used in Russian, has no connotations related to the classic "social" bandit so perceptively analyzed by the historian Eric Hobsbawm.[58] The classic bandit, a dangerous inhabitant of forests and mountains, was the mortal enemy of authorities, the instigator and leader of peasant revolts, who eventually ended his life on the scaffold. In contrast, the current Russian usage refers to the stationary urban bandit well integrated into commercial activity but armed and always ready to resort to violence. He is well connected to local authorities and beloved of middlebrow fiction and the movie industry. Anyone who lived in a Russian city for more than a month would easily recognize this type by his physical proportion, gestures, speech, haircut, clothing, and, of course, his car: a BMW, Mercedes or huge 4x4.[59] This is, so to speak, the phenomenological aspect. His social definition, as we discussed at length at the beginning of this chapter, is that of a violent entrepreneur.

Unlike bandits, thieves are not engaged in violent entrepreneurship. The thief's major task is to steal (in a broad sense) and to avoid being caught. Thieves do not produce anything and tend to keep a low profile except in their own milieu. The bandit, on the contrary, considers himself a producer of certain services or at least makes such claims to his clients. His claim to being productive and his ability to affect business transactions is derived from his capacity to apply and manage organized force. This capacity must be conspicuous, since it represents the group's major market resource and the source of income. Hence the elaborate system of external symbolic attributes (gold jewelry, sports haircuts, leather jackets,) and an easily recog-

58. Eric Hobsbawm, *Bandits* (London: Delacorte Press, 1969).
59. In popular usage, the acronym BMW was taken to stand for *boevaia mashina vymogatelei,* combat vehicle for extortionists.

nizable assertive style of behavior. Thieves would be difficult to identify in urban public places, while bandits are easily recognizable.

The thief's income comes from the illegal secondary redistribution of property and consists of the appropriation, by illegal means, of the private possessions of other citizens or of state property. The bandit aspires to receive a share of other entrepreneurs' income, which, as he claims, has been produced under the patronage or with the participation of the organized group he represents. His income, therefore, is derived from the redistribution of profit and takes the form of either fixed tribute or profit share (tax). Since they are a type of entrepreneur, bandits seek a regular income on the basis of a long-term business relationship and often claim to maintain order and protect property, which is why they can sometimes come into direct conflict with thieves—for instance, forcing them out of city markets and nightclubs.

The ethos of thieves is a projection of the values and rules of prison life into civic ("free") life. Prison and labor camp records are the major source of thieves' authority, respect, and career advancement to the highest rank of thief-in-law. The bandits' mores were formed in civilian life and are more rational and practical, containing fewer prohibitions and constraints. Cooperation with representatives of the state is unproblematic for them, especially if it delivers concrete commercial benefits. The bandit's reputation and his rise to the elite position of *avtoritet* (authority) is built on the precedents of successful and stern use or management of violence; of central importance is the combination of an adept use of force and organizational skills. In contrast to thieves, who tend to rely on the force of argument, bandits rely on the argument of force. The nature of the *avtoritet*'s power is close to what is called "political power," which rests on coercive capacity.[60] The power of thieves is much more dependent on moral authority and tradition; it is an example of normative power.

Unlike thieves, many bandit groups ban alcohol and drugs. They cultivate a healthy lifestyle, strict discipline, and physical fitness maintained in specially rented gyms, which serve as one of the permanent meeting grounds for the group. If the system of thieves' values and mores ensures their capacity for group survival in the severe repressive conditions of the Soviet labor camps, the value system of the bandits is functionally subject to the reproduction of the group's capacity to participate in the economic life of society as violent entrepreneurs. Thus, if the world of thieves is a product of the strong repressive socialist state, the world of bandits emerges from the illegal use of violence under the conditions of weak-state capitalism.

60. See Gianfranco Poggi, *The State: Its Nature, Development, and Prospects* (Stanford: Stanford University Press, 1990), 1–18.

Conflict and Rationalization

The differences between the two criminal cultures created tensions and sometimes caused violent conflicts. Vladimir Kumarin, the current leader of the Tambovskaya crime group in Petersburg, is reported to consistently reject the *vory* ideology and to denigrate thieves, saying: "Why feed those parasites?"[61] Most *avtoritety* regard *vory* as relics of a bygone age and refuse to follow their rules. *Vory,* in turn, respond with a contemptuous attitude, disparagingly calling them *sportsmeny,* "sportsmen." Driven by fear and resentment, *vory* accuse *sportsmeny* of indiscriminate violence, lack of intelligence, and unjustified ambitions. In the city of Ekaterinburg, Handelman recorded a conversation with an old-style criminal who bitterly admitted that the new gangsters no longer paid his kind due respect: "What is going on now is terrible. The old values are gone."[62] Andrei Konstantinov cites a confession of the *vor v zakone* Yurii Alekseev ("Gorbatyi") describing how the old criminal tradition has degenerated under the pressure of those who "respect only force and not brains."[63]

Normative contradictions became intertwined with concrete conflicts of economic interest. Bandits were aggressive and flexible enough to quickly subject large segments of emerging private businesses to their control and to devise methods of earning permanent incomes. Thieves, in turn, tried to subject the new bandits to their authority by contaminating the latter with their ideology, mobilizing prison networks to confront the advance of bandits, and pointedly using strong-arm tactics. Konstantinov also cites a letter circulated by authoritative thieves: "All the right people should read this *maliava* [the letter], follow it, and inform others. All the right people should assist in the collection of the *obshchak* for the needs of thieves. All cooperatives should pay a cut of their money into the thieves' *obshchak*. All of that should be controlled by people from the prison world and in no way by sportsmen or other dogs."[64] Disputes over spheres of influence often turned into gang wars and a chain of contract killings. Consequently, a certain division was established, by which some regions fell under the influence of bandits and others became the domains of *vory v zakone*. Thus, three large industrial regions, Petersburg, Ekaterinburg, and, arguably, Novosibirsk, are known as *banditskie* and are accordingly exempt from the influence of *vory*. The latter, in turn, continue to hold strong positions in the far eastern and

61. Cited in Andrei Konstantinov, *Banditskii Peterburg 98* (Moscow: Olma-Press, 1999), 74.

62. Stephen Handelman, *Comrade Criminal: Russia's New Mafiya* (New Haven: Yale University Press, 1995), 88.

63. Konstantinov, *Banditskii Peterburg 98,* 88.

64. Ibid., 73.

southern regions of the Russian Federation.[65] In the Moscow region, after a series of ruthless wars, the two subcultures have reached an equilibrium and tend to cooperate.[66]

In the face of growing competition, the *vory* were led to adapt their normative system and organization to the new realities, where violence and commerce ruled. Thus many basic tenets of the *vory* gradually became mere slogans that concealed a changing practice. In fact, the first signs of corruption emerged much earlier, parallel to the corruption of the Soviet system under Brezhnev. In 1982, at a *skhodka* held in Tbilisi in Georgia, *vory* debated the sensitive issue of whether they should get involved in politics. The Georgian *vory* suggested expanding relations with corrupt officials, while the Russian "purists," led by Vas'ka Brilliant, insisted on the sanctity of the tradition. The schism widened over time, and many Georgian *vory* began to infiltrate the establishment, as did Djaba Ioseliani, who became the right-hand man of Georgian President Eduard Shevardnadze.[67]

The younger generation of *vory*, while calling for the revival of tradition, managed to change its substance. Prison life did not go well with their growing involvement in commercial activities. Consequently, they spent less time in the "zone," and the traditional source of their authority became less important. In addition, it became possible for young aspiring criminals to buy the title of *vor v zakone*—a classic sign of corruption for any traditional elite. Respect for the purchased title would naturally be low, but this could now be compensated for by concrete commercial influence. In 1991 a young *vor*, Leonia "Mackintosh," was co-opted to the board of directors of the Moscow bank "Stolichnyi," after which a considerable sum of money was siphoned off, allegedly into the *obshchak*.[68]

The changing function of the *obshchak* can also be viewed as evidence of the rationalization of the world of thieves. As the private banking sector began to grow in the early 1990s, *obshchak* money was increasingly capitalized. It was first deposited into existing or specially created banks and then invested into commercial enterprises. The impact of the changing social-economic conditions is reflected in the career of the *vor v zakone* Pavel Zakharov (Pasha "Tsiroul'"). Tsiroul' began his career in the 1950s in the clas-

---

65. Razinkin, *Vory v zakone*, 17; Konstantinov, *Banditskii Peterburg 98*, 74–77.

66. For bandits, the risk of imprisonment, that is, the possibility of being transferred to the realm where the *vory* exerted unconditional authority and could take revenge, was a significant argument in favor of cooperation. A purely bandit group could also co-opt a *vor* as a "lawyer" to represent the interests of the group in disputes with traditional criminals. The former leading Petersburg *avtoritet* Alexander Malyshev, for example, retained for this purpose thief-in-law Slava "Kirpich," a recognized expert on traditional criminal scholastics.

67. Serio and Razinkin, "Thieves Professing the Code," 76.

68. Razinkin, *Vory v zakone*, 64.

sic way, as a pickpocket, and was first convicted at the age of fifteen. His five subsequent prison terms lasted more than twenty years. By the late 1980s Tsiroul' became a leading *vor* in Moscow and the manager of the biggest *obshchak*. He built himself a three-storied mansion outside Moscow, where he kept five luxury cars and a van in the underground garage. In violation of another norm, he had a spouse who lived with him (though legally registered as his brother's wife). But it was the accusation that he had mishandled the *obshchak* that brought him into conflict with an influential orthodox thief, Vasia "Ochko." Ochko condemned Tsiroul' for lending communal money to businessmen and appropriating the interest for personal needs. The conflict between the two leaders, which was debated at several *skhodkas*, continued until Ochko's disappearance. In the meantime, Tsiroul' increasingly turned to racketeering, the drug trade, and commerce and became the leader of a powerful criminal group. In December 1994 he was arrested and spent more than two years in custody. Pavel "Tsiroul'" Zakharov did not live to see his trial and died in January 1997 from an overdose of drugs.[69] The most remarkable and highly symbolic event in the whole story is his written abdication of the title of *vor v zakone*, which, according to some sources, he submitted to the Moscow prosecutor general shortly before his death in an attempt to earn release from prison: "I ask not to be regarded as a *vor v zakone* because I was incorrectly crowned in 1953, with violations of thieves' laws and traditions."[70]

69. Modestov, *Moskva banditskaya,* 103–5; Trabarin, *Vory v zakone i avtoritety,* 98–125.
70. Cited in Trabarin, *Vory v zakone i avtoritety,* 125.

3.

The Violence-Managing Agency

Now that we have defined violent entrepreneurship as organizational solutions and action strategies that enable organized violence to be converted into money or other valuable assets on a permanent basis, we can look at criminal groups as violence-managing agencies. In reality, there are almost as many kinds of organized criminal groups as there are forms of illegal activity. Law enforcement experts would list groups of swindlers, car thieves whose work requires an especially well-coordinated division of tasks, organizations of robbers, drug-traffickers, and so on. In the practice of law enforcement, when a crime is committed by a person as a member of an organized group the penalty increases significantly. Accordingly, any group comprising three or more people who coordinate their illegal activities can be classified as an organized criminal group.

This is not how I have defined organized criminal groups. My research indicates that traditional criminal groups, such as swindlers, drug dealers, pickpockets, and so on, are often affiliated with a core group. In their language, this is expressed by such phrases as to "work with" or "work under" X. Core group X does not itself engage in traditional criminal activities, except for the illegal use of force and threats, but exercises protective and governing functions in relation to other groups. It regards other groups as "businesses" that must pay a share of their profit. Moreover, such businesses are not necessarily illegal. Several legal enterprises can also have an affiliation with the core group alongside purely criminal ventures. For the core group, both categories are regarded as taxpayers and objects of protection and governance. The nature of this affiliation we earlier called "enforcement partnership." Although the business of affiliated groups can vary across a wide spectrum of activities, from prostitution to multimedia production, the nature of the business of the core group remains constant: violent entrepreneurship. In this study, by organized criminal group or organized criminal society I mean the core group rather than its affiliated businesses, whatever their level of organization and relations with the law. The organized criminal group is thus defined with reference to its activity as a violence-managing agency. The analytical definition, which places the main emphasis on the group's capacity to manage organized force (and information), has its empirical referent in a specific organization, normative patterns, and practices that distinguish such groups from other enterprises. This, then, is the general methodological rule observed throughout this chapter: examine those aspects of criminal groups that refer to their capacity to manage organized force and thereby to earn a permanent income.

As violence-managing agencies, criminal groups can vary depending on the proportion of criminal to legal businesses they control. This is not a static parameter, however. The evolution of criminal groups sometimes leads them away from "working with" criminal business and into the sphere of legal commerce. At a certain point, this orientation becomes an important differentiating factor. In Russia of the 1990s, violence-managing agencies also differed by legal status and relation to the state. These two variables led us to classify violence-managing agencies as follows: private and illegal (organized criminal groups); nonstate (private) and legal (private protection companies); and state and illegal (units of state police and security forces acting as private entrepreneurs). There is also a fourth type, public and legal, which coincides with our understanding of the state. The remaining part of the book is structured by this classification and arranged chronologically to chart the actual developments in Russia throughout the 1990s. In this and the following chapter I will concentrate on criminal groups and leave the state largely out of the picture. Then I will gradually bring the state back in by shifting the focus to the other two types, namely, informal groups of state employees and private protection companies. Finally, I will account for the fourth type, the state, as it forms by suppressing or regulating the activity of other violence-managing agencies and seeking a monopoly over the use of force, justice, and taxation.

Organized Criminal Group

The language participants of criminal groups use to refer to their organizations is of course different from how the law enforcement agencies define them. The language of participants is part of their form of life and is instrumental in their daily activities. Its concepts are never clearly defined, and a great deal of meaning is implied without being spelled out. The substitution of objective definitions for the vague language of practice is essential for some social institutions, especially those that exercise justice or conduct scientific research. In the practice of law enforcement, definitions are by no means neutral, since they constitute part and parcel of the actions taken against crime. The term *associazione a delinquere* (association for criminal purposes), writes Blok, "was invented by the judicial authorities to facilitate the mass arrests of mafiosi during 1926 and 1927 carried out by Mori, Prefect of Palermo of the time."[1]

Members of organized crime, on the contrary, tend to avoid any fixed terms for their organization. The Sicilian mafiosi did not invent and rarely used the term "Mafia," while their colleagues in the United States, for instance, referred to their world and its traditions as "la cosa nostra" but did not designate any concrete organization.[2] Participants in Russia do use a number of terms that denote certain elements of the organization, such as *brigada,* the basic operational unit of a criminal group, but they never refer to the entire structure using a generic term.

Russian law enforcement agencies, by contrast, employ two generic terms: *organizovannaya prestupnaya gruppirovka* (abbreviated OPG), that is, "organized criminal group," and *organizovannoe prestupnoe soobshchestvo* (OPS), "organized criminal society." An OPS may comprise a number of relatively autonomous OPGs and is therefore larger than the latter. There is also a qualitative difference, in that the OPS has a strong direct involvement in the economic realm through multiple forms of ownership and it has connections with the political realm through informal patronage and even formal representation in legislative bodies. In this chapter I will discuss OPGs for the most part and refer to them simply as "criminal groups," in accordance with a more conventional term, *prestupnaya gruppirovka.*

Names and Origins

How do participants refer to criminal groups? Normally, they simply invoke the group's name in the plural, adding the ending (*-skie*) that signifies belonging and origin (e.g., *podol'-skie, uralmashev-skie*). The name of the group refers originally to a territory or to the nature of the ties that created

---

1. Anton Blok, *The Mafia of a Sicilian Village: A Study of Violent Peasant Entrepreneurs* (Oxford: Basil Blackwell, 1974), 144.
2. Diego Gambetta, *The Sicilian Mafia: The Business of Private Protection* (Cambridge: Harvard University Press, 1993), 138.

initial trust among members. Variations in naming patterns reflect differences in the original mechanisms of group formation. In Petersburg, for example, the first racketeering groups called *brigady*, "brigades," grew out of two sorts of primary ties: nonresident students' communes *(zemliachestva)* and sports schools. Thus, in 1988 several students who came to receive a higher education in the institutes of what was then Leningrad (including the Institute of Physical Culture) from the town of Tambov formed what was destined to become the most influential criminal group in Petersburg. The group was dubbed *tambovskie*. Many nonresident communes from other cities (Murmansk, Vorkuta, Perm', Kazan') also became centers of gravity for former sportsmen and other individuals willing to earn their livings through the use of force. Thus emerged *murmanskie, vorkutinskie, permskie, kazanskie,* and the like. Groups formed by Leningrad residents recruited local sportsmen (mainly boxers, weight lifters, and wrestlers) whose cohesion and trust had initially formed during their joint athletic careers. In contrast to the toponymical labeling of the migrant brigades, the names of local ones were derived either from the kind of sport (e.g. *bortsovskaya brigada*, the wrestlers' brigade) or from the name of the leader—hence *malyshevskie* (from A. Malyshev), *kudriashevskie* (from P. Kudriashev), and *komarovskie* (from Yu. Komarov). In the city of Nizhnii Tagil, a racketeering group took the name of the sports club "Fortuna" from which it emerged. Ethnically based groups, active in many Russian cities, were named after either a particular ethnic group (e.g. *azerbaidzhantsy, chechentsy*) or a regional group (*kavkaztsy*, the Caucasians). In some cases, group names contained an overt reference to a criminal subculture, such as the Ekaterinburg group led by thieves-in-law and called *sinie*, "the blue ones," or to war veterans, like *afgantsy*, the Afghans.

In Moscow, toponyms prevailed. The major criminal groups and, accordingly, their names, emerged in the late 1980s in peripheral Moscow districts, such as Solntsevo, Izmailovo, Liubertsy, and Orekhovo, or in the small satellite towns that surround the capital: Podol'sk, Balashikha, Noginsk, Koptev, and Dolgoproudnyi. The powerful Taganskaya group was named after a central district in the capital. Although it is generally true that, over a period of time, these districts served as the power base for various criminal groups, assumptions about the territorial confines of a criminal group's activities and about its strictly ethnic basis are not correct. As a criminal group expands, it admits new members unrelated to the place of origin of the group's founding core; likewise, its major business activities quickly transcend its original topography. The name remains, however. The irrelevance of a fixed territory is well illustrated by the widespread presence of criminal groups from the distant Siberian towns of Novokuznetsk and Kourgan in Moscow and from

Perm' and Kazan' in Petersburg. Over time, names like *solntsevskie* and *podol'skie* preserve as little actual connection to respective Moscow territories as *kourganskie* and *permskie* do to Siberian towns.

The nicknames of the leaders of criminal groups are derived in a similar manner. Among low- and mid-level members, traditional criminal nicknames referring to certain animals (elephants, cats, bulls, etc.), tools (sledgehammers, nails, bolts, etc.), or any other suitable object (e.g., "Broiler," "Antibiotic") prevail. They resemble the names of chiefs of Native Americans but are generally more prosaic and concise. A different pattern obtains among the upper ranks. Their nicknames tend to be derived by adding to one's given name a topographical adjective referring to a place of origin (this is not a strict rule, however). This is achieved by adding the ending *-skii* to the geographical name, a concise way to denote that person X comes from place Y. Thus we have Vitia Kourganskii, Vasia Brianskii, Fedia Krymskii, Stepa Ulyanovskii, and so on, referring to Kourgan, Briansk, the Crimea, and Ulyanovsk, respectively. The derivation pattern resembles that of the medieval gentry, whose "surnames," in themselves a privilege at a time when this institution was generally nonexistent, referred to the lands they owned and governed. Reference to the land was often expressed by adding the particle "of" in English or *de* in French, or the ending *-skii* in the Slavic languages. I am not suggesting that criminal group leaders sought to ennoble themselves by imitating aristocratic forms in their nicknames. A reverse assumption is more plausible: the "surnames" of the medieval warrior nobility functioned like nicknames.

Flags, Trademarks, and Reputations

Many criminal groups have gradually lost their original direct connection to some obscure suburb, sports club, ethnicity, or founding leader. But if the name of the group is meaningless in the sense that it does not represent anything, this does not mean it is useless. On the contrary, the importance of the institution of names becomes apparent when we look at their practical usage. In the practice of violent entrepreneurship, the names of criminal groups are used as "flags" and "trademarks" with specific reputations attached to them.

I noticed that, in some instances, when participants spoke about themselves or others joining a certain criminal group, they used a curious expression: "to stand up under a flag" *(vstat' pod flag)*. A *brigadir* of the Komarovskaya group said of group formation:

> First there is a core, then young people appeal to them, like, we want to stand up under your flag. They get admitted to the group. At the start, they receive

five hundred U.S. dollars per month each plus a car and a mobile phone for two. They may ask, what's the mobile for? The answer they get is: it's not you but us who need your phone, so that you can always be at hand. In 1990 *tambovskie* did everything but hang notices on billboards to recruit people under their flag. (20)

Flags are symbols of military units of various types and sizes; joining such a unit and fighting for it means identifying with its flag and pledging allegiance to it. In the case of criminal groups, which did not have actual flags of their own, "to stand up under a flag" means to join a criminal group and to fight for its interests. Since participants often perceive criminal groups as military units of sorts, the flag image makes sense. Bandits can also transfer from one group to another, as if changing regiments and, accordingly, flags. The association is especially relevant in the case of an emergency mobilization: "Normally they worked as loosely connected groups. But in case of emergency, in one day *kazanskie* could gather two or three hundred soldiers under their flag" (9).

But the identity and solidarity function of symbols, so profoundly analyzed by Emile Durkheim, is not the major reason criminal group names can be associated with flags. The role of group names is more important for intergroup relations than for in-group solidarity. It is in the practice of violent entrepreneurship, which involves frequent divisions of spheres of control, that the group's name actually functions like a flag. Imagine a fortress or a hill taken by an army: the necessary conclusion of the successful operation would be to raise its flag. This not only means that the captured territory has been (re)claimed by the victor; it signifies to all other possible claimants that sovereignty and protection have been established. In this case, the flag functions as a token of protection and deterrence. The raising of the Union Jack over the Falkland Islands, for example, did not just mark the end of the military operation but was meant to reestablish sovereignty and, since the flag represented the reconfirmed reputation of the British navy, to deter potential aggressors.

As soon as a criminal group has imposed a protective relationship on an economic enterprise, the business's management will use the name of that criminal group or of one of its leaders when threatened by another group. Such use is as routine, as is the search for "free objects" by every criminal group. The identification of an "object" as "free" occurs when the company staff cannot give the name of their protecting agency. If they can, and the name produces the proper effect, the criminal group retreats. Thus names of criminal groups (and sometimes, names of their leaders as well) serve as tokens of protection from one another.

The next logical step was to turn the immaterial name, which had to be used each time probing by a competitor occurred, as if a flag were being raised in the face of an approaching danger and then removed again, into a visible token of protection marking its object. In St. Petersburg at the very beginning of the 1990s, one could come across kiosks and shops that displayed a homemade plate, "Security provided by A. I. Malyshev," which referred to the prominent criminal authority and sent a message to rivals.[3] Later, this subtle but symbolic innovation was picked up by expanding private protection companies. They introduced adhesive labels with the name of the company and its telephone number, which were to be attached to the front door of an office or restaurant, so that undesirable visitors could identify the protection agency without bothering the staff.

The name of a criminal group or of a private protection company can function as a token of protection and a deterrent only if it communicates a certain reputation. Writing about the Sicilian Mafia, Gambetta emphasizes the importance of reputation in the business of private protection. By reputation he means a "good name" that plays the role of a valuable asset in commerce by ensuring the quality and reliability of a commodity or dealer and that acts as a guide for buyers.[4] Such a commercial reputation is a product of the permanent relations between a producer (or supplier) of a commodity and its buyers. Where violence is paramount, reputations are likely to originate from a different set of relationships. The purely economic explanation that Gambetta favors throughout his study tends to downplay another kind of reputation, a reputation for resolve. This is the quality attributed to a wielder of force that determines the credibility of the deterrent. In theories of international relations, a reputation for resolve is an important variable for explaining scenarios of conflict.[5] It emerges from relations between wielders of force and has little to do with clients or buyers. Whereas a reputation for resolve emerges through precedents of violence, a commercial reputation refers to peaceful economic activity and comes about when the business fulfills a different kind of promise. Formally, both are reputations in the sense that they represent beliefs that someone has an enduring characteristic confirmed by past behavior, which is used to predict future behavior. But, unlike conventional businesses, where the collective belief of clients (or customers) is crucial for a supplier to earn a good reputation, in the protection business clients are secondary. Here reputations are made in the realm where a plurality of violence-man-

3. Elena Topil'skaya, *Organizovannaya prestupnost'* (Organized crime) (St. Petersburg: Yuridicheskii tsentr Press, 1999), 58.

4. Gambetta, *The Sicilian Mafia*, 43.

5. Jonathan Mercer, *Reputation and International Politics* (Ithaca: Cornell University Press, 1996).

aging agencies are brought into a relationship of strategic competition rather than in the relationship between the provider and the customer (within the domain monopolized by the provider). In the case of the Mafia, the state in the international arena, or any other protection agency endowed with the unrestricted capacity to use force, a commercial reputation as a supplier of protection will largely depend on the reputation for resolve or other qualities enabling effective control of possible threats. The recognition of a protection enterprise by clients is the result of its being recognized by other wielders of force, since the reputation for credible protection is derived from the reputation for being a credible threat.

In the first place, then, the name of a criminal group carries a reputation for resolve. Initially, it is little more than the sum of individual reputations earned by the group's members in rather primitive clashes with similar members of other groups. These clashes help previously unknown aspiring bandits to improve their standing. In Petersburg in 1989–90, first reputations were made at Copper Lake, where bandits met to resolve disputes through violent contests. The Copper Lake duels are still alive in the collective memory of certain circles in Petersburg. Thus, one story tells of a dispute between *azerbaidzhantsy* and local bandits over an insignificant sum of money— "some two hundred bucks," the storyteller said. The bandit Vasia Brianski pulled out a gun, but a cool Azerbaijani displayed no fear and, pointing to his own forehead, said: "Okay, shoot me." The trick, which was intended to demonstrate to others Vasia's lack of resolve and thus win the contest, did not work. Vasia put the gun to the man's forehead and shot him (5).

The reputation of a criminal group gradually builds on the basis of precedents in the successful use of force and is referred to as *avtoritet* (authority), which, as mentioned earlier, also stands for a criminal group's leader. But brute force does not suffice for violent entrepreneurship, since physical protection is not its major element. As soon as individuals or groups have earned considerable *avtoritet,* they switch to more sophisticated activities in which *avtoritet* is no longer the aim but the means. *Avtoritet* gives one access and the right to participate in negotiations through which "questions" are solved, in particular, those concerning property disputes, guarantees to fulfill contracts, the distribution of business opportunities and profits, and the like. Then it becomes similar to a commercial reputation, drawing to an *avtoritet* businessmen who have created problems they cannot solve on their own. From the interview with a *brigadir:* "I think when you create a certain reputation for yourself, a certain image, people will come to you on their own. How do you think people get 'themes' [business opportunities], their businessmen, so to speak?" (13). The skill of earning a commercial reputation from the reputation for resolve is indispensable for violent entrepreneurship. As the age of simple protection rackets passed and criminal groups began to compete for clients as enforcement partners, the reputation of a reliable partner became increasingly important.

When a reputation becomes alienable from its physical bearer and is commodified, it turns into a trademark. In practical terms, the license to use the trademark means the right to introduce oneself as "working with" a certain criminal group or with *avtoritet* X. Such a license is supplied to a brigade or to an individual member by the *avtoritet,* the leader of the group, normally after the candidate has been tested in action. For example, for killing the managing director of Petersburg's northern Rzhevka airport, a certain Andrei F. received five hundred U.S. dollars in cash and the right to introduce himself as *murmanskii* (i.e., as belonging to the *Murmanskaya* criminal group).[6] The amount of money may seem surprisingly low, but what was really valued in this particular case was the acquisition by the young bandit of the right to exploit the trademark.

The license to use the name to conduct violent entrepreneurship, that is, to act as a commercial enforcement partner, presupposes an informal contract between the leader *(avtoritet)* and the unit *(brigada)* that acts in his name. The contract includes the obligation to pay into the common fund and to follow certain rules. A group that has no license from one of the established *avtoritet* will have little success in its business and will either be exterminated or turned over to the police. The latter will be glad to use the occasion to its own advantage to credit itself with a successful operation against organized crime.

The trademark also allows the leader to collect a kind of rent by franchising his name to brigades for their day-to-day business. Reference to the name is the crucial part of the business and presupposes an introduction ritual: "We are such-and-such" or "we work with X." The biggest name rental *avtoritet* in Petersburg was Alexander Malyshev, who by 1991 had managed to unite many smaller groups and brigades into a powerful *malyshevskaya* "empire," whose members used his name in exchange for a share of their profits. At this stage, the physical presence of the *avtoritet* becomes unnecessary. He can be abroad or in prison: the signifier of a reputation can function in the absence of its physical bearer. This is one of the reasons why some criminal groups do not disintegrate after their leadership has been put behind bars. Yet the duration of this mechanism is limited. In addition to its size and heterogeneity, there is another reason for calling the Malyshevskoe criminal society an "empire": like an empire, it eventually broke up into numerous relatively independent "principalities," which subsequently either exterminated one another or merged into more powerful groups.

6. *Operativnoe prikrytie* 2 (1997): 10.

The Structure of the Criminal Group

A criminal group can form either from the top down or from the bottom up, but because its structure is geared toward its activity and functions, the outcome of both processes tends to coincide. Racketeering groups of sportsmen initially emerged as brigades of seven to ten members without a clear hierarchy. The presence of a strong leader with ties to the underworld enabled the group to grow and form an initial hierarchical structure of its own. In other cases, small groups joined large established criminal groups. A group of sportsmen from the far eastern town of Vladivostok, for instance, migrated to Moscow, where it joined the growing Orekhovskaya group and became known as *dal'nevostochnaya brigada* (the far eastern brigade).

Brigade leaders constitute the key element of any criminal group; they are as important as the officer corps in the army. A *brigadir* is responsible for the discipline in his brigade and for all of its operations. How does one become a *brigadir*? Vadim joined the Komarovskaya criminal group in 1992 as a rank-and-file soldier *(boets)* but was promoted in just a few months. In response to my question about how he became a *brigadir,* he recalled the following episode:

> Once we guarded a cargo train that had two platforms with expensive cars for Nazarbaev [the president of Kazakhstan]. Each car was worth sixty to seventy thousand U.S. dollars. The train suddenly stopped in an open field. Some bandits pulled up and wanted to unhook the car platforms. And there were many of them. We pulled out guns and started shooting along the train to keep them off, just to win some time, because we had managed to connect by radio to a nearby military helicopter unit and to call a helicopter. When it appeared they understood it wouldn't work out for them and retreated. After that I was given my own brigade. (20)

Brigadiry are directly subordinate to an *avtoritet,* one of the leaders of the group, whose rank is comparable to that of a general. Many criminal groups have an absolute leader who stands above the *avtoritety,* but some are managed by several equal *avtoritety,* each of whom has a number of *brigadiry* under his command. Thus, the leadership of the Koptevskaya criminal group in Moscow consisted of two brothers named Naumov and a former special forces officer, Sergei Zimin. Somewhat exceptional in their structure are criminal groups in the city of Kazan' in Tartarstan. According to an expert who used to work in the local anticrime police unit, each of the existing ninety-seven criminal groups consists of several brigades, while the leadership is made up of a council of brigade leaders *(sovet brigadirov)* (9).

Representatives of the traditional criminal culture, the *vory v zakone,*

tended to build their groups from the top down. First there was a core consisting of an authoritative *vor* and his close prison associates, each of whom,
upon release, became his representative supervisor *(polozhenets or smotri-
ashchii)*. The latter, then, recruited their own *brigadirs* and soldiers. The
composition of brigades could vary from former sportsmen to ex-convicts,
but the *brigadir* of a *vor*-led criminal group was always a former convict and
adept at the *vory* ideology.

Each large criminal group also comprises "technical subdivisions" responsible for car maintenance, armaments, and communication equipment.
These three components are the standard "means of production" of a criminal group, since they enable its mobility, firepower, and coordination in the
use of force. Apart from that, each group has a number of closely associated
businessmen whose relationship with the group is different from that of regular clients (see figure 2). They are responsible for the group's own investments in legal enterprises and are normally made executive directors or
major shareholders of companies created from the criminal group's money.
Their biographies are "clean," of course, though their real affiliation is well
known in business circles. *Avtoritety* normally become deputy directors or
executive security managers of such companies. In addition to this structure,
connections to corrupt state administrative and representative bodies make
an organized criminal group what is classified by law enforcement as an organized criminal society.

Elimination Contests

In the early 1990s the number of criminal groups grew dramatically. According to official statistics, their number rose from 952 in 1991 to 4,300 in
1992 to 5,691 in 1993, and reached the peak of 14,050 in 1995. By comparison, this figure was only 50 in 1988.[7] These widely cited figures are apparently based on a somewhat broad definition of criminal group, not sensitive to size, profile, influence, or other important parameters. The first line
in table 1 below includes all possible criminal groups, including those with
only three or four members. One way to improve the accuracy of statistical
accounts of these elusive entities is to introduce additional variables, such as
"international," "interregional," and "corrupt" ties that characterize larger
and more influential groups. As a result, the numbers drop significantly and
display a different dynamics.

What was happening to the criminal groups represented by these figures?
In 1989–91 suburban criminal groups aggressively moved into the cities to

---

7. Yakov Gilinsky, *Organizovannya prestupnost' v Rossii: Teoriya i real'nost'* (Organized
crime in Russia: Theory and reality) (St. Petersburg: Institut Sotsiologii, 1996), 77.

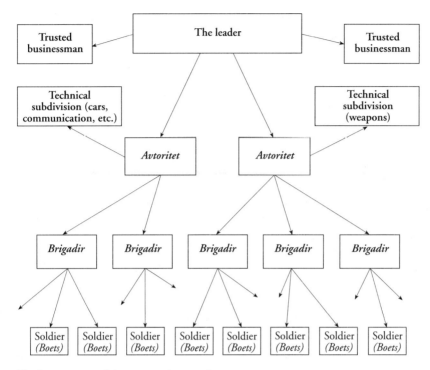

Fig 2. Structure of the organized criminal group

Table I. Organized Criminal Groups Uncovered by Law Enforcement Agencies

	1993	1994	1995	1996	1997
Number of organized criminal formations uncovered	5,691	12,849	14,050	12,684	12,500
Number of participants	27,630	50,572	57,545	59,389	60,000
Criminal groups with ties:					
International	307	461	363	176	222
Interregional	1,011	1,258	1,065	589	354
Corrupt	801	1,037	857	424	—

Source: Azalia Dolgova, ed., *Organizovannaya prestupnost'-4* (Moscow: Kriminologicheskaya as-sotsiatsiya, 1998), 258.

gain control of growing commercial opportunities. Smaller towns such as Kazan', Kourgan, Perm', and others exported their growing numbers of rack-eteers to Moscow and Petersburg. Some groups failed to establish permanent domains in large cities. *Kazanskie* and *permskie,* for instance, failed to find a permanent niche in Moscow but succeeded in Petersburg. Apart from these new violent groups of *bandity,* led by *avtoritety* and guided in their activities by sheer economic rationality, there were a large number of *vory v zakone* operating, who sought to use the authority of traditional criminal values and the power of old prison networks to secure their share and oppose the expansion of the new bandits.[8] *Vory* achieved uncontested influence in eastern Siberia and in the far eastern and southern parts of Russia, got a firm hold in Moscow, but lost ground in Petersburg and Ekaterinburg. Originally, ethnic groups, especially Azerbaijanis, Chechens, and Georgians, were also active in most major cities. Their settlements were traditionally strong in Moscow; Georgians had the highest ethnic representation in the ranks of *vory v zakone*, while Chechens relied more on their own clan structures.

Thus, instead of a well-coordinated and uniform criminal system in which each subunit had its own clearly circumscribed territorial or business domain, there was a rather heterogeneous, diffuse mosaic where territories and businesses were divided in many different ways among criminal groups of different territorial, ethnic, institutional, and historical origin. Although groups often claimed control over certain territories, the subjects of their divisions, rivalry, and cooperation were opportunities rather than territories or spheres of the economy as such. Hence there was no single feature common to all criminal groups except the means available to them, that is, organized force. Explanations of the activities of criminal groups, therefore, should be sought not in the groups themselves, in their legal status, or in the people that compose them, but in their interrelations and practices, determined by the opportunities opened by the emerging market and the failing state.

The many groups that formed to seize new opportunities quickly became engaged in open and covert struggles with one another. However broad, the opportunities were limited, and those criminal groups that did not grow stronger became weaker and were gradually either eliminated or subsumed by more powerful rivals. In 1992–93 the city of Perm' in the southern Urals experienced a violent conflict between the expanding criminal group led by the Georgian thieves-in-law and an allied front of Slavic groups directed from the Nizhne-Tagil'skaya colony by the authoritative thief Nikolai Zykov ("Yakutenok"). The Georgians lost and had to leave the region, while the Slavic groups consolidated and expanded under Yakutenok's leadership.[9] The elimination contest of 1992–95 periodically erupted into massive armed showdowns, such as the one between the *balashikhinskaya* and *podol'skaya* groups in Moscow in May 1992.[10] Some expert data on the dynamic of violent dispute resolution in 1991–97 are represented in table 2

8. The exact number of *vory v zakone* is unknown. Experts give different estimates, from 250 to 1,500.

9. Federico Varese, "The Emergence of the Russian Mafia: Dispute Settlement and Protection in a New Market Economy" (Ph.D. diss., Oxford University, 1996), 205–6.

10. For details, see Nikolai Modestov, *Moskva banditskaya* (Moscow bandits) (Moscow: Tsentrpoligraph, 1996), 149–60.

Table 2. Number of Registered Criminal Group Meetings with Violent Outcomes

Year	1991	1992	1993	1994	1995	1996	1997
N	144	305	610	690	630	620	600

Source: Azalia Dolgova, ed., *Organizovannaya prestupnost'-4* (Moscow: Kriminologicheskaya assotsiatsiya, 1998), 258.

above. For obvious reasons, the data cannot be substantively accurate but may be taken to correctly reflect the general tendency.

Because strong leadership is the major factor in a criminal group's consolidation and success, leaders rarely took part in day-to-day violence. Hence, carefully staged assassinations of leaders rather than gang wars became the routine method of violent competition. Anticrime police agencies were active against criminal leaders as well, often using to their advantage clashes between groups. The police were also used by these groups to remove rivals, if only temporarily. The "neutralization" rates of criminal leaders in 1986–97 are represented in the figure below.

Of the original founders of criminal groups only a few survived. The elimination contest reached its peak in 1994.[11] On the whole, the period between 1992 and 1995 was marked by numerous wars, such as those between Slavic and Caucasian groups in Moscow and Perm', between local and migrant groups, or between groups headed by traditional *vory v zakone* and those led by new bandit *avtoritety,* in Petersburg, Ekaterinburg, and other cities. These conflicts were about opportunities, norms, and leadership. Whatever their causes and stakes, these violent conflicts steadily contributed to one general outcome—the formation of a smaller number of larger groups, better organized and firmly integrated into the structures of the market economy. This outcome may explain the decline in the number of large criminal groups with well-established connections, as indicated in table 1.

Patterns of Normative Culture

An account of the action system should distinguish between its goal and its sociocultural organization (structure). The latter can be reduced to a set of culturally determined meanings and institutionalized norms that give the action a sustained and recognizable character. The structure of social action typical to a certain community is linked, on the one hand, to the individual motivations of its members and, on the other, to the functions of the insti-

11. The term "elimination contest" is borrowed from Norbert Elias, *The Civilizing Process* (Oxford: Basil Blackwell, 1995), 2:354.

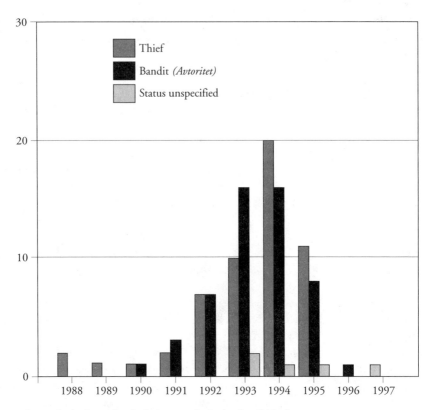

Source: Author's rough calculations on the basis of available data.

Fig 3. Assassinations (successful and attempted) and arrests of crime group leaders, 1986–97

tution to which this community belongs. An analysis of an action system, then, should articulate the correspondence between the structure of social action and its institutional function. This, in short, is the basic idea of the structural-functional analysis.[12] Values and norms form "patterns of normative culture" responsible for the integration and reproduction of human communities. Values provide some general orientations for broader communities, while norms are more particular sets of social prescriptions, distinguished from purely technical know-how, that regulate activities of professional groups so as to enable them to perform their specific tasks, for example, for doctors to treat patients, for scientists to produce knowledge,

12. For the best exposition of the structural-functional approach, see Talcott Parsons, "An Outline of the Social System," in *Theories of Society: Foundations of Modern Sociological Theory,* ed. T. Parsons, E. Shils, A. Naegele, and J. Pitts (New York: Free Press, 1961), 30–79.

or for the military to wage war.[13] What are the values and norms shared by violent entrepreneurs and how do patterns of normative culture enable protection and enforcement?

High Value of Force, Low Value of Life

Homer's poems glorify heroic deeds, which elevate those who accomplish them above mortals. These deeds consist of endless lethal contests between individuals, armies, or city-states, in which neither the original cause nor even the outcome matter as much as the drama of the fight and the cunning stratagem. Aggressive and violent behavior is not just the norm of the Homeric world, it is its ideal. Accordingly, the skill of warfare and the high level of aggressiveness, combined with a readiness to die, are the qualities most highly valued and praised.[14] In a similar vein, the medieval didactic literature of chivalry assures its reader that not only can man gain personal nobility by displaying bravery on the battlefield, he can acquire personal salvation as well. Saints' lives from the Carolingian period on fairly often add skill in arms and bravery to the characteristic of the "noble saint" to make him more like a warrior.[15] Even the modern codes of conduct of relatively peaceful gentlemen preserve many features of the earlier warrior codes.

Excellence in fighting skills naturally constitutes the supreme value for any warrior community, even though military capacity may be determined more by organization and state-of-the-art technology than by individual courage. No less important is a habituation to the permanent risk of losing one's life. The cultivation of a low value of life, expressed in a specific readiness to die, is as vital as perfecting fighting skills. A readiness to sacrifice one's life gives its bearer sufficient superiority to compensate for a deficiency in sheer physical strength. Not fighting for one's life but fighting despite the risk of losing one's life is what constitutes the core value of any warrior community. Durkheim observes that the low value of life in warrior communities results in the high level of what he terms "altruistic suicide."[16] In her rigorous study of the history of morality, the Polish sociologist Maria Ossowska demonstrates a strong structural continuity of knightly-aristocratic

13. For an exemplary application of the structural-functional analysis to science and the democratic social order, see Robert Merton, *Social Theory and Social Structure,* enlarged edition (New York: Free Press, 1968), 604–15.

14. Hans Van Wees, *Status Warriors: War, Violence, and Society in Homer and History* (Amsterdam: J. C. Gieben, 1992).

15. Malcolm Vale, *War and Chivalry: Warfare and Aristocratic Culture in England, France and Burgundy at the End of the Middle Ages* (London: Duckworth, 1981), 31.

16. Emile Durkheim, *Suicide: A Study in Sociology* (London: Routledge, 1951), 234, 238.

values in different eras and cultures and also notes a specific combination of a high valuation of physical force and contempt for death.[17]

This combination of values is geared toward the efficient use of force. It is thus no surprise that illegitimate communities whose chief activities are similar to those of the state warrior class or its modern successors adhere to a similar set of values. Studies of the Sicilian Mafia pay special attention to the resolute use of force and the permanent risk that earn mafiosi their honor and, accordingly, their status.[18] The values and norms adopted in Russia's bandit subculture of the 1990s, especially in those segments that grew out of sports and the military, also belong on the same spectrum. Their cult of physical might and their contemptuous attitude toward death are manifested in a somewhat primitive manner. The cult of aggressiveness is alive in numerous stories about the *avtoritety*'s extraordinary physical abilities. Thus, one of the leaders of the Kazanskaya criminal group in Petersburg, Marat Abdurakhmanov ("Martin"), had a reputation for being cruel and unpredictable. "They said that in a restaurant he could first smile at his interlocutor and the next moment break a bottle against the person's head."[19] A myth about the *avtoritet* "Kolia-karate" ascribed to him the ability to throw some kind of "energy punch," coupled with mastery of noncontact kung fu.[20] For many, socialization through fighting sports shaped their personalities in accordance with a warrior code that only became stronger throughout their careers as violent entrepreneurs. Sergei Mikhailov, known as "Mikhas'," the founder of the Solntsevskaya criminal group, gave an interview to a popular magazine soon after he had been acquitted by the Swiss court. Although he tried hard to portray himself as "just a businessman," Mikhailov could not help emphasizing his physical abilities. Asked what he would do if assaulted without bodyguards around him, he answered: "Then I will fight by myself. You do not know, but trust my word: I fight professionally. After all, I am a master of sports in freestyle wrestling."[21]

It is not just physical strength but the low valuation of life and the ability to put one's life in danger in a dispute that serve bandits as justification for their claims to superiority and domination. Roman, a former boxer and a veteran of several local wars, including Afghanistan and Bosnia, made a quick career as a violent entrepreneur, reaching the status of *brigadir* and as-

17. Maria Ossowska, *Rytsar' i burzhua: Issledovaniya po istorii morali* (The warrior and the bourgeois: Studies in the history of morality) (Moscow: Progress, 1987),

18. Henner Hess, *Mafia and Mafiosi: The Structure of Power* (Lexington, Mass.: Lexington Books, 1973).

19. Andrei Konstantinov, *Banditskii Peterburg 98* (Moscow: Olma-Press, 1999), 214.

20. Ibid., 119.

21. Sergei Mikhailov, "Ia stal zhertvoi kommercheskikh konkurentov" (I came to be a victim of business competitors), *Profil'*, 31 January 1999, 31.

piring to become an *avtoritet*. In the interview, he praises honor and repeatedly emphasizes the importance of overcoming the fear of death:

> I genuinely believe that in our country now the economy is created by people who have proven to everyone their contempt toward death. . . . In general, there are very few real people. Real people, who can solve questions by shooting and talking at the same time, are in short supply in this city. So lacking that even now anyone can, in principle, move up, it's not too late yet. I mean, any man who is ready to die at any moment. (13)

The repetition of the adjective "real" *(real'nyi)* is not accidental. This is a widely used word in the language of violent entrepreneurs, and one endowed with a strong positive connotation. It applies to someone who embodies the major values of this community and follows its norms. "Real" signifies "genuine" but also connotes "noble" and "powerful." According to the definition given by Roman, this is someone who is skillful and fearless in the use of force and is clever enough to conduct responsible negotiations ("who can solve questions by shooting and talking at the same time"). In fact, a "real" bandit, it is often said, possesses a particular set of traits: he is a normative bandit, an ideal type.

Normative Patterns

Norms reflect the values of a particular community or a professional group and regulate the behavior of its members to reflect the tasks of the given group in the social division of labor. Observations and interviews led me to classify the social norms observed by criminal entrepreneurs of violence into three categories: norms that relate to the use of force; those that regulate speech acts; and those that prescribe a certain attitude toward their own profession. I call them, respectively, "power resolve," "responsibility for speech acts," and "quasi-professional orientation."

Power resolve refers to a complex of norms relating to the use and demonstration of physical force. It implies a readiness to resort to violence; a conspicuous capacity to defend oneself and one's interests; and an active and assertive stance toward the environment. The "real bandit" code presupposes a "macho" style of behavior and resembles a primitive knightly code of honor. Behind the aggressive facade, however, the code recognizes the capacity to affect other peoples' behavior without recourse to open violence but by demonstrating the availability of force and the possible consequences of its application. The most important—but not always apparent—feature of this set of norms is that it restricts violence as much as it sanctions it. In fact, uncontrolled aggression and unjustified violence are regarded as serious offenses punishable by a fine or other penalty. Such behavior is called *bespredel* (literally "no limit" or "no holds barred") and those who adopt it *bespredel'shchik* or *otmorozok,* "frost-bitten," that is, insensitive and uncontrollable. Episodes of violence are always discussed within and among criminal groups. For a public accusation to qualify as *bespredel* and to win general acceptance, the case has to be supported by arguments appealing to more or less conventional norms of justice or precedents. The criminal group whose participants have conducted what are found to be *bespredel* has to pay compensation. If the side that has conducted *bespredel* refuses to negotiate the settlement, then the same set of norms will justify appropriate retaliation by the group that suffered "unjust" damage (this normally happens anonymously and some time later, but everyone gets the message). An entire criminal group may be accused of *bespredel* and exterminated on the determination of other groups. Some experts suggest, for example, that the assassination in June–July 1992 of the leadership of the young Balashikhinskaya criminal group in Moscow was carried out by several other groups after *balashikhinskie* continuously gave preference to violence over negotiations and were accused of *bespredel.*[22] As a matter of fact, *bespredel* became, over time, a much more serious and consequential accusation than the lack of resolve.

Interestingly, the word *bespredel,* once purely jargon, has now firmly entered everyday vocabulary. Its occasional use, in keeping with its original usage, has become common among some members of the Russian political leadership as well. Expressing his outrage at the bombing of Yugoslavia in March 1999, Russian Minister of Defense Igor Sergeev called the NATO action *bespredel.* Moreover, it turned out that the term conveniently fits the rhetoric used to justify strengthening the state. Thus, on 3 February 2000, in a brief televised speech, then acting president of Russia Vladimir Putin noted: "Without the legal system and the dictatorship of law, freedom turns into *bespredel.*"

The rule-governed use of force tends to reduce the level of actual violence within and among criminal groups and to increase its efficiency when applied to outsiders. Although participants in criminal groups are compelled by their code to demonstrate and occasionally prove their readiness to have recourse to violence, they know very well its destructive effects. The negatively marked concept of *bespredel,* then, helps to maintain the balance between the need to have a credible reputation for resolve, which requires a demonstration of force, and the spontaneous use of violence beyond the scope of economic rationality. The emergence and growing authority of

22. Modestov, *Moskva banditskaya,* 160.

rules relating to the use of force may serve as an additional explanation for the decline in the intensity of violence after 1995.

Responsibility for speech acts is a set of social norms that regulates the use of language by members of criminal groups and other private enforcers. It has the following requirements. The "real bandit" should be "concrete" *(konkretnyi)* in his statements, promises, threats, definitions, and other speech acts and should take full responsibility for his words. A bandit cannot say, "I did not really mean it," or, "I was just joking," because any of his words can at any moment be taken seriously by friends and adversaries alike. Thus some material effect will be attached to his words. If a threat, it must be carried out and, accordingly, will be taken "concretely," that is, as a material fact, by those to whom it refers. Likewise, any promise implies full responsibility for its fulfillment; in fact, every speech act is regarded as a kind of promise, and every bandit knows he is likely to be forced to fulfill the promise or face the consequences of his failure to deliver. The norms shared by criminal groups endorse a range of severe punishments, either physical, including death, or financial, for an inability to "answer for one's words." Likewise, every insult has a corresponding punishment. The Petersburg gang of Andrei "Malen'kii" (arrested by the RUBOP in July 2000), for instance, was notorious in criminal circles for an especially brutal system of punishments that involved cutting off fingers and executing members who had broken the rules.[23] In any case, a "misfire" of a serious speech act leads to the loss of authority. The ethos of responsibility for speech acts endows words with material force and equates them with deeds.

Likhachev's analysis of the traditional criminal oral culture of *vory*, written in the 1930s, was inspired by the French anthropological studies of primitive societies. Thus, when Likhachev observed that words in the thieves' milieu were endowed with material qualities, he was inclined to interpret this as an expression of a magical attitude toward the world typical of primitive peoples.[24] In the case of bandits, who display a similar attitude, Likhachev's interpretation would be only half-right. For bandits, I argue, the heightened responsibility for speech acts that endows them with material force is related to bandits' role as business mediators who give guarantees and enforce contracts. The conventional view usually associates bandits with violence—an image they themselves try hard to maintain. Yet in practice,

23. Valentin Grechaniuk, "Andrei Malen'kii kak fenomen rossiiskoi yakudzy" (Andrei Malen'kii as a phenomenon of Russian yakudza), *Vash tainyi sovetnik* 2 (November 1999): 25.

24. Dmitrii Likhachev, "Cherty pervobytnogo primitivizma vorovskoi rechi" (Primitive features in the speech of thieves), published as an appendix to *Slovar tiuremno-lagerno-blatnogo zhargona*, ed. Danzik Baldaev (Moscow: Kraia Moskvy, 1992), 360–61.

their code enables them to do business primarily with words rather than fists or guns.

The best way to elaborate this point is to turn to the famous work by the philosopher of language John Austin, *How to Do Things with Words,* and its sociological application by Pierre Bourdieu. In brief, Austin singled out a class of utterances whose role is not to describe a state of affairs or state some fact but to perform an action. He termed them "performative utterances" or "performatives."[25] The phrase "I do," uttered during a marriage ceremony, or the words "I name this ship Mr. Stalin," pronounced while smashing a bottle against the stern of a vessel, or a promise "I bet you sixpence it will rain tomorrow," are ways of doing things rather than saying about them. Many performatives, notes Austin, are contractual ("I bet," "I promise") or declaratory ("I declare war") utterances.[26] Further on, Austin makes it clear that the material effects of performatives are connected not to their particular linguistic form or even to the particular circumstances of their utterance. Their effects are derived from what he calls "illocutionary force." His reflections lead him to conclude that a great many utterances can function as a kind of performatives irrespective of their linguistic form, provided they possess illocutionary force.

According to Bourdieu, Austin, because he was still too much concerned with the linguistic properties of performatives, did not give a satisfactory explanation of the origin of their illocutionary force.[27] The performative utterance implies an overt claim to possess a certain power, argues Bourdieu. It is the power of a social institution that gives the words of its representative illocutionary force, enabling him or her to "do things with words."

> The limiting case of the performative utterance is the legal act which, when it is pronounced as it should be, by someone who has the right to do so, i.e. by an agent acting on behalf of a whole group, can replace action with speech, which will, as they say, have an effect: the judge need say no more than "I find you guilty" because there is a set of agents and institutions which guarantee that the sentence will be executed.[28]

The capacity to "do things with words," that is, to replace acts with speech, which may appear to be a linguistic property or an individual gift in fact rests on a whole set of background institutional arrangements and practices.

25. John Austin, *How to Do Things with Words* (Cambridge: Harvard University Press, 1962), 2.

26. Ibid., 7.

27. Pierre Bourdieu, *Language and Symbolic Power,* trans. Gino Raymond and Matthew Adamson (Cambridge: Polity Press, 1991), 74–75.

28. Ibid., 75.

Now we can better understand the mechanism of enforcement partnership. We can see the distinction between robbery and violent entrepreneurship, for example, and sense the difference between a protection racket and an enforcement partnership. Violent entrepreneurship is not violence per se that is bluntly converted into whatever a robber can get from his victim's pocket, but is rather violence socially organized to produce a set of speech acts that have a market value by virtue of their ability to govern transactions. When two enforcement partners meet, they exchange words, and the commission they receive is more or less the monetary value of their words. Yet they claim to have done certain things (endorsed contracts, defined the terms of fair exchange, made an exchange relationship permanent). This is possible because behind their words is a whole structure composed of the respective criminal groups, their reputations expressed in their names, the regalia by which bandits recognize one another, and the web of norms they embody and that tacitly connect speech acts to the lurking machinery of violence.

When enforcers meet, they give guarantees for or on behalf of businessmen whose word is not sufficient to sustain economic exchange. It is indeed not uncommon for businessmen to get caught in a web of unfulfilled mutual obligations and to have to appeal to enforcement partners to get their money back. Men of commerce are generally seen as too irresponsible and characterless to be trusted—so characterless and unworthy that exploiting them is often experienced by bandits as almost a moral obligation. Their moral inferiority in the eyes of bandits stems from their inability to defend themselves and from their fear of losing their lives (or suffering physical harm). Bandits, on the contrary, put their lives at risk (and constantly emphasize this fact!); their lives are their bond, because there is a brutal system enforcing guarantees. The mutual guarantees of enforcers work because their word carries the force of law. Bandits qua enforcers are preoccupied with assigning guilt and, accordingly, indebtedness, to men of commerce, who are supposedly unable to keep their promises. And bandits are particularly good at collecting debts. Payments they receive for substituting their guarantees for those of economic subjects or for compelling their clients to fulfill mutual obligations appear as pecuniary expression of their moral domination. Concrete pecuniary interest aside, the social result that the brutal enforcement games help to bring about is, to use Nietzsche's famous line, "the breeding of an animal which is entitled to make promises."[29]

---

29. The line is taken from the opening sentence of the second essay in Nietzsche's *Genealogy of Morals*, which gives an account of the origin of guilt and responsibility: "The breeding of an animal which is entitled to make promises—is this not the paradoxical task which nature has set itself with respect to man?" Friedrich Nietzsche, *On the Genealogy of Morals*, trans. Douglas Smith (Oxford: Oxford University Press, 1996), 39.

Quasi-professional orientation is a curious set of attitudes that "real ban-dits" hold toward their work. These attitudes are a variation on the famous "leisure class" ethos, so perceptively described by Veblen. Members of the leisure class, whom Veblen also calls "predatory men," are forbidden to en-gage in any productive activity, their occupations being war and government (and later also sports).[30] Likewise, the code of bandits includes a moral pro-hibition to engage in work, that is, to be a businessman or clerk. The bandit lives off what he "collects." That is to say, the bandit claims the right to "col-lect" (tribute) simply by virtue of being what he is, that is, by virtue of his status rather than his labor. Handelman cites a criminal authority boasting: "You can make money without doing anything."[31] Another aspect of this norm articulates the superiority of a bandit over a businessman and thus by definition obliges a businessman to pay the bandit. It is incompatible with the bandit's honor to pay out to anyone, since he should only "collect." When at a meeting of two groups it turned out that one of the members of *malyshevskie* was involved in commerce, Alexander Tkachenko ("Tkach"), the leader of the *permskie,* uttered an insult that led to a conflict: "Now we have to collect from you" (5). "You owe me by definition" is a typical ban-dits' line, directed at men of commerce. Bandits believe they get their money for their personal abilities and reputation. Konstantinov quotes the confes-sion of an *avtoritet*: "I am not afraid of being killed. . . . I receive my money for my name, and this is very important for me. . . . They can kill me, but it is impossible to collect from me."[32]

But does the conspicuous rejection of utility that constitutes their shared distinction prevent bandits from producing real services and performing useful functions? To engage in a practice, people do not necessarily have to understand its true nature. Moreover, a collective refusal to admit the true nature of a certain activity may constitute part of the activity itself. In his ac-count of archaic economies of exchange, Bourdieu makes a strong case for the necessity of what he calls "collective misrecognition." An important form of exchange in many societies and a social bond would be rendered im-possible if an anthropologist were to reveal and make participants admit the "sincere fiction of disinterested exchange" that covers up the practice of gift-giving.[33] "If the system is to work, the agents must not be entirely unaware of the truth of their exchanges, which is made explicit in the anthropologist's

30. Thorstein Veblen, *The Theory of the Leisure Class* (New York: Penguin, 1994), 2–15.

31. Stephen Handelman, *Comrade Criminal: Russia's New Mafiya* (New Haven: Yale Uni-versity Press, 1995), 14.

32. The words were spoken by Ruslan Koliak ("Lupatyi") of the Tambovskaya group. Kon-stantinov, *Banditskii Peterburg 98*, 276, 278.

33. Pierre Bourdieu, *Outline of a Theory of Practice* (Cambridge: Cambridge University Press, 1977), 171.

model, while at the same time they must refuse to know and above all to recognize it."[34]

For representatives of the leisure class, be it the gentry of the past or modern-day men of honor, sustaining a collective misrecognition of the nature of their activities, as distinct from those of salaried professionals, is an important part of their social reproduction as a dominant group. For warriors to admit they get paid for concrete work would make them equal to other groups, since in that case they would be dependent hirelings, compelled to work and therefore unfree. Their sense of honor compels them to do things for free rather than admit to accepting payment for a service. Historically, the downgrading of the social and political position of the military gentry and its subordination to the power of owners of capital (of "civil" society) proceeded, above all, through the dispelling of the fiction of the leisure class and its replacement by the ethos of professional service.

We can now see why *bandity* as criminal enforcers tend to cling to the rhetoric of the leisure class and deny providing any professional service, and why any explicit comparison to a man of commerce or a clerk is regarded as an insult. Admitting their utility would not only make them equal to and overtly dependent on the businessmen who pay them to provide certain services, but would also lead them to be regarded as the same as law enforcement employees, who are their natural enemies. For violent entrepreneurs, the quasi-professional orientation expressed in leisure-class rhetoric helps to coordinate the social and economic aspects of existence. Furthermore, the importance of the name and, accordingly, the claim to be entitled to revenue by virtue of respect alone hide as much as they reveal. An authoritative bandit indeed gets his fee for his name and respect, that is, for his reputation. But it takes effort to earn and maintain a reputation. Before the reputation can work for the bandit, he must first work for the reputation. A genuine belief in a special privilege attached to the name does not prevent its bearer from doing a substantial amount of specialized work to earn a living. One respondent mentioned that, at a certain point, their leader handed each *brigadir* a personal organizer to help them cope with the growing workload (3).

Practices

In their day-to-day activities, violent entrepreneurs use many technical terms that refer to their "doings." Some have been assimilated into everyday language and acquired a wider circulation, while others are still confined to

34. Ibid., 6.

the bandits' professional parlance. To avoid confusion, I should stress that technical terms are not "contractual" or "declarative" speech acts that keep the business world spinning, but a set of names for the conventional practices of violent entrepreneurs. By practice I mean the "how" of fairly common human activities. For example, all human beings have to eat, but eating practices display stunning variations across history and cultures. The same is true of practices of child-rearing, acquiring knowledge, executing criminals (and punishing in general), courting, teaching, and so on. Here I turn to ethnography to account for some basic practices of violent entrepreneurs. The most convenient way to structure the multitude of practices is to group them according to key technical terms: *probivka, naezd, strelka, razborka, razvodka.* Wherever possible, I will provide translations, though each of these terms can be understood only against the background of the set of practices as a whole. To say, for instance, that *strelka* means "meeting" is to say almost nothing at all.

Probivka

In the practice of violent entrepreneurship the acquisition of information about business enterprises and their protective arrangements has a strategic importance. It also saves time and effort. Simply speaking, a violent entrepreneur should know who is who in the area or, as they say, "who works with whom." Information about new companies is valuable in that it may bring in new clients. Information about one's partners can also help one to assess reliability and predict behavior. In case of a dispute, knowledge can replace firepower and help "solve a question." The side better equipped with information about its opponent—or capable of convincing others thereof—has a higher chance of winning a dispute. On the other hand, it is common for violent entrepreneurs to operate under conditions where information is scarce and the level of predictability low. Is this shop really protected by FSB officers or is the manager just trying to fool us? Who stands behind protection company Z? Will the adversary use violence or is he likely to seek a compromise? What is the value of the assets of company X, which failed to repay the debt? Who are its major shareholders? *Tambovskie*? Damn, this is getting serious.

Getting answers to these and similar questions and processing the information occupy much of a violent entrepreneur's daily routine. The practice is called *probivka,* "probing" or "penetrating." When a BMW with tinted windows stops by a new shop or the office of a newly opened company and its passengers pay a visit to the manager to find out, in this case more or less politely, with whom he works and what he would do if any business problems arose, this is an elementary case of *probivka*. Cruising around the city to identify new companies took a great deal of time for rank-and-file bandits at the beginning of the 1990s. Accordingly, only those companies that attended carefully to their protection were eager to get an office in a notable, centrally located building. Finding a cellar office space in the yard of a backstreet house not only saved small companies office rents but also allowed them to reduce protection costs. This also explains why business editions of the Yellow Pages were so thin in those years— once a company begins to advertise itself, a *probivka* will be quick to follow. Criminal groups actively introduced their agents into local administrations and banks to collect information about newly registered businesses and their accounts. As informants supplied names and addresses to the leaders, the latter composed operation assignments for each brigade, and brigades set out to conduct *probivkas*. This is more or less how things worked on the ground level until the mid-1990s.

The practice becomes much more complex in the case of sophisticated transactions and disputes. It requires access to specialized databases and recourse to methods of business intelligence. Formal details about regional businesses can be obtained from the registry division of the regional administration. More intricate data have to be sought either in the MVD's or the FSB's restricted access databases (this is called *probit' po bazam dannykh,* to probe with the help of databases): hence the value of acting or former state security and enforcement employees with access to such databases. In this case, *probivka* involves gathering, processing, and analyzing information that the object of interest would not want to publicize. If, at an early stage, specialists in *probivka* were ordinary bandits or state security employees acting on an informal basis, since 1993 the business has become increasingly professionalized and has been taken over by private protection companies.

Naezd

Criminal groups have worked out a variety of methods for putting pressure on businessmen. Primitive methods of intimidation are constantly replayed in middlebrow gangster and Mafia movies, which are especially favored by young racketeers and, according to some of them, often serve as manuals. *Naezd* (literally, a "run-over" or assault, harassment) is the term for all kinds of demonstration of force that involve explicit threats and potential or actual damage. In the words of Konstantinov, "*naezd* is a kind of psychological and sometimes physical assault on a businessman, mainly to stimulate his sincerity and demoralize him."[35] It ranges from an unpleasant visit to an office by a group of formidable thugs who crush office equipment, harass

35. Konstantinov, *Banditskii Peterburg 98,* 127.

personnel, and spill gasoline, threatening to burn down the whole damn thing, to sudden visits by fire inspectors or the tax police in camouflage, with the manifest intention to close down the company. Understandably, *naezd* is practiced to intimidate someone and thereby elicit the desired behavior. Regarded as a somewhat "extreme" and less respected method, *naezd* is used to establish tributary relations, to speed up the repayment of a debt, to put pressure on competitors, and so on. In the late 1990s the term was picked up by the mass media and appeared in the lexicon of leading businessmen and state officials. Thus, visits by the state tax police to the offices of the Most business group in Moscow in summer 2000 were called *naezd* in the Russian media.

Strelka

Having "probed" a businessman or company, a criminal group obtains the names and coordinates of its protecting agency (in the unfortunate case where there is none, a protection offer or *naezd* is likely to follow). The next step is to verify the client's claim to have a "roof." If members of the group know the "roof makers" personally, they will call them up to ask whether this *baryga* (a derogatory term for "businessman") really pays them. Otherwise, they will set up a meeting with representatives of the alleged "roof" to see who they are and to solicit a confirmation. It is taken as a rule (which is not always observed, however) that a bandit does not lie to another bandit (bandits may lie to businessmen), especially in a face-to-face conversation and in the presence of others. Cheating would be regarded as an insult and treated accordingly. Hence many cases require personal meetings. According to the rules, every bandit or group has a right to call another bandit or his group for a meeting. A refusal is not acceptable. In the language of violent entrepreneurs, such a meeting is called a *strelka*.

All forms of violent entrepreneurs' activities regarding disputes, guarantees, agreements, conflicts, and so on, are carried out through multiple *strelkas*. That is why *strelka* is the most frequent daily event of a violent entrepreneur. A typical bandit *avtoritet* might spend days in his Mercedes rushing from one *strelka* to another and coordinating meetings and appointments set by his brigades. Thus one cannot imagine a more convenient solution or a more fortunate coincidence than the massive introduction of mobile phones in the 1990s, which made it possible to coordinate multiple *strelkas*. For a brief period, the mobile phone came to be perceived as the bandit's symbol.

There are a number of rules pertaining to the *strelka*. One cannot ignore or miss a *strelka*. Not only does the failure to show up for a *strelka* automat-

Setting a *strelka*. A scene from the life of bandits in the early 1990s. By permission of the Agency for Journalistic Investigations, St. Petersburg.

ically mean defeat; it also damages one's reputation. A late appearance is also highly disapproved of and puts the latecomer in a disadvantageous position from the start. The most remarkable feature of the *strelka* is its semiotics. When setting up a *strelka*, participants do not negotiate many details, but there are subtle signs that make it possible to predict its possible scenario. All violent entrepreneurs are remarkably sensitive to these signs and know how to read them, since those who fail do not live long. Most important, one has to be able to predict the probability of a violent outcome and to prepare accordingly. How many people should be taken to the *strelka*? Should they all be armed and ready for a shootout? What if the police interferes and arrests us with all those guns? Is it worth the risk? What does the reputation of those guys who set up the *strelka* tell us?

How do violent entrepreneurs make decisions? Their decisions are, of course, a matter of experience and practical sense. It is intuition that often saves their lives, not rational assessment. Nevertheless, several major criteria can be set forth. First of all, the nature of the question awaiting resolution and the reputation of the opponent have to be considered. Certain criminal groups, like the Chechens in Moscow in the early 1990s and *kazanskie* in Petersburg, were known as extremely aggressive and uncompromising. A *strelka* with them was less likely to proceed in a friendly manner. Furthermore, where a *strelka* is held often serves as a sign of its possible outcome. If the sides want to avoid violence and assure one another of that intention, a *strelka* will be held in a populated public place, such as a square, café or hotel bar where the use of firearms is difficult and risky. In a less conspicuous place, and especially in suburban areas, the sides may set a limit on the number of cars (they count vehicles, not people) taking part in the *strelka*: "Five o'clock, westside park entrance, one car each." But if the setting is something like "fifty-fifth kilometer of the (Moscow) ring road" or "six o'clock by Copper Lake," with no other details agreed on, one would be either a fool or an exceptionally brave man (this is also, by the way, how reputations are made) to come alone and unarmed. Sometimes, several criminal groups may come to a *strelka* involving dozens of cars and over a hundred participants. A high concentration of violent people does increase the probability of a shootout; but, if all sides are adequately prepared, the mechanism of deterrence is likely to work. In general, the art of handling a *strelka*, that is, the ability to settle a dispute at a *strelka* without recourse to violence (*gramotno provesti strelku*), a kind of bandits' diplomacy, has a higher value than shooting skills.

Razborka

A violent clash with or without gunfire is commonly called *razborka* (a "sorting-out"). In some cases, *razborka* is a planned action, when two or more fully armed groups get together at an agreed-on place and exchange automatic gunfire. One such *razborka* took place at twilight on 6 May 1992 in Butovo, a peripheral Moscow district near the ring road. The Balashikhinskaya group had six Kalashnikovs and a few pistols. Their adversary, adequately armed, consisted of an assembled team of *podol'skie, izmailovskie, chekhovskie,* and the group of Seriozha the "Beard," over a hundred people all together. First, the leaders simply talked, but tensions grew, and after someone fired a shot, a full-scale *razborka* began. The outcome was three dead and five severely wounded.[36] One of my respondents reported cases where, to avoid heavy casualties, each of the two groups that arrived for a *razborka* put forward its strongest man for a duel (normally without firearms) and agreed to count the result of the individual fight as the outcome of *razborka* between the groups.

Razborka is the ultimate and most costly method of dispute settlement. Interviews and conversations left me with the impression that only a small proportion of *strelkas* end in *razborkas*, but, unlike routine *strelkas*, every shootout, like any extraordinary event, is widely discussed and remembered for a long time. A famous *razborka* happened on 12 August 1993 in the city of Nizhnii Tagil in the Urals. The casus belli was an attempt by an Azerbaijan criminal group backed by local sportsmen from the *Fortuna* club to establish a monopoly over the local city market. The other major group, which resisted the attempt, bore the name of the Afghan veterans' club Gerhat-Ural. Nizhnii Tagil is famous for its tank-building plant Uralvagonzavod, the largest in the world in area, according to the Guinness Book of World Records. A group of former Afghans hijacked a T-90 tank as it was returning to the factory from a test range and drove it into the city. The tank stopped at the office of the company Gong to pick up other members of the group and headed across town to the market to settle the score with rivals. The local police force was alerted and had to use its own armored personnel carriers to erect a roadblock near the Winter Sports Palace, where the tank was finally stopped just short of its destination. No shots were fired in this *razborka,* but no one dared dispute the Gerhat-Ural's claim to victory. Ironically, for lack of a suitable article in the criminal code applying to tanks, the person who drove the tank, one Vlasov, was charged with car theft and convicted.[37]

An even more incredible *razborka* episode, which happened in 1991, was told to me by a person who played the leading role in its preparation. I am still skeptical about the truthfulness of the story, but since an independent inquiry is hardly possible, I found no way to disprove Gennadii's story of a

---

36. Modestov, *Moskva banditskaya,* 155–56.
37. *Syshchik* 2 (October 1993): 2.

razborka he claimed to have organized. The group to which my respondent belonged was in a conflict with a criminal group from the town of Pskov, south of Petersburg. A *razborka* was imminent.

> Gennadii: We told them to come to a place called Tolmachevo, a village approximately halfway between the two cities. We said they should exit the highway not far from the bridge, by the Luga River, drive past an abandoned youth camp to the riverbank, and wait near a garbage dump. Before that I found my old friend, who was a wing commander of a jet fighter squadron stationed in Siverskaya, forty to fifty kilometers from there. For some five hundred or seven hundred bucks, I don't quite remember now, it was something insignificant, he promised to arrange for a jet fighter to do some kind of maneuver, you know, they target this bridge when they imitate ground attacks, as the guy said. [At that time, Su-17 supersonic ground attack fighters were stationed at the Siverskaya airbase—V. V.] We agreed on the time, and what the plane was supposed to do was a kind of very low-level flight and a vertical climb over that place by the dump. Apparently, the pilot did all that, the idea was to scare them and cover them with garbage, you know, that jet exhaust must have been strong enough. I don't know what happened to those other guys, but they no longer bothered us. We just phoned them and asked whether they wished to continue. . . . For a while after that, a rumor circulated that we have been providing the "roof" to an airbase *(kryshevali aerodrom)*. (5)

Razvodka

The term *razvodka* refers to a key stratagem of violent entrepreneurs. It can be translated as "dupe" or "frame" but also has the connotation of "divorce," *razvod*. One of my respondents defined *razvodka* this way: "It is a way to make a client understand what he really wants" (19). An elementary *razvodka* is a way to increase the amount of protection tribute by exaggerating the danger and thereby justifying additional payments. Typically, it goes like this. Criminal group X provides protection to enterprise Z, which pays X regular tribute. X wants to increase payments, but since relations between X and Z are generally regarded as a partnership or even a friendship, X cannot apply direct pressure. Instead, it secretly contracts another criminal group, Y, to conduct a rough *naezd* on Z's premises, demand payments, and perhaps even expropriate some of its property. Y does this, and the management of Z, understandably, gives an emergency call to X to report an outrageous assault. X declares it is mobilizing and sets up a *strelka* with Y to solve the problem. Then X and Y stage a *razborka* whereby some members of X suffer injuries. X presents the "injured" to the management of Z and explains that Y are *otmorozki,* and the only way to solve the problem is to shoot them all. The businessmen, who are themselves scared to death by that time, readily agree to bear the cost of war and give their "protectors" additional money for "guns and medicine." Finally, to the joy of Z, X reports a happy ending to the operation against Y, gives half the revenue to Y, after which X and Y celebrate a successful *razvodka*. In its simplest form, *razvodka* is a way to increase the rate of extraction by covertly managing external threats instead of making direct threats.

The practice of *razvodka* allows us to see the difference between extortion (bogus protection) and genuine protection and, at the same time, the elusive character of this difference. Imagine that X and Y did not enter into the secret agreement, and that Y, which might well be a brutal migrant gang trying to fight for its niche in the city, acted on its own, calling X to action and drawing them into a real, not phony, *razborka*. In other words, the same thing might well happen without a conspiracy, simply by virtue of the multiplicity of threats emanating from various violent groups. Understandably, any conspiracy of this type is logically possible when the situation it imitates is probable in the first place. Deliberate "framing" *(razvodka)* is possible only when some frame already exists. The conspiracy only exploits the logical interdependence of threat and protection and the fact that anyone who is caught in a situation of "more than one threat," that is, where no monopoly of force exists, can be easily framed. The fact that *razvodka* exist does not mean that the business of private protection can be reduced to a number of individual conspiracies, but, on the contrary, underscores the structural conditions that make that business self-perpetuating.

Let us take another example of what may qualify as a "classic" *razvodka*, drawn from a different setting and involving aims other than direct pecuniary benefits. On 11 February 1942 the former French liner *Normandie*, converted by the U.S. Navy into the troop carrier *Lafayette*, was set ablaze in New York's Hudson River harbor. At U.S. Navy headquarters, this was taken as a case of Nazi sabotage, since naval intelligence had long been suspicious that German- or Italian-speaking dockworkers were signaling to offshore enemy submarines. The New York authorities knew that the only agency capable of preventing further sabotage was the Mafia. This led Washington officials to devise a secret emergency plan called "Operation Underworld" and to sanction the navy to contact Mafia bosses Frank Costello and Meyer Lansky. They, in turn, let the authorities know that only Lucky Luciano, who was at that time serving his thirty-year prison term in Dannemora Prison, could really ensure that the docks were safe. A secret deal was agreed on. For his help, Luciano was transferred to the more comfortable Great Meadow Prison. Soon after the war, he was released for his patriotic service to the government.

As Carl Sifakis has put it, "It was the Mafia that struck the match to the *Normandie*."[38] The truth was revealed in the posthumous memoirs of Lucky Luciano and confirmed in Lansky's confessions to his Israeli biographers. The *razvodka* was masterminded by Luciano's underboss Albert Anastasia, and approved by Luciano himself. The Mafia conspiracy, it turns out, led the state authorities to devise another conspiracy that, in turn, enabled the Mafia to get what it wanted. But who can be sure there was no third conspiracy, whereby Luciano and Lansky made up the whole story to fend off allegations that they lent assistance to the government to control sabotage? After all, this was wartime, the Nazi threat was not a myth, and the government's control over immigrant workers was weak. With the other participants dead, there is no one to confirm or disclaim the story of the two Mafia bosses.

The appeal to conspiracy theories obviously leads to an infinite proliferation of so-called conspiracies and explains little. What is obvious, however, is that the authorities sought to use the Mafia to govern dockworkers and the Mafia used the authorities' incapacity to govern in order to govern them in turn (to make them understand that what they really wanted was to have Lucky Luciano released). The Mafia manipulated the Nazi threat (a real one at the time) to affect the behavior of the U.S. government, but if the government could have effectively controlled the threat itself, no Mafia "frame" would have been possible. Thus, the conspiracy (the "agency") matters less than the structure of the situation as a whole. Similarly, an elementary *razvodka*, which can now be seen as a form of indirect governance (as opposed to direct coercion), is simply a conscious use for one's own benefit of an already existing structure created by interdependencies of multiple ("more than one") violence-managing agencies.

38. Carl Sifakis, *The Mafia Encyclopedia* (New York: Facts on File, 1987), 242.

4.

Bandits and Capitalists

T here is a good deal of bias and confusion in the statistics reflecting the degree of criminal control of the new Russian market economy. The most widely cited data were provided by the MVD in January 1994, based on estimates by the Russian Government Analytical Center for Social and Economic Policies. It claimed that criminal gangs controlled or owned (the study was not specific in its terminology) forty thousand businesses, including two thousand in the state sector. The majority of businesses in Russia (up to three quarters) paid illegal protection money.[1] The Analytic Center of the Academy of Sciences provided even more alarming data, stating that 55 percent of the capital and 80 percent of the voting shares of private enterprises had been transferred into the hands of criminals.[2] These and similar estimates inspired the authors of the U.S. Center for Strategic Studies report on Russian organized crime to claim that "roughly two-thirds of Russia's economy is under the sway of the crime syndicates."[3]

Later and more sober analyses, such as the study of privatization in Russia conducted by a group of U.S. scholars, established that these figures were either exaggerations or in fact related to small businesses only. Thus, the forty thousand businesses mentioned in 1994 were four times the number of

1. Cited in *Economist* 19 (1994): 57–58.
2. *Nezavisimaya gazeta,* 21 September 1995.
3. W. Webster, *Russian Organized Crime: Global Organized Crime Project* (Washington, D.C.: Center for Strategic and International Studies, 1997), 2.

medium-sized and large enterprises that were privatized at that time and twice the number of large enterprises in existence.[4] "Many big privatized firms are unprofitable, and even organized crime wants a risk-adjusted return," write the authors of the study. "It is hard to imagine why organized crime would want to control weak firms that are cutting employees, reducing capacity, confronting serious cash flow problems, and struggling to supply the kindergartens, housing and hospitals their employees need."[5]

Estimating the degree of control criminal groups exercised over the economy without a prior understanding of the goals and forms of control may indeed yield distorted results. The separate acts of collecting protection fees, enforcement partnerships, and stock ownership all imply a degree of control but each act is different in its nature and scope. The consequences of control for criminal groups and for economic enterprises also vary depending on the nature of the business and the economic behavior of particular criminal groups. Control is dialectical and may involve mutual influence, so that a criminal group may itself become dependent on the economic assets it has managed to seize, especially if it intends to receive ongoing revenues from their use. Not only may the degree of control of criminal groups over the private economy in Russia differ from what the data suggest, but its nature and consequences may vary significantly from case to case. Furthermore, as criminal groups and economic enterprises evolve, so does the nature of relations between them. It can also be plausibly assumed that an expansion of the ownership of economic assets may transform the structure and action patterns of a criminal group, and, conversely, that the establishment of criminal control may affect the cost structure of a given enterprise.

In fact, these assumptions emerged from observations and conversations in the course of my research. But, given the nature of the research subject, a systematic test of such assumptions was hardly possible. Without understanding the economic dimension of the activities of violence-managing agencies and of their evolution in the changing political-economic context of the 1990s, however, we risk missing a major aspect of the genesis of capitalism. I resolved the difficulty, at least in part, by using the case study approach, which compensates for the lack of scope with an attention to detail. The choice of cases was strongly determined by the possibilities of access to the field. Where choice was possible, however, I focused on cases that had been typical but became exceptional, that is, I gathered data about criminal leaders and groups that had begun like many others but that, over time, had become economically much more successful than the others. Thus far I have

4. Joseph Blasi, Maya Kroumova, and Douglas Kruse, *Kremlin Capitalism: Privatizing the Russian Economy* (Ithaca: Cornell University Press, 1997), 116.
5. Ibid., 119.

focused on the violence potential of criminal groups as well as their interrelations, structure, and practices relating to that potential. I now turn to their economic policy.

The Career of a Violent Entrepreneur

How does one become a violent entrepreneur? Legends about people who have risen to prominence often mention signs attesting to these people's future extraordinary abilities that manifested themselves in their early years. The myth of Hercules, for instance, has him strangling snakes while still in the cradle. Retrospectively, early signs of professional fitness are considered proof that one is predestined for glory. Stories about underworld celebrities are no exception. While still a schoolboy, the would-be New York Mafia boss Lucky Luciano earned money and respect by offering younger and smaller Jewish boys his personal protection against beatings on the way to school. If they did not agree, he would beat them. One slender kid refused to pay, and Luciano attacked him but got an unexpectedly tough response. The kid's name was Meyer Lansky, the future boss of the Jewish Mafia and Luciano's lifetime friend.[6] One of my respondents, an active member of the Chechen diaspora in Petersburg, began his career in a similar way. He mentioned during an interview that to earn pocket money he used to sell protection to his schoolmates who were involved in petty commerce. While still a student, he worked in the security service of the Grand Hotel Evropa and, in addition, provided informal protection to the American Medical Center in Petersburg. "I can speak English, have honest eyes and a broad smile. And they, like all foreigners, are scared of bandits—pushy and brutal. I wore a suit and a tie and could use a company Volvo. They paid me three hundred dollars per month, and there wasn't very much work" (1).

In different social circumstances, the same personality traits and abilities can lead to different careers. Someone who has been brought up in the tradition of the priesthood and who displays a remarkable gift for this vocation, for example, may nonetheless become a militant materialist and revolutionary, as happened to many young Russian intellectuals in the 1860s. But even if one's gifts do not absolutely determine one's destiny, the spectrum of career choices is not unlimited. A movie actor can, in certain circumstances, become a politician, but he is unlikely to succeed as an accountant should he decide to change professions. Max Weber has termed a specific type of dispositional connection between personality traits and their likely (but not

6. Carl Sifakis, *The Mafia Encyclopedia* (New York: Facts on File, 1987), 200.

necessary) forms of social realization "elective affinity."[7] In his classic study, he charts an elective affinity between the Protestant ascetic and the early capitalist entrepreneur. Henner Hess also tries to establish an elective affinity (to my mind, he does not do so very convincingly) in discussing the role of traditional Sicilian character in the emergence of the Mafia in Italy and the United States.[8] Gambetta's economic model, on the contrary, eschews subculture as an explanatory device and focuses on the general properties of the market of protection and on respective sets of standard choices that require no theory of socialization. Suggesting, quite correctly, that there is little specifically ethnic (in this case, southern Italian) in the origin of the Mafia, Gambetta is nonetheless led to admit the importance of subculture as skills and expectations.[9] While having very little to do with ethnicity, subculture plays a major role in breeding potential violent entrepreneurs. When something goes wrong with their institutional reproduction, a boxing club, a Sicilian village, a prison camp, an army regiment, an ethnic diaspora, and even a police department can become subcultures producing violent entrepreneurs. The obvious disparity among these institutions may lead one to assume that subculture is therefore arbitrary and that there is something else—for instance, social and political conditions—that really matters. Yet some occupations, such as academic; some sports, such as table tennis; and some locales, such as the Russian agricultural village (unless in a Cossack region!) are less likely to breed violent entrepreneurs than the secret service, a boxing club, or a mountain village in Caucasus. Subculture also matters in that it affects the social trajectory of violent entrepreneurs and their capacity for group reproduction. Former members of the military turned private enforcers are more likely than ex-convicts to join a private protection company or even return to state service. Thus Weber's principle of elective affinity may be seen at work at the level of subcultures. Individuals socialized into a certain subculture, that is, molded and equipped by it, may be mobilized for purposes unforeseen and even restricted by that subculture, yet depending in key ways on its norms and skills.

Several subcultures in Russia produced individual dispositions and skills that are also required for violent entrepreneurship. Sports clubs, especially those in fighting sports and the martial arts made an especially significant contribution. I would estimate that three out of five middle-and upper-ranking members of Petersburg criminal groups specializing in private en-

7. Max Weber, *Protestant Ethic and the Spirit of Capitalism* (New York: Scribner's, 1958), 90–92.

8. Henner Hess, *Mafia and Mafiosi: The Structure of Power* (Lexington, Mass.: Lexington Books, 1973).

9. Diego Gambetta, *The Sicilian Mafia: The Business of Private Protection* (Cambridge: Harvard University Press, 1993), 10–11.

forcement have athletic backgrounds. Criminal groups in other cities, especially Moscow and Ekaterinburg, display a similar tendency. Former sportsmen are as prominent in illegal enforcement as former state militiamen and security forces are in the private security sector. This pattern requires little explanation. A combination of qualities, such as competitiveness and team spirit, physical aptitude and willpower, readiness to use force and to sustain injury, leadership and discipline, make a sportsman particularly fit for violent entrepreneurship. Still, these qualities are not sufficient to ensure an individual or a group a successful career in private enforcement. Of all sportsmen, only a fraction become violent entrepreneurs and only a few achieve success. The following case studies are intended to provide some clues to understanding how this happens.

My first meeting with Vitalii took place in a hotel bar in summer 1998. Our mutual acquaintance referred to him as an *avtoritet* and defined his status as "a general but not a marshal"(5). As befit his status, he had two bodyguards (one of them was also the driver of a Mitsubishi Pajero and the other performed secretarial functions) and wore a massive gold necklace, a gold cross, and a gold bracelet. He was of medium height, but his physique attested to the master of sports title he possessed in freestyle wrestling. That first interview revolved around issues regarding the formation and activities of criminal groups as well as his prison experience, which was still a fresh memory. A year and a half later, I asked, through the mutual acquaintance, if I could meet Vitalii for another interview to talk about his career as the leader of a criminal group. Two more meetings, in the same hotel bar and in his office, followed. By then, his hair had grown to a respectable length and the gold regalia were gone. On the back wall of his office hung a large poster of the leaders of the Medved progovernment movement, which prevailed in the last elections: Minister of Emergency Situations Sergei Shoigu, the leading anti-Mafia cop Alexander Gurov, and the Greco-Roman wrestling champion Alexander Karelin. Having noticed my surprise, Vitalii pointed to Karelin's autograph on the poster and said: "My colleague, so to speak." I did not ask what exactly he meant by that.

I had to learn speed writing because a tape recorder was ruled out. I explained that, as a sociologist, I was interested in general patterns, schemes, and examples and that I had no interest in who killed whom and sought no information that would put him or myself at risk. During the interviews, I could ask any question, but my respondent answered only those he wished. It was agreed that he would simply ignore the questions he considered inappropriate. As with other similar respondents, although I had an interview plan and a set of prepared questions, the conversation often took random turns. Sociologists call such a conversation "a semistructured interview."

Vitalii was born in 1962 into a Leningrad working-class family. He began attending a sports school at the age of five, and, when he turned seven, was admitted to a special sports class affiliated with the High School of Sports Mastery (ShVSM). This meant regular practice in addition to the standard primary school curriculum. "We practiced until 8–10 P.M. We all knew each other well, practiced and went on competition tours together—wrestlers, boxers, sambo wrestlers, judoists.[10] Putin, by the way, also practiced judo in that school. I was in the freestyle wrestling section." Vitalii finished secondary school in 1979 and a trade college the following year. When in 1982 he got out of the army, he was invited to join the Dynamo team. "In fact this meant that I went to work in the militia. You know perhaps, Dynamo is the MVD club and you get formally enrolled and receive a rank. They paid 170 rubles salary plus dinner coupons I could sell, so it added up to no more than 300 per month altogether. I realized I wouldn't be able to save enough that way to buy a car." In 1985 Vitalii decided to end his career in sports, but the MVD authorities did not let him formally leave the militia until he had obtained a medical certificate that allowed him to be decommissioned. Thus, after fifteen years, he finished his wrestling career and formally left ShVSM. In practice, however, it was as though he had graduated from sports, having received special training and acquired a network, an informal team of wrestlers, boxers, judo wrestlers, and the like.

"Then I went to work in the Eliseev supermarket [a prestigious shop on Nevsky]. Many people went to this shop, and this gives you an opportunity to be aware of what's going on [Vitalii is implying a particular public related to the shadow economy rather than ordinary shoppers]. By then I already understood that your social origin does not matter, and if you manage to translate your ideas into economy, you can get huge dividends. One simply has to be creative." Infected with the spirit of entrepreneurship, Vitalii began seeking areas were it could be applied. These were the years when Gorbachev's restrictions on alcohol trade were still in force. Officially, no alcohol could be sold after 7 P.M. Consequently, illegal trade flourished. Taxi stands, student hostels, and shops in private apartments were in the forefront of the business. "We decided to expropriate the vodka trade from the state, so to speak. That is, to consolidate and take control of the alcohol trade after seven. First, we had to establish wholesale supplies and take control of the retail trade. We would visit the director of a supermarket and propose that he sell us, say, four trucks of vodka per month." The basic scheme was to buy vodka from the state at the regular retail price via corrupt shop directors. The retail price of a bottle doubled after 7 P.M. Vitalii's group pocketed the

10. "Sambo" stands for the Russian *samooborona bez oruzhiya,* the art of self-defense without weapons.

difference and paid directors their cut. If shop directors were not willing to sell part of their vodka supplies through the back door, Vitalii made them "an offer they couldn't refuse." "Some of those directors were unprepared to do business. Sometimes we had to convince them. Once we had to overturn his car. But generally, they agreed. It was not hard to calculate how much they got from one truck. He had thirty thousand rubles per truck, not bad for the time [the price of a prestigious car was ten thousand]. Then he saw that we paid him properly and on time, solved his questions, and did not harass him. And he'd be glad to work with us."

The rise of a new group, which at that time was called the *bortsovskaya brigada,* the wrestlers' brigade, did not go unnoticed in the underworld. Traditional criminal elements approached sportsmen to bring them into their system of relationships and values.

> Sometimes we were approached and they [the criminals] would ask: what kind of life are you living? And we would tell them, no particular life [meaning no particular code]. Where possible, we tried to avoid brutality. But no one can resist an organization. I created my own organization. Everyone knew his place and responsibilities. No drugs, regular meetings, regular training. Brigadiers elected the leader themselves. I do not particularly enjoy the power and try not to show it too often, but in our work you must show that you are responsible for everything.

Thus, on the one hand, there was organization, discipline, fitness—a kind of paramilitary structure. On the other hand, the leader, a graduate of a trade college, sought commercial opportunities and adapted the organization to set up and manage commercial projects. "I looked for free themes [commercial opportunities not seized by other groups]. I was not interested in themes that did not bring in money. And we did not engage in theft or outright swindling. It's dirty money and it could get you into trouble. I do not like when money lies idle. It has to be invested somewhere. At one point we set up private sewing workshops where people made clothes, put on trendy labels, and then sold them. Serious changes happened in 1989. Then cooperatives began and we rushed to do what everyone else did—protect trading spots, put up our *kommersanty,* build kiosks. Then we bought out a supermarket for seventy thousand rubles." At this point I asked whom he meant by "we." Vitalii's reply: "'Plastilin,' the wrestlers 'Pozdniak' and 'Chum,' the boxer 'Vopros,' and Kolia-the-Nose, also a boxer. And they had their own teams. In the beginning, we had only about thirty people." Thus initially, Vitalii's enterprise consisted of five *brigadirs,* each with five or six people under his command. Later, another *brigadir,* Denis, a former hammer thrower, joined the group. Vitalii also had a deputy adviser, who was a master of sports in judo and a Leningrad University graduate. From certain remarks and information from other sources, I concluded that, originally, the group had been loosely attached to the large Malyshevskoe criminal society but became fully autonomous in the 1990s.

The nature of the activities of Vitalii's group was very much like that of other similar agencies. It controlled a city market and a number of private shops and cafés. The sportsmen provided physical protection, enforced contracts concluded by their clients, and settled disputes. Vitalii emphasized his role as a manager capable of organizing and rationalizing the business that the group took over. In 1990–91, for example, the group supervised prostitution in the city center, which the Tambovskaya group had previously controlled and had decided to abandon. Although quite profitable, prostitution was regarded as an inferior business, capable of downgrading the relative status of the group, since it lived off "women's income."

> We took over the Tolmachev street business [a gathering place for prostitutes in the late 1980s]. *Tambovskie* did not do much there except collect. We set up a security brigade there and told the girls to remember names and addresses in case they were mistreated or not paid. When they complained, we took action, and they felt safe, and people knew we wouldn't just drop it. And we had a lot of new offers to work under our supervision. We earned a kind of reputation. With all that we then turned to debt recovery and wholesale warehouses. Then we decided we should start production. We bought a farm near Pskov. Some Caucasians claimed the land was theirs. We said, What do you mean it's your land? Your land is mountains, so go there. There were some tensions but eventually we drove them out. We set up a cattle farm and supplied meat to enterprises in exchange for their products, those goods we felt we could sell for cash. This is how we built up economic ties. Then we drew partners from Moscow, they added investments and we set up a meat-processing plant.

From another member of the group I learned about transfers of management that were practiced in the bandits' milieu. When the *avtoritet* of the Tambovskaya group, nicknamed "Anzhei," was put behind bars, he suggested that Vitalii manage, "for half" [of the profit], a business that Anzhei had controlled before his arrest—the Olgino Motel on the Petersburg-Helsinki route. Vitalii agreed. "You should have seen what a mess was there under *tambovskie*," says Gennadii.

> Prostitutes, drugs, thieves, a real mess. Drug traders were ousted immediately. Then Vitalii sat down to calculate how many prostitutes were needed to satisfy the demand. I don't know how he estimated that, but he came up with a figure. All the rest were driven out. Then he turned to the restaurant and bars. Once we see pickpockets arrive. And we tell them, no guys, you won't be

working here, and kick them out. Next day a *vor v zakone* comes: how come you don't allow them to steal? And Vitalii says, They're not stealing from the hotel clients. They're stealing from me and from Anzhei, who is in the zone. Because if Finnish tourists get their wallets stolen they won't pay for drinks, they won't pay prostitutes. You think I should let them steal my money?(5)

In 1992 the leaders of the group, including Vitalii, were arrested and charged with extortion. This, in brief, is what led to the arrest. The group protected a professional swindler, one Lev Levin. When Vitalii went to Moscow, the local bandits asked him to help them find a person who had embezzled 65 million rubles from Elektrobank and was suspected of hiding in Petersburg. It turned out this was Levin, who had cheated the Moscow bank and, by not reporting the loot, his Petersburg patrons as well. Vitalii started to press Levin to return the money, but eventually Levin turned himself in to the Anti–Organized Crime Directorate. There was another extortion episode and a witness, the group's car mechanic, who owed money and fled. He was later caught by members of the group and handcuffed to a pipe in a toilet and left "to think about how to repay the debt." But he managed to unlock the handcuffs and escape. Turning himself over to the police was his only way out.

Vitalii was sentenced to eight years in jail, and his associates received a lighter sentence. He was released in under six years, at the end of 1997. The arrest was a real setback for the group, especially given that, in 1992–95, violent entrepreneurs were actively dividing up potential business spheres. The group, however, managed to preserve its major ventures with the help of those members who remained free. There is an informal rule that forbids bandits from seizing economic enterprises from someone who is serving a prison term. Violent entrepreneurs nonetheless do their best to avoid arrest and imprisonment, since these cause serious economic damage by impeding prospective contracts and disrupting existing ones. In the case of Vitalii, however, it should also be remembered that the years he spent behind bars were also the wildest in Russia's recent history and cost a great number of people like himself their lives.

At some point in the conversation, a man entered the office to greet Vitalii and pass him some papers. He introduced the man as Gurgen. This visit changed the direction of the interview. "Gurgen is my *kommersant*. I have been working with him since 1991, he is a specialist." It has become common for an economically minded *avtoritet* to have a number of trusted businessmen. They are not regarded as mere taxable subjects but are treated as genuine business partners. They manage investments while the *avtoritet* protects investments, enforces related contracts, and seeks new opportunities. Each holds half the business's stocks and occupies formal managerial positions. Thus, Gurgen turned out to be the executive director of a holding company that owns and manages three large city markets (Torzhkovskii, Poliusrovskii, and Southern), while Vitalii's official position is deputy director.

In Vitalii's story and in the very office where the story was told there was much evidence of the rationalization of the criminal group's activities. Vitalii talked about the importance of professionals and of formal relations. "Now is the time of professionals. Everyone still does everything according to human relations, but it ought to be done as it should [by that he meant duties as opposed to favors]. Instead there are only close people." He turns around and points to tables and graphs hanging on the wall by the Medved poster and tries to explain. As the criminal group became involved in investments and management, close personal relations, which had hitherto constituted the basis of group cohesion, had to be transformed into formal duties and a clear hierarchy, which no longer depended on specific people and their previous distinctions in "combat."

> You see, now we have all those graphs and timetables, all positions are specified, anyone can see who does what and how much. In May 1998 we only had 50 percent of the stock in this market. Now we have 100. Actually we began with a 25 percent share and gradually bought stocks from employees. As for the southern market, we won a tender, honestly, our project was chosen as the best one by the city authorities. Money is an instrument for realizing one's ideas. Like recently, we got interested in a factory, invested our money, and the factory began to work.

Then I asked Vitalii if business relations had changed in recent years and in what direction.

> There are less cheats. I personally think that cheating is bad. But when a contract is signed, we, the roof, meet their roof, their partner and negotiate. And I do not care who is their partner, it can be anyone, even the Cossacks. We establish who they are, and find out, for example, that they have a certain X, a former boxer I know, we practiced in the same school. I phone him, ask questions, he gives his guarantees, and I trust him. This is the informal way and it's passing. We can also take the legal way. We have a lawyer, former deputy procurator of the city. He was convicted for accepting bribes from the Chechens. We helped to get him released and now he works with us. So then we draw up a long contract and observe all the formalities and in case things go wrong we'll go to court. I am not interested in increasing my wealth if it

involves high risk. Like Eldar *malyshevskii,* he embezzled money and is now compelled to live on the mattresses.

At this point Vitalii suggested an excursion to the market. This also meant that time was up, and we left the office.

The attitude Vitalii demonstrated throughout the interview can be summed up by the popular term *khozyain,* which means simultaneously "master" and "manager." The term has strong positive connotations of rule, responsibility, and protection but refers to the management of the economic domain, the *khozyaistvo.* An archaic word related to a well-off peasant household, it is still widely used to refer to successful regional governors, city mayors (Moscow mayor Yurii Luzhkov is regarded as an exemplary *khozyain*), enterprise directors, and local oligarchs. Despite its traditionalist undertones, the concept can accommodate advanced forms of corporate ownership and management, because its traditionalism refers neither to particular spheres nor to technologies of management but to the sovereignty of the manager and the economic effects of management. A *khozyain* is a local strongman who supplies order and promotes growth. During the interview, Vitalii mentioned the Krasnoyarsk aluminum baron and informal regional ruler Anatolii Bykov as someone for whom he felt great respect. A former boxing coach, Bykov (nicknamed "Tolia-byk" and "Chelentano") had a stunning career, moving from local racketeering brigade leader to director of the TANAKO holding company, which at that time owned a regional aluminum and energy complex. Bykov is often called the *khozyain* of the region (currently under arrest after the clash with the Krasnoyarsk governor Alexander Lebed). "After I got out of prison I lived in Krasnoyarsk for a while," says Vitalii. "Bykov is highly respected there as a genuine *khozyain.* There are no criminal gangs in the region because Bykov drove them out. He managed to subject to his rule a city with a population of a million and put things in order."

In the context of rapid change, the idea of *khozyain,* master-manager, became associated with pragmatism—the *khozyain* readily disregards the means for achieving sovereignty if its effects on the local economy and order are positive. In other words, how one manages the property is more important than how one has acquired it. This attitude, typical of early capitalism (and of the transitional stage, since there is no shortcut to late capitalism), inevitably presents Russia's central authorities with the uncomfortable dilemma of choosing between rational-economic and legal approaches to a whole new breed of local masters-managers. Should they be incorporated into the new structures of economic governance at various levels? Should their de facto economic position be recognized de jure or should they be purged by the rule of law? In the absence of a clear position by the central authorities on this key issue in the second phase of Russian reforms, the dilemma finds its resolution on the local level.

The Evolution of a Violence-Managing Agency

I have called "violence-managing agency" any human community that commands organized force and manages this key resource in such a way as to make it the source of a permanent income, eventually by establishing control over a local economy. Violence and coercion are powerful instruments used in the competition between violence-managing agencies, but they are not sufficient for long-term survival. The need to secure gains led some groups to adopt a new strategy for increasing their economic involvement. Their leaders also sensed that economic investments and participation in local politics could make them less vulnerable should the state policy toward crime be more actively applied. This, in turn, compelled them to make two important adjustments: to introduce a more efficient property regime for the enterprises they controlled and to change their status vis-à-vis the law and public opinion. Their criminal reputation, so helpful during the earlier phase, was no longer conducive to their changing aims. I will illustrate this tendency by focusing on the evolution of two violence-managing agencies from racketeering gang to local financial-industrial group: the Tambovskaya and the Uralmashevskaya groups. By the year 2000 they had become influential political-economic players in the northwestern and Ural regions, respectively.

Tambovskie

Vladimir Kumarin was born into a peasant family in a small village in the Tambov region. Unlike many of his future associates, he did not earn any high sports titles, though he played football and attended a boxing club. As he recounts in his autobiography, published by Konstantinov, he came to Leningrad in the late 1970s determined to receive a higher education and become a specialist.[11] Nonetheless, Kumarin soon left the Leningrad Institute of Mechanics and Optics to work as a bouncer in newly opened bars, a typical move for sportsmen in the mid-1980s. "We provided security in the bar and settled conflicts. Many interesting people appeared there and we of course rubbed shoulders with them. There we first met Novoselov, for example, now the deputy speaker of the city Legislative Assembly."[12] At that

11. Andrei Konstantinov, *Banditskii Peterburg 98* (Moscow: Olma-Press, 1999), 351.
12. Ibid., 354.

time, the rare and well-known bars in the city were centers of gravity for people with shadow incomes. Debts and conflicts were routine, and bouncers were pulled in to settle disputes and enforce order. "Almost all of my acquaintances went through the school of bars: Malyshev, Arthur, 'Krupa,' Pasha Kudriashev, Cheliuskin. We all boiled in the same pot," says Kumarin, enumerating the future leaders of racketeering gangs.[13]

Kumarin gradually made a name for himself, and became even more notorious after he spent two years in correctional camps for hooliganism. In 1988 he met another Tambovian, Valerii Ledovskikh, a graduate of the Leningrad Institute of Physical Culture and master of sports in boxing. This was the formative event for the Tambovskaya criminal group (popularly *tambovskie* or *tambovtsy*). There were a few more young people from the same town who joined the two founders. Other members of the quickly growing collective had no relation to Tambov whatsoever. It was not until the first shootout in 1989, when the former militiaman Sergei "Broiler" Miskarev (see photograph in chapter 1) killed the bandit Fedya Krymskii for assaulting cooperative traders whom "Broiler" had claimed to protect, that the undifferentiated racketeering milieu split into separate gangs with distinct names. *Tambovskie* became one such name. The gang rose to prominence after a series of TV reports the same year by the famous journalist Alexander Nevzorov, who gave the name wide publicity. In the words of Kumarin: "Nevzorov began producing one TV report after another about the horrible *tambovtsy*—for us this was like advertising. After that people started coming to us. Of course there were occasions when we lured people artificially, I won't deny that."[14]

The group expanded rapidly. By 1990 its leadership also included Mikhail Glushchenko ("Khokhol"), the former boxing coach and future deputy of the State Duma; the Gavrilenkov brothers, authoritative leaders of the Velikolukskaya brigade; Alexander Efimov, the future director of a large private protection company; Oleg Shuster, a future businessman, master of sports in judo and, for a short period, the owner of local TV channel 11; and the rising *avtoritety* Vasia Brianskii, Stepa Ulyanovskii, and Bob Kemerovskii. Each had a number of brigades under his command. Different experts estimate the group's overall numbers in 1990 at between three hundred and five hundred. At that stage, *tambovskie* did not have any particular specialization, but simply expanded their protection to every possible form of commercial activity, from prostitution to the importation of computers.

In 1990, as a result of the special police operation, seventy-two members of the Tambovskaya criminal group, including its founders, Kumarin and

13. Ibid., 355.
14. Ibid., 359.

The leader of the Tambovskaya criminal group, Vladimir Kumarin (center), and his associates at a baptismal ceremony. By permission of the Agency for Journalistic Investigations, St. Petersburg.

Ledovskikh, were arrested and convicted. Kumarin was sentenced to four years. The operation did weaken *tambovskie* but did not undermine the criminal world to any significant extent. Rather, it changed the balance of power in favor of the Malyshevskaya and other rival groups. In 1991–92 Alexander Malyshev became a stationary bandit with headquarters in the international Pulkovskaya Hotel and managed to consolidate the protection business by incorporating a large number of autonomous brigades, including some of the former *tambovskie* members. In 1992 the newly created Northwestern Anti–Organized Crime Directorate (RUBOP) turned against *malyshevskie* and arrested the leader and his close associates. According to Konstantinov, the vacuum in the leadership created by the arrest of the "emperor" resulted, in 1992–93, in a wave of clashes and murders. According to some estimates, thirty-five upper- and middle-ranking bandits were killed in those two years.[15] Many smaller groups later broke away from *malyshevskie* and continued on their own. Because the actions of law enforcement agencies could not affect institutional conditions that sustained the growing realm of illegal protection and enforcement, their efforts only triggered internal reconfigurations of the realm, leaving untouched its capacity for self-reproduction. Thus, as soon as *malyshevskie* suffered a setback, another force rushed in to profit from it and to change the balance of power in its favor. Continually reinforced by fresh supplies of young fighters from the town on the Volga, the Kazanskaya criminal group quickly built up its presence and influence in Petersburg.

15. Ibid., 144.

The phenomenon of youth gangs in Kazan' still requires an explanation. At the beginning of the 1980s, when the level of public safety in the Soviet Union was still high and crime rates low, Kazan' and another neighboring Tartar town, Naberezhnye Chelny, had already been divided up by dozens of youth gangs and was periodically shaken by gang wars. Each gang was named after and tied to a certain city neighborhood. The gangs were primarily engaged in hooliganism, robbery, and fights with one another. For the majority, active gang membership rarely continued after the age of twenty or so, but an efficient mechanism for recruiting new eleven- and twelve-year-olds never allowed the membership to drop. Another distinguishing feature of youth gangs in Kazan' was the absence of sportsmen in their ranks and their explicit contempt for the cult of muscle. Instead, they made broad use of knives, stilettos, metal rods, truncheons, and other traditional weapons. Accordingly, the use of drugs and conventional forms of crime prevailed (9). With the growth of private entrepreneurship, gangs turned to racketeering, but the scale of private business in Kazan' did not match the size of the "protection" offer. Hence, after the first gang leaders from Kazan' settled in Petersburg, the gangs began sending their brigades to the northwestern region for short-term shifts. Several *avtoritety* coordinated dozens of relatively independent brigades, each making money for the main gang in Kazan'. In case of conflict, however, they acted as a unified force. After spending several months to a year in the city on the Neva, those who survived returned to the town on the Volga and were replaced by a fresh contingent.

These tactics enabled *kazansksie* to rapidly increase their influence in Petersburg in 1993–94, at the expense of local groups. Their tactical strength, however, turned into strategic weakness. Over the long term, the reliance on brutal criminal methods, active involvement in drug trafficking, and the system of rotation impeded their integration into the local political-economic structure. Citing unnamed representatives of *tambovskie*, Konstantinov asserts that *kazanskie* were excessively cruel and predatory on the businessmen from whom they collected protection money: "They are completely irrational, they rip off their own businessmen and do not let them develop."[16] Such an attitude may indeed have followed from the system of rotation, which gave preference to short-term gains over sustained "stationary" protective relationships. Since their home base was in Kazan', the *kazanskie* would have had little interest in long-term investments in Petersburg. After one RUBOP officer had been shot dead and another wounded by *kazanskie* bandits in April 1995, the law enforcement agency launched an unprecedented retaliatory operation targeting the leadership and businesses of the

16. Ibid., 216.

criminal group.[17] From the interview with a RUBOP officer: "*Kazanskie* lost their position after they shot two RUBOP employees in 1995. RUBOP raided the city and arrested a lot of bandits, especially from *kazanskie*. It deliberately put heavy pressure on all of them, so that *kazanskie* would be blamed and also punished by others. By that time Noil, their leader, had been killed and they had no center. They knew no limits and their groups would come from Kazan' and grab whatever they could, while their businessmen left them or went bankrupt."(22) Other experts have also confirmed that *kazanskie* were heavily involved in swindling, robbery, and the drug trade, which eventually made them relatively more vulnerable to anti-crime campaigns (4, 9). It would also be logical to assume that *tambovskie* and *malyshevskie* secretly offered a helping hand to the authorities in purging the city of violent, uncontrollable types.

In the meantime, many *tambovskie,* including Kumarin, returned to the city. A further trajectory of the group was strongly affected by the internal conflict that broke out in 1993. According to the RUBOP version publicized in a TV documentary (whose accuracy Kumarin later confirmed), one faction of *tambovskie,* led by the Gavrilenkov brothers, expropriated over one million U.S. dollars' worth of imported wine from a businessman who worked with another faction led by Kumarin.[18] Instead of returning the revenue from the sale or sharing it, they simply killed the businessman and then contracted the killing of Kumarin. On 1 June 1994 an assassin fired twenty-eight shots at Kumarin's car, killing his bodyguard and severely wounding the leader of *tambovskie.* Although he spent many hours in a coma and lost his right arm, Kumarin survived the attack and was sent to a hospital in Germany to recover. After a private investigation, the killers (Runov and Gavrisenkov) were found and interrogated. To save their own lives (only temporarily, as it turned out), they volunteered to settle the score with the Gavrilenkov team. A mutual hunt began. Consequently, during the following year, Nikolai Gavrilenkov ("Stepanych") and two other members of his brigade, Anzhei and Kosov, were murdered. Nikolai's brother Viktor was also shot at but, unlike the British lawyer John Hyden, who happened to be sitting next to him in the hotel bar, he survived the automatic gunfire.

Having survived the internal war, Kumarin consolidated the leadership of the Tambovskaya group and began to create a new structure that would allow it to transform itself into a legitimate financial-industrial group. By the

---

17. Vadim Khimich, "Rasstrel mashiny RUBOPa. Sorvavshiasya razrabotka" (The shoot-down of the RUBOP car: An investigation that misfired), *Operativnoe prikrytie* 1 (1997): 23–25.

18. *Banditskii martirolog,* a documentary by Marina Kozlova, available on videotape as *Vne zakona* (Outside the law) (St. Petersburg: Dubl video, 1998).

end of 1994 the group had already invested in the timber trade, computers, and entertainment facilities, and had set up a number of banks. Many of *tambovskie*'s business projects were realized through the Shevtchenko brothers. Viacheslav Shevtchenko, who became the deputy of the State Duma on Vladimir Zhirinovsky's party list, and Sergei Shevtchenko, the deputy of the Legislative Assembly of Petersburg, were made owners of the Nord holding company, which controls the nightclubs Hollywood Nights and Golden Dolls on Nevsky, a network of shops, the FM radio station Petersburg-Nostalgie, and a large distribution network of print media.[19] In 1995 Mikhail Glushchenko, another founding leader of the Tambovskaya criminal group and a close friend of Zhirinovsky, became a deputy of the State Duma. Another influential city deputy, Viktor Novoselov, Kumarin's friend from the 1980s, was responsible for regional political protection. These are only the most prominent figures among the army of managers and officials that the group began to propel into business and politics. The coercive potential of the group, which was the responsibility of Ledovskikh, was legalized through the creation of a number of private protection companies: Delta-2, Concord, Condor, and Kasatka (22).

The chief interest of Kumarin, however, was the energy sector of the northwestern region, especially the fuel trade. At the beginning of the 1990s a Siberian oil giant, Surgutneftegaz, became the largest fuel operator on the Petersburg market. Through subsidiary companies it established a network of fuel depots and gas stations that provided the city with key energy products. With little control over prices and supply, the city authorities were seeking ways to reorganize the regional fuel market. The need became especially pressing after the acute fuel crises of 1994, for which the authorities blamed the monopoly policies of the Siberian supplier. To shield the city from unpredictable decisions by the oil monopoly, the city authorities sought to encourage greater competition on the fuel market by inviting in other dealers. There was another, parallel solution, which *tambovskie* quickly realized would allow them to capitalize on the economic problems of the region and, at the same time, to assist the authorities in resolving them. They decided to sever relations between the local distribution infrastructure and the Surgutneftegaz mining and refining facilities and to link the city to alternative suppliers. The plan involved surreptitiously seizing the Surgutneftegaz facilities and resolving the inevitable conflicts—activities for which the criminal group was particularly well suited. Exploiting tensions between Surgutneftegaz and its Petersburg representatives, making lucrative offers,

19. "Kto takie bratiya Shevtchenko i pochemu imi interesuiutsia bortsy s orgprestupnostiu" (Who are the brothers Shevtchenko and why do they interest the anti-criminal police), *Vash Tainyi sovetnik* 7 (April 2000): 16–17.

and using strong-arm tactics and sophisticated setups, *tambovskie* began subjecting Surgutneftegaz subsidiaries, which owned the major fuel depots and gas stations, to their control. In the meantime, following the Moscow example, the Petersburg city authorities set out to create a home-based company that would protect the interests of local fuel consumers. In September 1994, the city administration and leading businessmen, including those known to work for *tambovskie,* set up a new company, the Petersburg Fuel Company (PTK). By the beginning of 1998 all the companies and fuel facilities set up by *tambovskie* or former Surgutneftegaz subsidiaries were officially incorporated into PTK.[20] After adopting his mother's maiden name, Kumarin (now Barsukov) became the vice president of the holding company, with vice governor of Petersburg Yurii Antonov as its president.

The tactics of *tambovskie*–PTK have achieved the goal of displacing Surgutneftegaz. The fuel infrastructure of the city was annexed and firmly linked to the largest regional oil distillery, KINEF. Afterward, PTK set out to expand its regional activities (albeit in competition with other operators, such as Balt-Trade, Neste, and LukOil). In 1999 it won the tender for refueling the city's public transport system, built a vast network of modern gas stations, and thus became the largest regional fuel operator. The sustained effort of the *Tambovskaya* criminal group (now called an "organized criminal society" by law enforcement) to achieve control over segments of the regional economy was largely successful, but the consequences of success were somewhat insidious. For the criminal group, PTK has turned out to be a kind of Trojan horse. The more the group got involved in owning and managing economic enterprises, the more it became subject to powers other than those operating in the milieu of criminal enforcers. *Tambovskie* came to be increasingly dependent on professional managers and accountants. Its economic interests and dependence on the powers of the economic sector and business culture have made the criminal reputation of its members a negative asset. PTK now tries to be as law-abiding as possible and, as a result of the growing interdependence, increasingly relies on state bodies for protection. "PTK has a clear structure and is absolutely transparent to the city as taxpayer," claims its president and the city's vice governor, Antonov.[21] The chief security consultant of PTK, according to RUBOP information, is the former head of the Northwestern Chief MVD Directorate, Sergei Bukhanevitch (22). In an effort to refashion himself as "businessman Barsukov," Kumarin claimed in his interview that he had developed new goals

20. Kirill Metelev, "Khozhdeniya po neftianomu Piteru," *Operativnoe prikrytie* 1 (1998): 28–33; Konstantin Shmelev, "Tambovskaya vetv' piatoi vlasti," *Obshchaya gazeta,* 20–26 August 1998, 4.

21. *Lichnosti Peterburga* 1 (2000): 8.

and had changed his understanding of life. "In June 1998 I became the vice president of the biggest holding company—the Petersburg Fuel Company. We have lots of new tasks and problems to solve: to draw up the budget, create a joint accounting office, consolidate the holding company's management. Big changes have happened in my life," concludes Kumarin-Barsukov.[22]

The positive mood of 1998, which reflected the emerging pact between the new financial-industrial group and the regional authorities, waned by the end of 1999. Initially, a number of important people associated with *tambovskie* were murdered or arrested. In October 1999, the deputy Novoselov was blown up in his car. At the beginning of 2000, one of the leading businessmen of the group, former deputy S. Shevchenko, was arrested and charged with extortion, while Kumarin's right-hand man, Pozdniakov, was killed. In the meantime, the approaching elections of the head of the Petersburg executive branch generated a massive media campaign against the Governor Vladimir Yakovlev to prevent his reelection. The slogan "Petersburg—the criminal capital of Russia" was taken up by the governor's rivals, reportedly backed by Moscow financial circles wishing to promote an alternative candidate. The attack on the people associated with *tambovskie* was seen by many as the flip side of the election contest. But this time, the challenge, in itself a regular feature of Kumarin's career, resulted in an unusual response, which testified to his readiness to accept different rules of the game. The title of his article published by one of the city newspapers, "Tambovians, like Petersburgians, Are Simply Citizens of Russian Towns," reflects the author's intention to clear *tambovskie* of the association with the criminal group and reincorporate them, as it were, into a wider civic body of "Petersburgians"—a kind of unmaking of the criminal group's name. In a fairly straightforward manner, Barsukov expresses his outrage at "those who call Petersburg the criminal capital." Then he argues that *tambovskie* no longer exist and goes on to legitimate his business on the basis of the public good that PTK has done for the city. He notes that 90 percent of public transportation runs on PTK-supplied fuel and that the city owns a 14.5 percent share in the twenty-five thousand–strong holding company.[23] After Yakovlev's rivals failed to come up with a strong alternative candidate and the governor won by a wide margin, the media campaign receded, but Barsukov was compelled to leave the executive post at PTK. This could have been a temporary solution and we may yet witness his return. The resignation can also be viewed as a realization of the principle of separating owner-

22. Konstantinov, *Banditskii Peterburg 98*, 390.
23. Vladimir Barsukov, "Tambovians, Like Petersburgians, Are Simply Citizens of Russian Towns," *Smena*, 20 April 2000, 4.

ship from management, since his leaving the post did not entail a loss of control.

Uralmashevskie

Like many other gangs, Uralmashevskaya received its name from its territory—the district adjacent to the giant machine-building plant Uralmash in the city of Ekaterinburg in the Urals. In police reports it was referred to as the Uralmashevskaya criminal group; informally it was called *uralmashevskie*. Henceforth I will use both names interchangeably.

By the late 1980s the district represented a typical Soviet working-class suburb of an industrial city, and, as in many similar districts, the favorite pastime of its young people was attending sports clubs and fitness centers. Among the founders of the criminal group were the brothers Grigorii and Konstantin Tsyganov, the wrestler Sergei Vorobiev, the skier Alexander Khabarov, and boxers Sergei Terentiev and Sergei Kurdiumov. They all grew up in the same neighborhood, were trained at the sports club sponsored by the machine-building giant, and gradually recruited a few dozen young toughs into the gang. Initially, the core of their local political economy was the district cooperative market, also named Uralmashevskii. Then they established control over private shops and companies in their territory and began to produce alcohol illegally. At the end of 1991, the Uralmash plant, like many other enterprises across the country, was hit by a cash deficit after the government had tightened monetary policy. The plant had difficulty selling its products (mainly mining equipment) and was unable to pay its employees. The leaders of the gang offered the management cash in exchange for a number of properties belonging to the enterprise, including the massive factory club building. The latter became the office of Intersport, the sportswear company founded by K. Tsyganov, and, naturally, one of the gang's headquarters. Then, in addition to functioning as an informal protection agency, the Uralmashevskaya criminal group assumed the role of an investment company. Like hundreds of similar racketeering groups in Russia, it collected a fee of 20–30 percent of the revenue of the companies it claimed to protect. But, unlike others, it quickly started to invest profits, which increased incomes and the degree of control. This strategy would later bring the group decisive competitive advantages.

The aspiration to expand and exploit the growing number of business opportunities promised by the sweeping privatization of the economy inevitably brought *uralmashevskie* into conflict with other gangs. In 1992 a ferocious gang war broke out in Ekaterinburg. One rival force was the so-called *sinie* (the "blue ones," a reference to the color of tattoos), a criminal society composed of ex-convicts with extensive prison records brought up in the old traditions of the Soviet criminal underworld. They aspired to dominate the region and control its commercial opportunities on the basis of their past record opposing the Soviet power. They belonged to the so-called *vorovskoi mir*. Violence was not their major method; on the contrary, the code restricted violence to special cases that required a collective decision by the criminal elite. *Vory* were not entrepreneurs of violence, and although the new realities urged them to adapt and adopt the racketeer's methods, they eventually lost in the ruthless competition with the "sportsmen," as they disparagingly called the new gangsters. The latter were better organized; they endorsed discipline, banned drugs and alcohol, and relied on the use of force to settle disputes—all of which became invaluable assets in times of open warfare. The new Ekaterinburg gangsters no longer paid the old criminal authorities due respect and were unwilling to adopt their code. Conflicts between the old criminal fraternities and the "sportsmen" erupted in many other Russian cities, and, as in most other places, the Ekaterinburg sportsmen emerged victorious, having killed some leaders of the *sinie* and driven the remaining ones out of legal business into the traditional criminal niches.

The Uralmashevskaya's major enemy, however, was the new and no less powerful Tsentral'naya (central) gang, which emerged at the same time and in the same way but this time around the central market of Ekaterinburg. Its leaders were Oleg Vagin and his close associates, former boxer Mikhail Kouchin and the karate master Vladimir Klementiev. Throughout winter 1992 and spring 1993 almost no night in the city passed without an exchange of gunfire. The tactics of the gang war were aimed at destroying both the "military" and the "economic" potential of the rival gang—either by knocking out upper-and middle-ranking leaders, causing damage to businesses, or killing businessmen who worked under the gang's protection. *Uralmashevskie* lost one of its leaders, Grigorii Tsyganov; its major businessman, the investment broker Viktor Ternyak, president of Europe-Asia Company; and a great many less prominent members. Soon they settled the score by ambushing the leader of *tsentral'nye,* Vagin, his bodyguards, and their major businessman, Igor Tarlanov. Kouchin escaped death by being arrested in March 1993 but was killed soon after his release in 1994. By the beginning of 1993 the list of the dead upper-ranking gang members contained fourteen names. The Uralmashevskaya group proved stronger and was able to dictate the conditions of peace to the weakened Tsentral'naya and its new leader, Klementiev. The subsequent redistribution of the spheres of influence did not favor the Tsentral'naya: it remained in gambling, the hotel business, and retail trade, while the Uralmashevskaya expanded into the copper industry, energy, and communications.

The elimination contest of 1992–93 served to strengthen the victorious *uralmashevskie* and to limit the activities of their rivals. The now dominant gang also invested in its public image by conducting charity campaigns supporting the social infrastructure and youth sports clubs, and by subsidizing local public transportation, which earned its leaders some public support. The local police organizations continued to regard it as a criminal association and launched an assault in spring 1993. When the police finally arrested Tsyganov for extortion, public protests followed, and the head of the regional Interior Ministry Directorate had to call a press conference to explain that they had arrested the godfather of organized crime. By then, the police had begun to refer to the Uralmashevskaya not as a group (*gruppirovka*) but as an "organized criminal society" whose membership exceeded three hundred.

In response, two days later a leading Ekaterinburg entrepreneur, Andrei Panpurin, the new president of Europe-Asia Company and the director general of the Ural Brokerage House, called another press conference, during which he put forward an alternative view of the situation, referring to the group not as Uralmashevskaya, a gang name, but as the more neutral Uralmash. "Uralmash is a financial group, not an organized criminal society," asserted Panpurin, stressing its "socially useful activities." Then he explained the source of the group's economic success: "In contrast to others, Uralmash has the most civilized and democratic style of work. Nobody stifles businessmen, many problems were resolved, and their fear of partnership disappeared." Then he described the role of Tsyganov as "the stabilizing figure for the enterprises that cooperate with him. Tsyganov has maintained the balance of power, which may be disturbed with his arrest."[24] After a few months Tsyganov was released.

Thus Panpurin hinted at a certain economic policy introduced by the group and aimed at creating conditions for investment and growth, which appealed to an increasing number of businessmen and brought them into partnership with the Uralmash group. With the key resource of organized force and a local monopoly, the group could also provide firm protection and enforcement for its own investments and those of its partners—the most valuable service under conditions where the state is inoperative. A member of *uralmashevskie* told me in an interview that the group survived because of its economic success, as its members came to realize that force should be used to assist the growth of business rather than simply to steal: "Others, especially *sinie,* turned out to be unprepared for the new realities.

24. *Vechernii Ekaterinburg,* 29 May 1993.

They only knew how to milk [the business], and it did not occur to them that one should invest." According to the police data, the group established more than two hundred companies and twelve banks, and obtained shares in another ninety companies. The financial-industrial group Uralmash invested heavily in the copper processing holding company Evropa, the major regional oil processing facilities Uralnefteproduct, mobile phone and paging companies Uralwestcom and Continental-Link, car trade, and beer breweries.[25] At the same time, police analysts reported a steady decline in the number of criminal offenses committed by Uralmash members.[26]

By the mid-1990s, Uralmash had become a regional political-economic unit consisting of economic enterprises and a "superstructure" that protected property and enforced contracts, relying on its own force and reputation. Wielders of force became owners of capital, but their informal status no longer matched the scale of their activity. The group was firmly integrated into the regional economy and participated in external economic relations. It is thus no surprise that Uralmash sought to forge links with the regional government to secure its economic gains, while the government could no longer disregard the new force in the domain. The first signs of an informal pact emerged in 1995 when Uralmash supported Eduard Rossel' in his successful election campaign for regional governor. Rossel', in turn, stated in a public interview that, to his knowledge, Uralmash members no longer had any problems with the law. He admitted that what really mattered for him were the investments and other contributions that the members of the group were making to the regional economy. "I gave them the order to invest in the building industry of the region," says Rossel'.[27] Thus emerged the outline of a deal that would be repeated in other regions of Russia: former gangsters investing in the legal regional economy, paying taxes, and respecting the law and official regional governments guaranteeing the safety of their capital and accepting them as legitimate businessmen. The leading members of Uralmash joined the civil movement Preobrazhenie Urala (the Transfiguration of the Urals), which had been created to mobilize support for the governor. In summer 1996, on the eve of the presidential elections, Khabarov, one of the founding leaders of the Uralmashevskaya gang, organized The Workers' Movement in Support of Boris

25. *Spravka v otnoshenii OPS deistvuiushchikh v Sverdlovskoi oblasti* (Report on Organized Crime in Sverdlovsk Region), manuscript of the Regional Directorate of the Federal Security Service (UFSB), 1998, 2.

26. *Obzor struktury organizovannykh prestupnykh formirovanii Sverdlovskoi oblasti* (Review of organized criminal groups in Sverdlovskaya oblast'), report by the Sverdlovsk RUBOP (Ekaterinburg, 1999), 8.

27. Cited in Piotr Nikolaev, "Kto zakazyvaet murku?" *Nezavisimaia gazeta,* 11 June 1999, 4.

Yeltsin, for which he later received a personal letter of gratitude from the re-elected president and a watch with a personal dedication from the governor. "I am really proud of that watch," Khabarov later confessed. "It was no undeserved gift. They distinguished me. They acknowledged me as a human being, yeah? This is worth remembering."[28]

In 1997 two founding members of the Uralmashevskaya group took part in the special election of Duma deputies as candidates of the Socialist Party, but that debut was unsuccessful, even though the group managed to get one of its members elected to the regional legislature. In summer 1999 they again backed the governor in his successful reelection campaign. Shortly before, they had witnessed an unprecedented event: on 6 May 1999 the former racketeering gang was officially registered as a political organization, the Social-Political Union Uralmash. The abbreviation OPS, which had been used by police organizations to refer to an "organized criminal society," was now redefined as *obshchestvenno-politicheskii soiyz*, "social-political union," and registered by the regional branch of the Ministry of Justice. The witty reappropriation of the label was no doubt intended to demonstrate the power of the new organization and its changing nature and relation to the law. Nearly half of the twenty-three founding members are the same well-known original members of the Uralmashevskaya gang, the others consisting of "white collars," who, as the PR manager of OPS Uralmash put it in a conversation I had with him, "never held anything heavier than a calculator in their hands" (9). The union's website contains a brief historical narrative—selective and legitimating. In the wild early days of the reforms, so the tale goes, a stern group of sportsmen decided to become businessmen. They managed to withstand the pressure of "criminal elements" and protect their business and that of their partners when the state was unable to provide protection and settle disputes. *Uralmash* responded to the attempts of certain dishonest police officials to fabricate criminal allegations by investing in the local economy, filling the market with goods and services and solving the problem of youth unemployment. Apart from the enormous effort to rescue regional industry and protect it from "negative external interventions," the group supported sports and culture and organized the policing of their native *uralmash* (official name—*Ordzhonikidzevskii*) district "to protect the citizens from hooligans."[29] The general tone of the site, including the platform of the newborn political organization, is firm and assertive, as if presenting the reader with an extended report of its contribution to regional economic and civic life. In an effort to increase public support, members of Uralmash or-

28. Cited in Sergei Mostovshchikov, "Konets banditizma v Rossii," *Ekspert*, 12 June 1999, 53.
29. http://www.ops-uralmash.ru, accessed 15 June 2000.

ganized an antidrug campaign called City Without Drugs, relying on private policing and violence to drive drug dealers out of the city and force addicts to undergo a harsh withdrawal program.[30] What some ten years ago was the racketeering gang Uralmashevskaya has now completed its transformation and become the OPS Uralmash, a political organization with ambitions of becoming a party that defends the interests of regional industry—a substantial part of which is the property of its members.

Yet, as a survey conducted by Ekatcrinburg sociologists in the autumn of 1999 has revealed, public opinion is not as malleable as OPS Uralmash leaders would like. A substantial proportion of the sampled population, 75.9 percent, perceived the group as a "criminal structure" and a "union of bandits striving for power"; 60.2 percent also agreed with the formulation that OPS Uralmash "is a group of businessmen seeking popularity for private commercial gains"; 27.6 percent considered it a "group of businessmen trying to improve the city's condition"; and 38.8 percent agreed it is "the most influential economic and political force in the city." During the March 2000 elections to the regional legislature, Vorobyev, one of the founding members of the gang, ran against the district head of administration, Cherkesov. Although the latter won by a narrow margin, the most significant fact about this election is that the electorate was sharply polarized by age: the younger voters supported the OPS Uralmash candidate, while the older age group voted for Cherkesov, who represented the old administration.[31]

The Uralmashevskaya racketeering gang has thus undergone an evolution. Specialists in violence—former athletes—created an organization, a violence-managing agency that allowed them to extract tribute from local businesses by offering protection. Having established territorial control, the agency waged war against competing violence-managing agencies. It survived and won the elimination contest, expanding both its territory and its commercial opportunities. Having attained a monopoly among informal enforcers, *uralmashevskie* consciously chose an economic policy of reasonable taxation and reliable protection of property, thus creating a relatively secure environment and competitive advantages for its business partners. In the longer run, protection rents and reputation resulted in the accumulation of capital and further economic expansion. Uralmash turned into a financial-industrial group. Parallel to that development, it concluded an informal pact and then established institutionalized relations with the legitimate regional government. Finally, it made an effort to legalize its political and eco-

30. Patrick Tyler, "Russian Vigilantes Fight Drug Dealers," *New York Times,* 4 March 2000.

31. Socium, Center for Sociological Research, manuscript of the *Otnoshenie naseleniya Ekaterinburga k OPS "Uralmash"* project (Public attitudes toward OPS Uralmash), 2000.

nomic power by registering as the Social-Political Union (OPS) Uralmash and actively sought to achieve legitimacy with support from the local population. While its success on this front has so far been modest—impeded by the memories of the past gang wars—nothing suggests it will not be able to achieve this goal over time. If this happens, it will finally unmake itself as a racketeering gang or criminal organization, and few will be willing to remember the early stage in the genealogy of capitalism in the city on the Europe-Asia divide.

Vertical Disintegration

In November 1998, in an interview given to a major weekly magazine, one Moscow criminal *avtoritet* made the following claim: "Over the last two years we [i.e., criminal groups] have been the biggest investors in the Russian economy. One cannot imagine the country's economy without our investments."[32] Although exact figures on investments of this kind are unlikely ever to be established, such claims should not be dismissed. As wielders of force become owners of capital, and especially in cases where they take part in its management, their ability to control their domains comes to depend on the logic and rules of economic activity. To put this dialectic in concise form, the more criminal groups strive to control the emerging markets, the more the markets control and transform these groups. The acknowledgment by wielders of force of the rules of the economic domain, from the simple principle that violence, in the long term, is costly, to a more complex dependency on functionally divided management structures and on the impersonal force of the market, transforms criminal groups into legal business enterprises.

To varying degrees, such a transformation is evident in each of the three cases explored. The groups began as typical racketeering gangs, then turned into well-organized criminal groups that taxed economic subjects and provided protection and enforcement. At earlier stages, many were involved in shadow or criminal businesses, managing and supervising illegal trade operations. Illegal trade and protection rackets provided the primary source of capital accumulation. Then the groups extended their protection to legitimate enterprises, primarily small and medium-sized ones. Ownership was informal; tributary relations were the main instrument of the realization of property rights that rested solely on informal agreements and depended on the policy of each concrete criminal group. There is evidence that those criminal groups that acted in a more predictable manner, created a balanced

32. Alexander Ryklin, "Bratva na nervakh," *Itogi,* 8 December 1998, 16.

informal property regime, and provided competitive advantages for affiliated businessmen and especially for those entrusted to manage the group's finances, became economically more successful than those involved in purely criminal businesses, swindling or excessive extraction.[33] For the majority, the widespread criminal tactic was to gain control over enterprises for the purpose of stripping them of their assets and transferring the revenue to offshore accounts. Having successfully managed a few operations of that kind, a large number of criminal leaders have now settled in the West. Others, probably a minority, invested some of their revenues in Russia, using the groups' reputation and violence potential to protect investments. Investments were further facilitated by the development of stock markets and new forms of ownership. By the late 1990s, criminal groups increasingly turned to formal ownership, actively accumulating stocks and setting up holding companies. This, in turn, required an army of accountants, managers, and other specialists and new forms of organization geared toward capital accumulation rather than coercion.

If, from the very beginning, criminal groups had been operating in a well-regulated environment, their expansion would have been limited and their activities confined to the traditional criminal niche. This, however, was not the case in Russia in the early 1990s. Initially, criminal groups did not encounter much competition from other enforcers, and even less from state authorities. Hence criminal groups were less constrained by the legal framework of the state than by the structure created through their own interactions. As this structure was extended and forced on some segments of the legitimate economy, it also became part of the nascent market order. Another emerging market order was constituted by state regulations, which for a long time were unstable, arbitrary, and poorly enforced. Although the informal order was for a time more efficacious and economically productive than the formal one, especially for small and medium-sized businesses, the formal order could not be disregarded by criminal groups and their businessmen when they turned to the legitimate economy. At a certain point, alliances with local authorities became necessary for the efficient protection of investments. However weak and fragmented the rule of law, state justice and enforcement remained a potent instrument of authorities at various levels and as such could not be ignored by other participants.

The order created by illegal private enforcers and the one that emerged at various levels of the state administration were, by definition, in conflict with

33. Varese's respondents in Perm' also distinguish between predatory "black" protection and more effective business-friendly "white" protection. Federico Varese, "The Emergence of the Russian Mafia: Dispute Settlement and Protection in a New Market Economy" (Ph.D. thesis, Oxford University, 1996), 149–51.

each other. Sporadic anti–organized crime campaigns were an expression of that conflict. Conversely, the tactical convergence of interests and the possibility of agreeing on common rules of the game at a local level made compromises desirable and possible. The restructuring of the regional fuel trade by Petersburg authorities brought the Tambovskaya group to dominance. The Uralmash constantly claims to protect the interests of local industry from foreign and Moscow capital. It supported Rossel' for regional governor in 1995, after he had been removed by the Kremlin in 1993, and also supported his reelection in 1999. Covert and sometimes even public deals between local authorities and financial-industrial groups occurred in many other regions of the Russian Federation, including Moscow. Shortly before his arrest in Switzerland in autumn 1996, Mikhailov, formerly known as the leader of the Solntsevskaya criminal group and now a businessman, won the tender to modernize the Moscow water supply facilities and participated in the project of building a gas pipeline from Turkmenistan to Ukraine. As a matter of fact, his career, which involved an even greater range of international economic activities, shares many features with the three cases already considered and could be taken as further evidence of the transformation of criminal groups into legitimate business enterprises. The confusing "not guilty" verdict of the Swiss court and the 450,000 U.S. dollars it was subsequently compelled to pay Mikhailov in compensation for his "unjustified" imprisonment do not so much compromise law enforcement as reflect the growing orientation of former shadow entrepreneurs of violence toward new economic and legal rules.

What happened to criminal groups as their leadership became involved in legal business? Police experts have noted a tendency that can be called "vertical disintegration." Leaders of criminal societies undertake to improve their public image through charity and investments. Elena Topil'skaya, the author of a study on organized crime, notes that their PR efforts have gained priority over domination of criminal organizations and concludes that "an authoritarian consolidation of organized criminal groups from the top down, as happened in the United States, is unlikely in Russia."[34] As the leadership of economically more successful groups integrates into the legal business world and develops relations with political authorities, many of the mid-level and especially rank-and-file members of their groups become obsolete. Former criminal authorities now prefer to retain lawyers and hire state police and security to enforce contracts and protect their businesses. They do keep a small number of brigades of thugs, but only for special tasks. Their regular activities are increasingly protected by state justice and en-

---

34. Elena Topil'skaya, *Organizovannaya prestupnost'* (Organized crime) (St. Petersburg: Yuridicheskii tsentr Press, 1999), 69.

forcement agencies (4, 26). "Now I do not need that many people," says Vitalii. "Now I rely on professionals from 'Typhoon' [The Ministry of Justice special task force], which is more efficient" (23). Another respondent, who, at the time of the interview, was himself seeking a way to leave the criminal group, asserted that "young people are no longer that eager to join criminal groups. If they do, all they want is to get some money to start a business of their own" (20).

As a result of internal differentiation, some members of criminal groups have become businessmen, others, having lost their jobs and their place in the organization, have joined conventional, "disorganized" crime. The latter has become the primary target of police operations, along with those criminal groups that continue to operate primarily in the shadow and illegal economy. For many former *avtoritety*, criminal leadership has turned out to be a means of rapid social advancement within the span of one generation. Of working-class origin as a rule, many violent entrepreneurs have now become part of the upper middle class.

5.

The Privatization of the
Power Ministries

Thus far, our discussion has largely left out the state. This was justified not least by the need to focus more sharply on the logic of interaction between violence-managing agencies and the structures that resulted from this interaction. It was appropriate to treat Russia's early 1990s as a "state of nature" or a system resembling that of states in the international arena in that the Russian state indeed failed to provide governing order and security. Consequently, agencies operated in a weakly structured environment and were more affected by structures created through their own interaction than by state laws and regulation. A multitude of small private monopolies corresponding to the domains of various protection agencies coexisted with state institutions. In such a field of interaction, the violence potential (or protective capacity) of economic enterprises and, conversely, the economic potential of violence-managing agencies acquired particular significance. As within any other system of self-help, organized violence in Russia's emerging markets became a valuable resource, and access to it produced differentiated outcomes within the national economy. A number of existing institutions and groups, previously unrelated to the rule structure of the economy but equipped to use force, supplied cadres for new private force-wielding organizations that dealt in private protection and en-

Material from this chapter appeared in a different form in Vadim Volkov, "Between Economy and the State: Private Security and Rule-Enforcement in Russia," *Politics and Society* 28, 4 (December 2000): 483–501.

forcement and, accordingly, governed the redistribution of the income of economic enterprises.

But how can one possibly leave the state out when dealing with a country in which the state played a key role for several hundred years? Given the size and power of the state in the Soviet Union and in previous times, stripping the state of any significance during the post-Soviet transition might seem to be a gross error. The state could not possibly have disappeared overnight, even after the radical reforms of 1992. Given that several influential studies have now underscored the role of state structures in revolutionary change, narratives in which the state is absent and claims about self-emerging social orders should be treated with suspicion.[1] The legacy of the Soviet state must have exerted a strong influence on transition paths. Yet the influence of the state is not easy to detect. The role of the state is often seen by scholars in negative terms in connection with corruption and rent-seeking as the conversion of administrative capital. The opportunistic behavior of bureaucrats at various levels and arbitrary administrative actions have only further underscored the way the state has withered away as a public governing institution.

In this chapter I address an important but largely overlooked aspect of the effective legacy of the Soviet state. The conundrum of the strong influence of the absent state, I argue, can be partly resolved by looking at the quiet conversion of large segments of state "power ministries" into a private protection industry. The high coercive potential of the former Soviet state, which became redundant with the major international and internal changes, was unlikely to disappear overnight but rather altered its institutional form. The conversion of the state's coercive and information-gathering capacity into a marketable asset required new organizational forms compatible with the changing economic system, in which the state was no longer the primary owner. Private protection and security companies thus emerged, staffed by former state security and police employees. Their spectacular growth occurred in 1993–96. Thus far I have focused on illegal enforcers and have largely ignored these new key players. It is now time to introduce the new players, observe their interaction with the old ones, and understand the outcomes.

The creation of a private security industry did not appear on the agenda of those who designed Russian reforms. Rather, a combination of short-term political decisions aimed at reducing the power and capacity of the old Soviet state security institutions, adaptive responses of the state security

---

1. See, for example, Theda Skocpol, *State and Social Revolution* (Cambridge: Cambridge University Press, 1979); and Karl Polanyi, *The Great Transformation: The Political and Economic Origins of Our Time* (Boston: Beacon Press, 1965).

personnel to these policies, and the institutional demands of emerging markets led to the rapid formation of this new business sector. Unlike the privatization of the economy, which was the primary reform plan from the start, the privatization of protection and enforcement came as an unintended and ambiguous development. In exploring this process, I also want to highlight the mechanism of unintended consequences that led to the proliferation of legal private protection agencies and to assess their impact—also largely unintended—on the institutional environment of the postsocialist economy.

The Soviet "Power-Wielding Ministries"

As in most other modern states, the political leadership in the Soviet Union maintained a strong centralized control over organizations that constituted the core of the state—the armed forces, the security service, and the police force. Unlike some Western nations, where the government and the coercive apparatus were made accountable to the class of property-owners and, to some extent, to a larger body of citizens, the Soviet state was exempt from the direct control of civil society. From the 1930s on, the national economy was under state ownership and state control, while the highly disciplined one-party system gave the political leadership virtually unlimited decision-making powers. State control over the economy and society, the one-party political system, and the pre- and postwar international context were among the factors that determined the size and political importance of the Soviet coercive organizations.

The People's Commissariat of Internal Affairs (NKVD, the predecessor of the MVD), was set up on 8 November 1917, immediately after the revolution. The "worker-peasant" militia was created simultaneously and became the major police force, which it has remained until the present. Beginning in 1918, the militia was under the dual subordination of the NKVD and local administrations. Since then, tensions between central and local control have caused periodic reorganizations in favor of one or the other.[2] In 1931 the dual subordination ended, but in 1960 the central ministry, by then the MVD, was abolished, giving priority to its republican branches. In 1962, in the spirit of Nikita Khrushchev's reforms, the republican MVDs were renamed "Ministries for the Protection of Public Order." After Khrushchev's removal, the new leadership reversed many of his initiatives and, in 1968, restored the central ministry under its previous name.

---

2. For a history of the Soviet militia, see Louise Shelley, *Policing Soviet Society: The Evolution of State Control* (London: Routledge, 1996), 26–33.

The history of the KGB began on 20 December 1917 with the creation of the Extraordinary Committee for the Struggle against Counterrevolution and Sabotage, the VeCheKa. In 1922 the VeCheKa was attached to the NKVD and became its State Political Directorate (GPU). Since then, the history of state security organizations and of the interior ministry has been one of periodic mergers and divisions, at the discretion of the Party leadership. Each time the head of state sought to strengthen his authority, he would unite the two organizations into one huge ministry, as Joseph Stalin did in 1934–41 as Lavrentii Beria did in 1953, after Stalin's death, and as Yeltsin attempted unsuccessfully to do in 1991–92. Since 1954, the Ministry of Security, renamed the Committee for State Security (KGB), has remained organizationally and operationally independent from the MVD. Like the latter, it was formally under the jurisdiction of the Council of Ministers. In reality, all power ministries were tightly controlled by the Party leadership.

From State to Private Security

In the late Soviet period, the Ministry of Defense, the MVD, the KGB, and the Ministry of Foreign Affairs were informally termed *silovye ministerstva,* "force-wielding" or "power" ministries. The term gained wide currency and semiofficial status in post-Soviet Russia. In the new post-Soviet idiom, it also became common to shorten *silovye ministerstva* to the concise *siloviki,* "wielders of force." Throughout Soviet history, control over power-wielding ministries was the top priority of Party leaders, since it was key in the exercise of political power, and the loss of such control carried the risk of one's removal from power. The same attitude persisted through the post-Soviet transition. The participation of the key power-wielding ministries and their chiefs in the failed attempt to remove Mikhail Gorbachev in August 1991 confirmed that the weakening of control over force-wielders could lead to open political revolt on their part. The heightened attention of the post-Soviet leadership to the power-wielding ministries was expressed in constant reshuffling and sporadic reorganizations that undermined their coherence and operating capacity.

Reforms in State Security

On 22 August 1991 the huge statue of Felix Dzerzhinsky, the founder of the Soviet security service, was triumphantly toppled by a crowd of people in front of the KGB headquarters in Moscow, in the aftermath of the failed coup d'état. This event was the culmination of a spontaneous popular protest against the party-state rule. The act was deeply symbolic: the KGB embodied the coercive power of the state, and the conspicuous popular violence toward it signified defiance and liberation. In the mass consciousness the state and its coercive organs represented a major obstacle to liberal reforms, an obstacle that was then symbolically removed.

Reforms of the state security ministry followed. Their aim, as Vadim Bakatin, Yeltsin's appointee as head of the KGB, openly admitted, was to fragment and decentralize state security organs to diminish their power.[3] Having failed to unite the two power ministries under his control—the decision was deemed illegal by the Constitutional Court in January 1992—Yeltsin switched to the policy of "divide and rule." During the three years after the disintegration of the Soviet Union, the security ministry was reorganized and renamed three times, each time under a new chief. Several former KGB directorates were transformed into separate agencies under federal or direct presidential jurisdiction. By the end of 1993, the formerly united organization was split into five separate agencies: the External Intelligence Service (SVR), the Federal Agency for Government Communications and Information (FAPSI), the Federal Counterintelligence Service (FSK), the Chief Guard Directorate, which included the Presidential Security Service, and the Border Guard Service. In 1995 FSK was renamed the Federal Security Service (FSB).[4]

These reorganizations led to a fragmentation of the state's force-wielding and surveillance capacity. Under the new federal law of 12 August 1995, all the above agencies except the FAPSI, plus the MVD, the Tax Police, and the Federal Customs Service were designated to carry out detective and operative work and to keep their own paramilitary units. In comparison to the Soviet period, the number of agencies entitled to perform these functions grew from three to seven. By mid-1995 Russia had fourteen state internal intelligence, security, and law enforcement agencies.[5] The new division of spheres of competence and jurisdiction was poorly defined, and the agencies competed with and duplicated one another, weakening their overall coordination. Both the FSB and the MVD, for example, currently have directorates for fighting organized crime and others for fighting economic crimes, and all four target the same criminal activities. Consequently, the efficiency of state security and law enforcement agencies has decreased significantly.

The restructuring of state security was accompanied by personnel reduc-

3. Vadim Bakatin, *Izbavlenie ot KGB* (Getting rid of the KGB) (Moscow: Novosti, 1992), 77.

4. Vladimir Korovin, *Istoriya otechestvennyx organov bezopasnosti* (A History of the Russian security organs) (Moscow: Norma, 1998), 80–86.

5. Michael Waller and Victor Yasmann, "Russia's Great Criminal Revolution: The Role of the Security Services," in *Understanding Organized Crime in Global Perspective: A Reader,* ed. Patrick Ryan and Georges Rush (London: Sage, 1997), 198.

tions. The negative public attitude created moral pressure that devalued the status of this profession, while the shrinking state budget and inflation devalued wages. All this strongly induced security officers to seek alternative employment. More than twenty thousand KGB officers resigned or were discharged between September 1991 and June 1992. A significant number left after the crisis of October 1993, including members of the special elite antiterrorist units Alpha and Vympel. In 1992 Yeltsin ordered that the 137,000-strong central apparatus of the former KGB be reduced to 75,000 (a 46 percent reduction) during the restructuring. While a substantial proportion of the former staff of the central apparatus was transferred in 1992–93 to the newly established bodies (SVR, FAPSI, etc.) and to regional FSB directorates, 11,000 had to leave state security permanently.[6] By 1995 the number of operatives with seven to fifteen years of professional experience had decreased by a factor of five.[7]

According to expert sources, besides these obvious factors, which caused an exodus of state security employees and their entry into the private sector, there were more subtle operative considerations that moved in the same direction. The new tasks set before the state security agencies included the struggle against organized crime and the promotion of state interests in the rapidly privatizing economy. One method of acquiring the information needed to fulfill these tasks was the direct infiltration of private businesses (4, 7). Thus, while it is possible to distinguish analytically between the search for a new job by former state security employees and their new operative assignments, an empirical distinction between the two phenomena has become virtually impossible.

Formally, the basic structure of the MVD did not change as radically as did that of the KGB. Anticipating social disorder, the Soviet leadership strengthened specialized divisions and MVD troops. As early as 1987, a special task police force, OMON, was created to counter possible mass turmoil. Two years later, it was thrown into action in the capitals of several Soviet republics. In 1992, in response to the rise of organized crime, the MVD set up a system of twelve Regional Anti–Organized Crime Directorates and special operation detachments (SOBR). At the same time, the shrinking central ministerial budget led to a gradual weakening of vertical control and the regional MVD organizations and personnel were subordinated to regional administrations. Since then, repeated declarations by interior ministers regarding their intention to restore centralized control have had little effect. In addition, the foundation of the system, composed of militia cadres, became

6. Evgeniya Albats, "Raport ob otstavke" (The resignation letter), *Izvestiya,* 2 March 1994.
7. *Belaia kniga rossiikikh spetssluzhb* (The white book of Russian special services) (Moscow: Obozrevatel', 1996), 76.

seriously eroded. Low salaries and morale in the MVD caused an even greater exodus of qualified cadres than had occurred in the KGB. In 1989, 83,500 employees were dismissed from the MVD, including 37,000 commissioned officers. More than 30,000 left the service in 1990.[8] This reflected an extremely high turnover rate rather than overall reduction, since the old cadres were quickly replaced by fresh ones. According to a rough estimate, in 1991–96 up to 200,000 were leaving the MVD each year, a quarter of them dismissed for violations of the law.[9]

Countermoves and Adjustments

The first organizational solution—a countermove—that enabled the FSB to address its new problems—personnel reductions, decline in material welfare, and the need for infiltration—was the creation of the institution of the so-called assigned staff *(prikomandirovannye sotrudniki)*. Article 15 of the federal law on the organs of the federal security service maintains that, "in order to carry out security tasks, the military personnel of the organs of the FSB, while remaining in service, can be assigned to work at enterprises and organizations at the consent of their directors irrespective of their form of property."[10] This provision allowed thousands of acting security officers to hold positions in private companies and banks as "legal consultants," as the position was modestly called. Using their ties with the state organizations and information resources of the FSB, they performed what has become known as "roof" functions—protecting against extortion and cheating by criminal groups and facilitating relations with the state bureaucracy. Expert estimates suggest that up to 20 percent of FSB officers are engaged in informal "roof" businesses as *prikomandirovannye*.[11]

A long-term solution for the commercial use of the personnel and of the informational and technical resources of the KGB and MVD was found by legalizing the informal security and rule enforcement business. The legal framework for such activities was provided by the federal law on private detective and protection activity" adopted on 11 March 1992 and the special government decree of 14 August 1992, which specified certain aspects of its application. Also on 14 August, the MVD adopted the "Regulations on Extradepartmental Protection," which allowed local directorates to set up special protection subdivisions and emergency response groups operating on a

8. Shelley, *Policing Soviet Society,* 56.

9. Azalia Dolgova, ed., *Prestupnost', statistika, zakon* (Crime, statistics and law) (Moscow: Kriminologicheskaya assotsiatsiya, 1997), 48.

10. *FSB Rossii* (The Russian FSB) (Moscow: n.p.: 1995), 18.

11. Alexander Lvov, "FSB na vol'nykh khlebakh" (Freelance FSB), *Novaya gazeta,* 13–19 July 1998, 6.

commercial basis. The latter solution provided local MVD branches with a stable source of extrabudgetary support and made them even less dependent on the central authorities.

Under the new law on private protection, private agencies were entitled to "protect the legal rights and interests of their clients" on a commercial basis. The law permitted private agencies to pursue a broad range of activities: to physically protect citizens and property, engage in security consulting, collect data on lawsuits, conduct market research, collect information about unreliable business partners, protect commercial secrets and trademarks, search for people claimed to have gone missing, recover lost property, and conduct investigations into the biographies of prospective employees of client companies.

It is relatively easy to get a license to set up a private security agency: the Department for Licenses and Permissions, set up at every regional MVD directorate, requires that every prospective head of a security agency have a higher-education degree and evidence of special qualifications or of three or more years of professional experience in state law enforcement or security services. The procedure was designed to facilitate the registration of former security and police employees. The central supervising authority is the department of the chief MVD directorate in Moscow.

The most widely cited data on the service backgrounds of the heads of private security agencies are those provided in 1995 by the executive director in charge of security for the Association of Russian Banks, V. Sidorov (former deputy minister of interior). According to Sidorov, half the heads of private security agencies are former KGB officers, another quarter are from the MVD, and the rest are from GRU (army intelligence) and other organizations.[12] These rough figures probably refer to the Moscow banking sector. According to an FSB expert, they are also likely to change as newly established private security schools begin training fresh cadres for the growing security industry.[13] Thus, exact figures for the entire private security sector as of 1 July 1998 are the following: out of a total of 156,169 licensed private security employees in Russia, 35,351 (22.6 percent) came from the MVD, 12,414 (7.9 percent) from the KGB-FSB, and 1,223 (0.8 percent) from other security and law enforcement organizations.[14] All in all, private security agencies have absorbed nearly fifty thousand former officers from state security and law enforcement bodies, who constitute over 30 percent of the

12. Ivan Zhagel, "Kakie liudi i vse—v okhrane," *Izvestiya,* 26 January 1995.

13. Mikhail Aleksandrov, "Uchastie organov FSB Rossii v konsul'tativnoi deyatel'nosti i podgotovke kadrov dlia negosudarstvennykh struktur bezopasnosti" (The participation of the FSB in consulting activities and in the training of cadres for nonstate security structures), *Mir bezopasnosti* 6 (June 1999): 23.

14. *Biznes i bezopasnost' v Rossii* 2 (1999): 34.

total number of licensed employees. Their influence is hard to overestimate, since most of them, especially former members of the KGB, occupy key managerial positions in the sector. The reemployment of state security officers has been partly managed by the professional association Business and Personal Security created by former FSB employees in 1992. Between 1992 and 1994 the association helped to retrain and employ more than four thousand former state security service employees, half of whom became heads of private security agencies.[15]

Private Security Agencies

The law defines the licensing procedures for three types of security agencies and their personnel: *chastnoe detektivnoe agentstvo,* private detective agency, *chastnaya sluzhba bezopasnosti,* private (company) security service, and *chastnoe okhrannoe predpriyatie,* private protection company. Detective agencies normally perform narrow and specific tasks requested chiefly by private individuals for their private matters. Consequently, autonomous detective agencies are few (just over a hundred for the whole country), and their services expensive. They are beyond the scope of this discussion.[16]

Private Security Services

All enterprises, independently of their size and form of ownership, were allowed to establish a special security subdivision, the private security service (PSS). These were set up in large numbers by private and state enterprises and financial institutions for physical and economic protection and information gathering and analysis. Large banks and companies, especially those assigned to deal with state financial assets or strategic resources, were organized and staffed by former high-ranking state security officers. To give just a few examples, V. Zaitsev, one of the former commanders of Alpha, the special unit of the KGB, became head of security at the Stolichnyi bank; Mikhail Gorbunov, who used to serve in the Chief Directorate of Intelli-

15. "Klienty nami dovol'ny. Interviu s Igorem Borisovym i Yuriem Rudakovskim" (The clients are content with us: Interview with Igor Borisov and Yurii Rudakovskii), *Sekiuriti* 2 (1995): 5.
16. There are several cases where private detective agencies are subdivisions of large PPCs. This reduces costs and gives the companies additional legal rights in conducting surveillance.

gence of the Soviet Army (GRU), went on to be head of security at Inkombank; former KGB deputy chief Philip Bobkov heads the corporate security service of the Most financial group.[17] With thirteen thousand employees, the largest PSS of Gazprom, the natural gas monopoly, is headed by former KGB colonel Viktor Marushchenko and consists of forty-one subdivisions at the company's installations across the country.[18] The majority of PSSs, however, are much smaller. Many of them were created to secure a one-time deal or simply to legalize armed bodyguards for the company's boss, and they continue to exist chiefly on paper.

Private Protection Companies

In contrast to PSSs, private protection companies (PPCs) are autonomous from their clients and act as independent market agents supplying services on a contractual basis. The first PPCs, such as Aleks in Moscow and Zashchita in Petersburg, were set up even before 1992, in advance of the applicable legislation. Originally, many future PPCs started as private guards or informal security services for particular business projects. For example, a Petersburg PPC Severnaya Pal'mira, headed by the former colonel of military counterintelligence Evgenii Kostin, was initially set up as a security service for the city market of construction materials, Muraveinik. Later it became an independent supplier of security for a number of construction companies, such as Business Link Development and Com & Com, and for the official Peugeot dealer in Petersburg, Auto-France.[19] This case represents a typical evolution pattern of a PPC: originally tied to particular clients, it became an autonomous supplier of services on the market.

The corporate principle that sustains the identity of employees in the state security ministries is also closely observed in the private security sphere. Many successful PPCs were founded by tight-knit communities made up of former officers in special task units who sought to convert their skills and reputation into a marketable asset. Not least, attempts by the central government to use special antiterrorist units as instruments in internal political struggles during the crises of August 1991 and October 1993 frustrated offi-

17. Olga Kryshtanovskaya, "Nelegal'nye struktury v Rossii" (Illegal structures in Russia), *Sotsiologicheskie issledovaniya* 8 (1995): 96.

18. "Sluzhba bezopasnosti RAO 'Gazprom': Sostoyanie i perspektivy razvitiya" (The security service of RAO Gazprom: The present condition and future development), *Biznes i bezopasnost' v Rossii* 2 (1997): 6.

19. Evgenii Kostin, "Ia ne vizhu sebia v drugom kachestve," *Lichnosti Peterburga. Bezopasnost'* 1 (1998): 36.

cers and led many to quit the service and consider new employment.[20] That was the case for the former commanders of the KGB special antiterrorist unit Alpha I. Orekhov and M. Golovatov left the unit to set up a family of protection companies whose names openly point to the original affiliation of the staff: Alpha-A, Alpha-B, Alpha-7, and Alpha-Tverd'.[21]

After the KGB antiterrorist unit Vympel refused to participate in the storming of the Parliament during the October 1993 crisis, it was transferred to the jurisdiction of the MVD. Of the 350 Vympel officers, only 5 decided to continue under the MVD; 215 found new employment in the FSB and other state security organs; and 135 left to work in private security.[22] Many of them were employed by the PPC Argus, set up by one of the former senior commanders of Vympel, Yurii Levitsky. Now Argus is one of the largest private security operators in the Moscow region. Other commanders set up a PPC under the original name of the former special unit (Vympel-Chest'). In St. Petersburg, the largest PPC, Zashchita, was established by former MVD employees and is known to actively recruit former RUBOP officers. A group of former officers in the Soviet army paratrooper divisions, who shared combat experience in Afghanistan, were behind Aleks-Zapad, a large private security operator in northwestern Russia. The original Moscow Aleks was created by police officers; its Petersburg division became fully autonomous in 1992 and was taken over by army personnel. In an interview with the author, Boris Markarov, the chief of Aleks-Zapad, mentioned the corporate principle of recruitment, admitting that he trusts "the army caste much more than the militia or the KGB" (10). Hence most large PPCs tend to preserve their corporate identity and resemble privatized segments of the state defense and security ministries. The chiefs of PPCs openly admit what they call "mutually beneficial cooperation" with state organs, meaning they exchange valuable information for money or equipment. Later, relations between state and private security forces were strengthened by new formal organizations, such as the special Consultative Council of the FSB, which consists of employees from the economic counterintelligence department and heads of the major PPCs.[23]

20. Vladimir Zhdanov and James Hughes, "Russia's Alpha Group Changes with the Times," *Transition,* 8 March 1996, 28–31.

21. "Vse problemy reshaiutsia mirno—s pomoshchiu 'Alfy'" (All the problems get resolved in a peaceful manner—with the help of "Alpha"), interview with I. V. Orekhov and M. V. Golovatov, *Biznes i bezopasnost' v Rossii* 9–10 (1998): 28–29.

22. Valerii Yakov, "Vysokie chiny otsenili 'Vympel' tol'ko posle ego razvala" (High officials appreciated "Vympel" only after it had been dismissed), *Izvestiya,* 3 March 1994.

23. V. M. Smirnov, "Opyt raboty FSB s negosudarstvennymi strukturami bezopasnosti" (FSB's experience in working with nonstate security structures), *Biznes i bezopasnost' v Rossii* 2 (1999): 22.

The Structural Dynamic

Soon after the adoption of the law on private security, the new business sector began to expand at an unprecedented rate, especially in Moscow and Petersburg. The law was adopted in 1992; the official registration of businesses started in early 1993; by the end of the year, there were already over 4,000 private security agencies in Russia. Then, until 1996, the overall growth rate was especially dramatic; the number of agencies almost doubled, reaching nearly 8,000. After 1996, growth continued, but the rate slowed (see table 3 and figure 4). By the end of 1999 the number of private security agencies reached 11,652, including 6,775 PPCs and 4,612 PSSs, while the number of licensed security personnel (i.e., those entitled to carry firearms) reached 196,266 (the total number of employees exceeds 850,000). Private agencies own 71,400 firearms.[24] In 1998, the city of Moscow had a total of 3,125 private security agencies and Petersburg had 816, which amounted, respectively, to 29 and 7.6 percent of their total number in the same year. No systematic data on the geography of security businesses have been made available so far. Cities with a lower concentration of businesses tend to have fewer private protection agencies, although other factors, especially the policies of local authorities, may also have a bearing in the matter. In 1997, the city of Cheliabinsk had 150 private protection agencies; Novgorod, between 50 and 60.[25] No data on the size and turnover rate of private protection agencies have been made public either. Large security companies are reported to have an annual turnover rate of between 500,000 and 1 million U.S. dollars.[26] Small protection companies tend to prevail; there are not more than several dozen large and truly influential ones for the whole country.

Several factors were responsible for the leveling of growth after 1996. First, the reshuffling of the state security system, which had generated the supply of jobless specialists, subsided. Second, the initial market demand for protection services was met, and the possibilities for extensive growth were exhausted. Third, MVD supervising bodies tightened control and inspection measures, closing down more than six hundred agencies each year after 1995 for violating regulations. In May 1995 the government in Moscow issued a decree ordering the regional MVD to increase control over the activities of private security agencies in its territory and to introduce an electronic accounting and identification system. At about the same time, similar measures were undertaken in Petersburg.

24. Data made public by Ivan Mayatsky, head of the Chief Directorate for Registration and Licensing of the MVD, *Biznes i bezopasnost' v Rossii* 2 (1999): 20.
25. Ivan Zakharchenko, "Okhrana v uezdnom gorode N" (Security in the provincial town N), *Operativnoe prikrytie* 4–5 (1997): 61.
26. *Ekspert* 2 (1996): 22.

Table 3. Growth of the Private Security Sector by Year

	1992	1993	1994	1995	1996	1997	1998	1999
Total number of agencies	0	4,540	6,605	7,987	9,863	10,487	10,804	11,652
Private protection companies	0	1,237	1,586	3,247	4,434	5,280	5,995	6,775
Private security services	0	2,356	2,931	4,591	5,247	5,005	4,580	4,612
Agencies closed down by authorities			73	690	622	978	1,364	1,277

Sources: Mir bezopasnosti 2 (1997) and 3 (2000); *Biznes i bezopasnost'* 2 (1999).

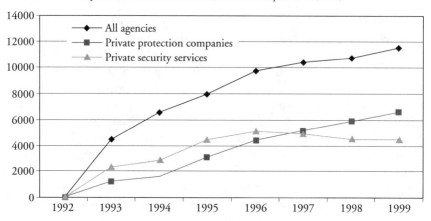

Fig 4. Growth of the private security industry in Russia, 1992–99

Figure 4 also indicates a structural trend: over the last three years, the growth of the private security industry was a result of the growth of PPCs, while the number of PSSs has gradually decreased. Ivan Mayatsky, head of the Directorate for Licensing and Permissions in the MVD, gave two explanations for this trend. First, many PSSs were created by banks during the period of their proliferation in the early 1990s. As some banks subsequently went bankrupt, their security services disappeared as well. Second, it proved more expensive for a bank or company to maintain a PSS than to contract an independent PPC, and gradually many turned to the more efficient option.[27]

This second factor seems to point to an important trend toward the externalization of protection. If, in the beginning, companies tended to inter-

27. Ivan Mayatskii, "Tak o chem zhe my plakali v proshlom godu: Pokhlebka pusta ili zhemchug melok?" *Mir bezopasnosti* 1 (1999): 2.

nalize protection by creating their own security services, later, many turned to external protection. Because of the economy of scale and better technical equipment, large PPCs are more cost-efficient. A PSS has a different advantage. As a subdivision of a private company or bank, it operates under two different authorities, public regulations and the private orders of the company's director general. The latter authority is naturally stronger, and, in cases where the two clash, the PSS is likely to circumvent the formal regulations of external (state) authorities. In contrast, autonomous suppliers tend to be less constrained by their customers (except when created by them). But because they produce services for sale rather than internal consumption, they are constrained by the rules of the market. According to the public claims of their managers, PPCs prefer to conduct their business on the basis of formal contracts and respect for the law. This, however, may be just a successful marketing strategy. Whatever the actual practice, the degree of autonomy of PPCs versus PSSs is greater by definition. The growth of PPCs and the decline of PSSs after 1996 may indicate that for customers, considerations of economy are becoming more important than the ability to directly manage force. If this is correct, then the outcome may be a growing differentiation between economic and security enterprises.

The "Roof"

With the entry of KGB and MVD cadres into the market as private agents, the age of the "roofs" reached its zenith. *Krysha,* "roof," is a key term in the contemporary business lexicon, referring to a private enforcement partner, criminal or legal, and signifying a complex of services provided to clients to protect them physically and minimize their business risks. Unlike some other business terms that have gained currency in recent years, *krysha* did not belong to the criminal jargon but came from the professional vocabulary of the intelligence service, where it signified an official cover-up—diplomatic or journalistic—of a spy. Yet the term was quickly adopted by racketeers and acquired criminal overtones. Everyday practice generated further linguistic innovations, coining verbs from the noun to designate the activity: *delat' kryshu* (to make a "roof") or simply *kryshevat'* (to "roof"). In addition to the influence of the secret service, the adoption of these terms also reflects a subtle shift in the understanding of relations between economic and protection enterprises. Earlier, in the criminal milieu, these relations were designated by the word "collect" *(poluchat')*, which connoted unidirectional extraction, even though real services could be provided. In contrast, "roof" emphasizes the use value of protection and justifies the payments received from clients.

Functions

I have defined the activity of private agencies that manage organized force as violent entrepreneurship—a set of organizational solutions and action strategies enabling organized force to be converted into money or other market resources on a permanent basis. PPCs were not the first to discover this entrepreneurial niche. Since the late 1980s, as the first cooperative and private enterprises began to emerge, organized criminal groups have moved in to demand tribute from private business, since the latter received virtually no protection from the state. As extortion became a standard practice, it turned into a protection racket—an institutionalized practice whereby tribute is collected on behalf of a criminal group that, in exchange, claims to offer physical protection from other such groups. As the private sector expanded and the volume of business transactions grew, criminal groups became engaged in more sophisticated activities such as debt recovery, contract enforcement, dispute settlement, and negotiations with the state authorities concerning registration, export licenses, tax exemptions, and the like. I have distinguished these activities from the protection racket and defined them as "enforcement partnership"—the function performed by a criminal group or other violence-managing agency deriving from the skillful use of force on a commercial basis and allowing certain institutional conditions of business to be maintained. To avoid confusion, let me repeat that the term "function" is used in a dual sense: as a business function (utility) and as an institutional function. Each particular enforcement partner performs a range of business functions for a set of affiliated economic subjects. The outcome of the interactive efforts of enforcement partners is the reproduction of a particular set of constraints that affect the behavior of participants in economic exchange. Although enforcement partners are generally aware of their business function, their institutional function remains largely beyond their grasp.

"Roof" is a descriptive (and slang) term for "enforcement partnership" (an analytical term). "Roofing" should therefore be distinguished from simple physical security. Physical security, which PPCs provide through private guards and security equipment on a contractual basis, is not the primary mission of these agencies. The actual practice of a successful PPC includes, first, the acquisition and analysis of information about prospective business partners, the supervision of business transactions, and, most important, the ability to engage in informal negotiations with other enterprises and their enforcement partners in case of physical damage, breach of contract, or failure to repay a debt. For instance, in 1992 the PPC Komkon, associated with the FSB, successfully recovered a large debt for the Petersburg branch of Sberbank Rossii, the biggest state-owned commercial bank, and subsequently became its permanent partner.[28] This informal practice of solving problems through negotiation between enforcement partners is extremely valued in business circles and is the basis for the reputation of the violence-managing agency, be it a PPC or a criminal group. Thus the enforcement partnership docs not just protect individual clients but is an activity and a function that relates to the institutional structure of the economy as a whole. What distinguishes the security industry in Russia of the 1990s from its no less numerous counterparts in other countries is that, in Russia, the activity of private protection agencies extended beyond mere physical or informational security and into the sphere of business transactions and civic property relations.[29]

By the mid-1990s private security had become a booming new business sector. The demand for PPC services increasingly came from state enterprise directors and from medium-sized and large companies. Understandably, the large established PPCs operate in those sectors that manage to survive and are capable of generating profits, such as the oil and gas industry, banking, communications, high technology, export-oriented production, and the like, including the majority of foreign companies. Among the clients of the security holding company Al'ternativa-M, for instance, are the large chemical consortium Rosagrokhim and the Gromov aerospace research and testing center.[30] In Petersburg, the PPC Staf, headed by former KGB major M. Timofeev, started by collecting debts from the clients of the telephone company Peterstar. Then it became the security and enforcement partner of PTS, the major state-owned telephone network, and of the private communication providers Peterstar and Delta Telecom. As a result, the PPC, which, as its chief has admitted, maintains close relations with the FSB, now supervises a vast regional communications network.[31]

28. *Operativnoe prikrytie* 6 (1996): 9.
29. In the United States in 1982, more than 1.1 million people worked in private security; estimates for 1995 place this number at 1.6 million. Britain has about 100,000 private security employees. Cited in Timothy Frye, "Contracting in the Shadow of the State: Private Arbitration Commissions in Russia," in *The Rule of Law and Economic Reform in Russia,* ed. Jeffrey Sachs and Katharina Pistor (Boulder: Westview Press, 1997), 132.
30. *Mir bezopasnosti* 9 (1997): 10.
31. Mikhail Timofeev, "Menia raduet, chto 'Staf' vospital nastoyashchie kadry" (I am glad that "Staf" has brought up real cadres), interview with Mikhail Timofeev, *Lichnosti Peterburga* 1 (1998): 54–55.

The Competition and Its Limits

In 1992–95 rapid privatization and the rise of private financial institutions brought large new segments of the economy, including medium-sized and large enterprises, into the sphere of free-market relations. The legal and institutional problems were still far from being resolved by the state powers. The physical and economic risks of conducting business remained very high. The amount of unpaid debt steadily increased. Criminal groups, so it seemed, were moving toward achieving full control of the privatized economy. However, it is precisely at this stage that the criminal syndicates encountered a powerful commercial rival, private protection and security agencies set up by former police and security employees. This is not to say that the law on private protection was designed as an anticrime measure. At the time, the state authorities had neither a strategy for institution building nor an anticrime program, and the legal provision on the business of private protection was adopted merely as a tactical solution to provide employment for the former staff of the "power ministries." In the broader structural context, it produced consequences that were not intended when the policy decisions were made.

Since criminal groups were the first to discover this entrepreneurial niche, they also set down the basic rules of the game that every newcomer to the field had to take into account. The head of the Petersburg Department of Licensing and Registration of the MVD, Yurii Buryak, frankly noted, "The business of private protection is impossible without relations with criminal structures. I do not mind *strelki*, they have been and will be. But I am strongly against what is called *razborki*."[32] To achieve success, private protection agencies have to navigate between the legal regulations increasingly tightened by the state authorities and the actual practice of private enforcement, which rests on informal dealings and frequent use of semi-criminal methods. This stems from the highly informal nature of business relations in Russia and the strong presence of criminal groups. These groups also strove to use the law on private protection to their advantage, creating their own PPCs to obtain licenses to carry concealed weapons and to legalize their protection services. Thus, in Petersburg, one of the oldest protection companies, Scorpion, was set up and headed by Alexander Efimov (nickname "Efim"), one of the leaders of the Tambovskaya criminal group. He established close relations with the local police and recruited its former employees to protect more than 120 companies. As a result of the RUBOP investigation, Scorpion was closed down by the authorities at the end of 1996 and

---

32. Yurii Buriak, "Ia ne sobiraius' komu-to ugozhdat'" (I am not going to please anyone), interview with Yurii Buriak, *Operativnoe prikrytie* 2 (1997): 33.

many of its employees were arrested. Its director managed to escape but was tracked down in Ukraine and arrested a year later.[33] In July 2000 Efimov was sentenced to six years in jail for extortion. Many other PPCs known to have criminal origins continue to operate. The PPC Adris, for example, which "roofs" more than a dozen companies, including the chain of ice cream shops Baskin and Robbins, is said to belong to the Malyshevskaya criminal group (1).

The use of force and intimidation to recover debts and settle disputes among businessmen is one of the major activities of criminal groups. Many PPCs are also involved in this business, using purely criminal methods. For example, in September 1996 the police arrested the director general of the PPC Barrs Protection, former KGB major Vladimir Zhukov, and his driver. They were accused of beating and threatening the director of Petrotrade, the PPC's client company, and demanding 35 percent of the company's shares and twenty thousand U.S. dollars in payment for an alleged debt. The case, however, was settled informally and the PPC staff members were released without being criminally charged.[34] In the last two years the MVD authorities have intensified their control, trying to eradicate the informal practice of debt recovery. They issued warnings and published a list of companies known to practice debt recovery, but these measures so far have not had any tangible effect.[35] According to FSB experts, about 15 percent of all private security agencies have connections with criminal groups.[36]

On the whole, despite many cases of PPCs' involvement in criminal affairs, the cumulative effect of their activities has been more positive than negative. While not being manifestly anticrime agencies, they nonetheless managed to weaken the economic base of organized crime and to limit its expansion. "To save a company from being taken under the 'roof' by a criminal gang is very hard," asserts Levitsky, chief of the PPC Argus. "That is why we are proud that none of our clients ended up 'under the mafiya.' If

33. Sergei Leonov, "Konets 'Skorpiona'—nachalo voiny?" (The end of "Scorpion"—the beginning of war?), *Operativnoe prikrytie* 1 (1997): 8–9; Konstantinov, *Banditskii Peterburg 98,* 282–86.

34. "Chastnye okhrannye predpriyatiya Sankt-Peterburga: Analiticheskaya zapiska Agentstva zhurnalistskikh rassledovanii" (Private protection companies in St. Petersburg: An analytical paper for the Agency for Journalistic Investigations) (St. Petersburg, 1998), 4–5.

35. V. V. Ivanov, "Iz opyta raboty Upravleniya litsenzionno-razreshitel'noi raboty v plane kontrolia za prakticheskoi deiatel'nostiu negosudarstvennykh okhrannykh i detektivnykh predpriyatii" (The work of the Directorate for Licenses and Permissions to control the practical activities of nonstate security and detective enterprises), *Biznes i bezopasnost' v Rossii* 2 (1999): 18.

36. Yulia Ignatieva, "Chopophobia. MVD stremitsia monopolizirovat' okhrannyi biznes" (The phobia of private security: The MVD strives to monopolize the protection business), *Obshchaya gazeta,* 9–15 November 2000, 4.

The chairman of the Liberal-Democratic Party, Vladimir Zhirinovsky, and members of the Tambovskaya criminal group: Alexander Efimov ("Efim") (convicted in 1998), Ruslan Koliak ("Lupatyi"), and Mikhail Glushchenko ("Khokhol"). By permission of the Agency for Journalistic Investigations, St. Petersburg.

the establishment of a [criminal] 'roof' is already under way, we get in contact with the leaders of the criminal group and talk to them in the language they understand."[37] On another occasion, Levitsky summed up the overall effect of the private security industry: "Several years ago all Russian businesses were criminalized. We could have become a 'bandit' state. Now, five years later, 'roofs' are [legal] security structures. We accomplished the task quietly, without revolutions and shooting."[38] Overall, the anticrime effects were achieved through a higher quality of services offered by PPCs at lower prices and through their active interaction with state law enforcement and security bodies.

Already in 1991, in pursuit of a supplement to their devalued salaries, informal groups of police and state security officers offered private businesses an alternative protection and enforcement solution and thus entered into di-

37. Yurii Levitskii, "Argus ne snimaet 'krysh'" (Argus does not dismantle "roofs"), interview with Yurii Levitskii, *Chastnyi sysk, okhrana, bezopasnost'* 9 (1995): 12.
38. "Okhrana i pressa: stolknovenie interesov" (Protection and the press: A clash of interests), *Operativnoe prikrytie* 3 (1999): 29.

rect competition with criminal groups. Those companies that managed to contract a police or KGB "roof" could stop fearing a visit by gang members offering their protection. The informal rule that "every businessman has to have a roof," well known to all entrepreneurs operating in the Russian market, was a peculiar way to acknowledge the burden of transaction costs, but it also presupposed multiple options and hence a competition between those who exacted these costs. Let us consider the basic noncriminal options, the logic behind the choice made, and the consequences.

The cheapest solution is to have or make a friend among the police, in particular in RUBOP. This gives the entrepreneur the opportunity to claim RUBOP as his "roof" and to ask the friend to help out when a criminal gang demands protection fees. The owner of a small network of pharmacies in Petersburg can be taken as a typical client of such an informal "friendly" police "roof." His payment for protection may consist of occasionally providing medicine for the policeman's parents (18). This solution pertains chiefly to small businesses and gives advantages to those who happen to have the right friends. Its reliability, however, is low, matching the low cost.

Hiring an acting or retired FSB officer as a manager or law consultant is another widespread "roof" arrangement that enables a company to avoid paying protection money to a criminal group. This "law consultant" acts as a kind of multipurpose fixer, shielding the company from criminal and bureaucratic extortion and mediating relations between private businesses and state authorities. Interview sources indicate that hiring (formally as well as informally) an FSB officer became a widespread practice in medium-sized companies, especially in Moscow. Such a "lawyer" would normally cost the company an equivalent of one thousand U.S. dollars or more per month. Thus, a Moscow-based company producing silicon medical equipment was approached by a criminal group from the city of Kazan', where the company's production site was located. Unwilling to find itself under criminal protection, the director urgently sought an alternative. First he hired a retired KGB colonel and later an acting FSB officer (*prikomandirovannyi*) as his company's "roof." Unfortunately, the officer was later killed in Chechnya performing his state service duties. Subsequently, the company signed a contract with a PPC (24).

A client company and a PPC normally sign a formal contract that specifies the range of services and their price. If the company requires armed guards, the price is calculated on the basis of the standard four to six U.S. dollars per guard per hour. An alarm system, including a hotline connection to an emergency response team, normally retained by the PPC, costs up to two thousand U.S. dollars. Obtaining regular information about another company costs one hundred to three hundred U.S. dollars per month.[39] Alternatively, the contract may resemble medical insurance with a monthly fee of two hundred and fifty U.S. dollars or more, depending on the size and nature of the business, paid to a PPC, whose help is requested only when a problem arises. If the problem is serious enough, such as a need to recover a debt or resolve a dispute, especially if the adversary is a criminal group, the deal is likely to be negotiated on a noncontractual basis and the fee, normally quite high, adjusted to the value of the disputed property, the level of risk, and the amount of work involved. But not all PPCs provide such services. They may instead assist the client in calling on state organs of justice to resolve the problem in a legal manner. In this case, the role of the PPC is to ensure that state courts deal efficiently with its client and to enforce their decision. Many PPCs have a subdivision that provides legal support to its clients and works with the state organs of justice. According to the codirector of the Petersburg PPC Avanpost, "Now one can make the state judiciary work more efficiently. If we need to help our client recover a debt, we have a legal option to seize the accounts of the debtor, which carries a potential damage incomparable with the amount of the debt. This is how we compel debtors to start peaceful negotiations" (12).

Notwithstanding the fact that the realm of private security and enforcement resembles a market, some serious limitations of choice remain, in particular, freedom in the choice of an enforcement partner. Once a company gets caught unprepared for a visit by representatives of a criminal group, yields to intimidation, and starts paying protection money, it is likely to develop a path dependency. Likewise, once a company has appealed to a criminal group to resolve a problem, it will probably continue under the protection of this group, and any attempt to break free will lead to severe sanctions. Understandably, a company is likely to engage or be engaged by illegal enforcers if it operates in the shadow sector of the economy, or in illicit trade. Criminal groups are known to lure clients by offering cheap start-up credits and loans, which subsequently allows the group to hold sway over the enterprise as a shareholder.

As interview sources indicate, the contractual nature of the relationship, a higher degree of predictability of behavior, and a higher quality of services make PPCs a more competitive security solution than the criminal group, given that the constraining factors mentioned above do not obtain. From an interview with the director of a Moscow-based trade-industrial company conducted in 1997: "Today it is beneficial, much more beneficial to deal with FSB than with some criminal group. . . . Talking to them is more eco-

---

39. Anna Kaledina and Tatiana Novikova, "Detektivnye rasskazy" (Detective stories), *Den'gi,* 23 June 1999, 28.

nomically beneficial and also more reliable."[40] Unlike criminal groups, PPCs normally do not interfere in the businesses of their clients, but neither do they provide loans. As mentioned earlier, clients of criminal groups are compelled to pay up to 30 percent of their profits, while the cost of recovering a debt is normally 50 percent of its value. The price of security and enforcement charged by noncriminal PPCs is negotiable and varies with the size and nature of the client business. But it takes the form of a fixed monthly payment rather than a tax on profits or turnover, as is the case of criminal protection. According to the executive manager of a middle-sized multimedia company that signed a contract with the PPC Zashchita, the protective arrangement was highly cost-efficient.

> According to the contract we paid them 350 U.S. dollars per month. This was just pennies. Our revenue then was 20,000 U.S. dollars per month. A great advantage was that they did not have the right to interfere in our business, to count, to audit. We simply bought a service. Basically, the service consisted in our having the right to cite them as our "roof" and call them in an emergency. . . . They also helped us to repay debts. They did not ask anything for small amounts, but from big debts they took a 40 percent fee. Like when our debtor, that Rosenbaum's company Velikii Gorod, which was controlled by the bandits . . . , when it went bankrupt, we had no hope of getting our money back. But Zashchita did that for us. (21)

Managers of large PPCs claim to provide a better quality of service due to the professional experience of their personnel. While maintaining formidable firepower, large companies rely on informational and analytic methods acquired during their managers' careers in state service. The major emphasis is said to lie not in direct physical protection or intimidation but in the preventive neutralization of potential conflicts and threats. The vice chairman of the security service at the Association of Russian Banks, A. Krylov, described the methods of legal enforcement partners this way: "To recover the debt one does not need recourse to violent means—it is enough just to demonstrate that you have information that compromises the debtor and the channels for its dissemination."[41] The director of Aleks Northwest claims his company has a database on all businesses in the region, allowing it to assess the reliability of its clients' potential partners before entering into business relationships.

More directly related to anticrime activity are those PPCs that provide a

40. Cited in Vadim Radaev, *Formirovanie novykh rossiiskikh rynkov: Transaktsionnye izderzhki, formy kontrolia i delovaya etika* (Moscow: Tsentr politicheskikh tecknologii, 1998), 208.
41. *Ekspert* 2 (1996): 20.

rare but increasingly in-demand service, the so-called removal of the roof
(sniatie kryshi). This task, involving great risk, consists of forcing the criminal group that controls an enterprise to leave. The PPC would then naturally provide alternative protection. It is very difficult for a company to
break free from a criminal group—the costs of such an action would normally exceed the benefits. Yet, in instances where the client company wishing to do so is not itself engaged in illegal business and has a high commercial potential, and the PPC is powerful enough and well connected to police
organizations, the company may decide to take the risk and force the criminal group out of business. This practice represents a truly extraordinary
profit-motivated private form of anticrime activity, whereby the manifest
commercial interest that drives the struggle for the client has the latent outcome of a relative decriminalization of business. Baltik-Escort, one of the
first active PPCs in Petersburg, was set up in April 1993 by former MVD
employee Roman Tsepov and former FSB officer Ivan Koreshkov. The core
of the staff at Baltik-Eskort was recruited from the ranks of the former special task police unit (OMON) stationed in Vilnius and Riga, the capitals of
the former Soviet republics. The PPC clashed with the Chechen gang over a
car maintenance company, Inavtoservis, whose management was seeking an
alternative protection arrangement. Far from peaceful, the competition
ended with the victory of the PPC, which thus acquired its first permanent
client. Then the company began to escort trucks carrying imported goods
from the West to Petersburg through Ukraine—a route controlled by criminal gangs and considered one of the most dangerous for drivers. This, maintains Tsepov, was the key to the company's subsequent commercial success,
since it earned Baltik-Escort the reputation of a tough and reliable security
partner (18). Now the PPC provides protection to more than twenty companies, including the Volvo dealer, the electric equipment plant Energo-
mashstroi, the computer firm Cityline, and to VIPs visiting St. Petersburg,
including the tycoon Boris Berezovsky and fashion model Claudia Schiffer
(18).[42]

Outcomes

The rise of the private security industry in Russia is a story of unintended
consequences. The first powerful impulse that began the process was a series
of reorganizations of state security services devised and executed on the basis

42. See also see the published interview with Roman Tsepov in "Esli zashchishchaem, to
zashchishchaem do upora" (If we start protecting, we protect til the end), *Lichnosti Peterburga*
1 (1998): 56.

of short-term political considerations, as Yeltsin and his government sought to strengthen political authority and neutralize possible threats to the new regime. The radical liberalism and anticommunism of the early 1990s made this policy fully legitimate. The early ideology of market reforms also endorsed radical limitations on the role of the state, assuming that the "invisible hand" of the market would bring about a new economic order as soon as conditions for the free play of economic interests were created. For the government, the strengthening of security and police institutions were seen as going against the conventional wisdom of market liberalism. Its energies were mobilized to achieve economic liberalization. In this context, the downsizing of the state security system quickly led to the proliferation of informal protective arrangements, as both discharged and acting security officers discovered a way to convert their skills into a marketable asset. While destroying the old Soviet system of coercion, which was designed to guard state property, the government did little to create institutions for enforcing the rights of new private owners. But former state police and security employees, not to mention criminal elements, also had no notion of institution building—most of them were just adapting to the new economic conditions. Violent entrepreneurship, whose methods had already been perfected by criminal gang members, was their major adaptive response. Instead of fighting against organized crime, many state employees got involved in the business and left the service.

On the whole, the law on private protection, adopted in 1992, can be seen as a successful example of a legal development whereby informal practices, in this case the private use of force and coercion, acquired legal status and became subject to state regulation. This was a rare instance where the adoption of a law reflected the effort to acknowledge, codify, and regulate an already existing practice rather that to create something from above, although we may add that the state was simply incapable of the "from above" strategy. The growth rate of the new, now legal, business of private protection and enforcement attests to the success of this legal initiative and to the huge demand it met. In conceiving of and pushing through the law on private protection, state security and enforcement employees were acting in their own immediate interests, just as the Russian leadership did when it reorganized the power ministries. Public reaction was mixed; it was often said that the new law worked for the benefit of criminal elements wishing to legalize their "roofs." The MVD authorities were quick to realize that PPCs were directly competing with the militia and especially with the so-called extradepartmental protection service, the commercial police in state uniforms.[43] In 1995, the ministry, then under Evgenii Kulikov, undertook ef-

43. In Russian, this organization is known as *vnevedomstvennaya okhrana*.

forts to discredit the private security business and protested in the State Duma with the intention of banning it altogether. In January, the legislature even passed on the first reading a number of amendments to the law on private protection, threatening to seriously limit the activities of private security agencies. Simultaneously, Kulikov created the Committee for Cooperation between Banks and Law Enforcement. In December 1995, the MVD and the Association of Russian Banks signed a cooperation agreement by which the MVD assigned to itself the responsibility for security in the banking sector.[44] Thus the minister hoped to recapture for the MVD the vital segment of the security market that had become the domain of KGB-controlled protection companies and security services. The former KGB responded with an open letter to the president and the chairmen of both chambers of the legislature, emphasizing the constructive role of the private security business in the development of civilized markets and warning against hasty decisions by the Duma. Signed by the presidents of associations of veterans who had served in the major special units of the KGB-FSB, including Alpha, Vympel, and Vesna, the letter explicitly argued that, due to the inability of state law enforcement agencies to protect private business, private security agencies were the only efficient check against organized crime, and, should they be disabled, criminal groups would instantly take their place and expand accordingly.[45] Eventually, the original law on private protection withstood the attacks. Having failed to repeal the law, the MVD reversed the tactic and demanded its consistent enforcement, instructing its regional divisions to tighten control and inspection to close as many private security agencies as possible. Hence the steep, almost tenfold increase in the number of agencies that lost their licenses in 1995 (see table 3). In the meantime, a group of lawyers and lobbyists began preparing a new, improved version of the law, which passed on the first reading in the Duma in 1997 but still awaits final adoption.[46] A new round of debates in the Duma in November 2000 showed that the confrontation between the MVD and the private security lobby remains heated.[47]

On the ground level, the private security boom has continued. The most important result has been the creation and legal recognition of new organi-

44. Kulikov's speech and the text of the agreement are published in *Biznes i bezopasnost'* 1 (1996): 8–11.
45. "Kogda okhrana 'strenozhena,' kriminalitet torzhestvuet" (When the guards are tied up, the criminal elements prevail), letter addressed to President of the Russian Federation Boris Yeltsin, Chairman of the Council of the Federation Vladimir Shumeiko, Chairman of the State Duma Ivan Rybkin, and Secretary of the Security Council Oleg Lobov, signed by S. Goncharov, S. Lysiuk, V. Rozin, I. Zevelev, and V. Velichko, reprinted in *Sekiuriti* 2 (1995): 3.
46. Major amendments are published in *Biznes i bezopasnost' v Rossii* 2 (1999): 14–17.
47. Ignatieva, "Chopophobia," 4.

zational forms and practices of private protection. Previously existing informal and illegal organizations began to refashion themselves in accordance with new organizational possibilities. In doing so, criminal groups and informal networks of state employees engaged in the "roof" business were compelled to obtain state licenses and take into account respective state regulations. This, in turn, made the murky sphere of "roof" businesses more legible for the state. The state supervising bodies gradually tightened control and increased sanctions for violating the regulations. There is evidence that the role of these regulations in private agencies has been increasing. According to the chief of a large PPC, "now a signal from a businessman that employees of such and such security company are putting pressure on him is enough for the law enforcement agency to take away that company's license."[48]

At the time of its adoption in 1992, the law on private protection appeared as a legal acknowledgment of the de facto fragmentation of the state monopoly of violence and justice; by the year 2000 it had become an instrument that gave the state at least some degree of control over violent entrepreneurship. Although few intended this result, it looks as though the state chose the lesser evil and brought its policies into agreement with its de facto capacity. Itself incapable of efficient protection and enforcement in the economic realm and facing the challenge of the criminal sector, the state appears to have been led to delegate these vital functions to its former employees on a private basis. This interpretation, though illuminating, is no more than a cognitive construct, since it introduces meaning and design where there were only power struggles, adjustments, moves, and countermoves. The current outcome, then, reflects a temporary balance of power rather than a realization of a plan or policy.

A remarkable consequence of the privatization of security and enforcement has been the growth of competition and its indirect effect on crime. Although arranging and paying for some kind of protection has clearly remained an imperative for economic subjects, the conditions of the deal have gradually changed. What the law achieved was to bring into being a market of private protection, which was a step forward from the protection racket arrangements of the early 1990s. The domination of illegal force wielders over clients and the serious limitations in choice—the criminal monopoly of force—began to wither away under the influence of several factors, including the legalization of the protection business. The proliferation of legal protection enterprises led to the diversification of supply and expanded the possibilities of choice, giving more power to clients. To be sure, neither the rules

---

48. Interview with Pavel Badyrov, chief of the PPC Skat, *Vash tainyi sovetnik* 8 (May 2000): 32.

nor the competition are perfect, and the presence of criminal elements remains high. But it is likely that the resulting degree of business security and governance has grown. Furthermore, in contrast to criminal groups that tax economic subjects but are themselves exempt from taxation by definition, PPCs were compelled to operate on a different economic principle: they sell concrete services on a contractual basis and are subject to state tax.

Competition and specialization have also increased the tendency already present in the activities of criminal groups—the transition from retaliatory to preventive tactics. Retaliation requires a substantial force ready to strike; preventive tactics put more emphasis on intelligence and information analysis and on legal competence. The latest trend in the protection business is the growth of informational and legal subdivisions and a reduction in the number of armed guards to the level needed to fulfill contracts for physical protection. The small armies that in the mid-1990s used to move around, backing up *strelki* or participating in *razborki,* are becoming redundant (2, 10, 17).

How stable is the present form of the private protection business? We have seen that criminal groups did not prove stable enough and began mutating under the influence of their changing economic agenda. If we extrapolate from current tendencies, it is easy to see the unmaking of criminal groups in the near future or a retreat into the confines of the traditional niche (drugs, gambling, prostitution, etc.), should they choose to remain faithful to the criminal subculture. It should be noted that weak reproductive capacity constitutes an important difference between Russian organized crime of the 1990s and the Sicilian Mafia, which managed to reproduce its structure and maintain its boundaries for several generations and for more than a hundred years.

PPCs initially emerged as an alternative form of a violence-managing agency engaged in violent entrepreneurship, by means of providing a set of institutional services in cooperation or competition with criminal groups. This form proved to be relatively competitive. Economic enterprises preferred to contract PPCs rather than criminal groups as soon as they had the choice; criminal groups also refashioned themselves as PPCs and formalized their relations with clients. Those that did not are gradually being pushed back into the shadow economy. To distinguish themselves from the front companies of criminal groups, PPCs operated by former security and police employees turned to traditional market methods for generating trust. They formed a number of business associations and leagues with closely monitored membership, achieved recognition by internationally established foreign security companies, and advertised their business records and trademarks. Through the network of professional journals, state supervising authorities began to publish lists of companies caught in illegal activities and connected to crime. A large segment of PPCs has publicly distanced itself from what are called "pocket security companies"—set up and fully controlled by large holding companies.

In theory, PPCs should have an interest in preserving the presence of criminal groups and other sources of business risk, since this sustains the demand for their services and helps them obtain respectable clients. At the same time, PPCs have an incentive to improve the quality and reduce the costs of their services. To elicit trust from anxious clients—whom the media has convinced that the Russian Mafia is everywhere—they never miss a chance to underscore their difference from criminal elements. This compels PPCs to act in a more predictable and civilized manner.

On the other hand, the prospect of staying in business has become more dependent on following state regulations. Consistently observing formal regulations, however, potentially undermines the original raison d'être for private security agencies—the protection of property rights and the enforcement of contracts. These agencies are valuable for the business insofar as they can "solve questions," that is, make informal deals. But if private security employees withdraw from dispute settlement and informal debt recovery, if they refrain from giving personal guarantees and participating in acts of intimidation, what are they left to do? There are several possible options. One, as we have seen, is to stop short of performing actual adjudication and use the legal institutions of the state to settle civic disputes between clients of PPCs. In this case, a PPC would provide legal advice and ensure, through informal connections, efficient treatment of its client by the state judiciary. But this, as Gambetta has noted, amounts to advertising a different protection agency, that is, the state.[49] The logical outcome of this practice is to transform the PPC into a consulting company. Another possibility is to concentrate on physical protection, security equipment, and business intelligence, in other words, on information and technology. This tendency has recently become more visible as well. Now PPCs get involved in the production, distribution, and maintenance of high-tech security equipment, create databases, and advertise their business analysts. The third direction is the same as that seen in the evolution of large criminal societies: investing in economic enterprises and shifting resources from protection to conventional businesses. In addition to the legal, technological, and purely economic paths, there is, obviously, a fourth way: reintegration into the state. Given the extensive state careers of many private security managers, their return to state service is not entirely unrealistic. At the beginning of 1999, the chairman of the League of Private Security Managers, I. Goloshchapov, predicted a radical reassertion of the state in the sphere of security and law enforce-

---

49. Private conversation with Diego Gambetta on 6 November 2000.

ment after the year 2000 and concluded that the long-term prospects for the development of the private security industry consisted of "the integration of the mass of chaotic protection enterprises into larger structures and the creation of state organs for their management."[50] By the end of 2000, the four possible evolution trajectories of the private security industry were already clearly visible. Which path will become the major one is still unclear. What is more certain is that the realization of these various possibilities has come to depend on the policy of another key player: the Russian state.

50. I.A. Goloshchapov, "Integratsionnye protsessy v srede negosudarstvennykh struktur obespecheniya bezopasnosti" (The process of integration in the sphere of nonstate security structures), *Biznes i bezopasnost' v Rossii* 2 (1999): 27.

6.

The Politics of State Formation

After the breakup of the Soviet Union, the former Russian Soviet Federative Socialist Republic became an independent state and most of the former republican governing structures acquired federal status. The formal attributes of statehood were either inherited from the Soviet Union or quickly created anew. Since that time, state officials and organizations have been issuing decrees, signing international agreements, and speaking on behalf of the state. In this sense, there was hardly a moment when the Russian state did not exist. When viewed from the bottom up, it is more difficult to see the presence of the state than from the top down. On the level of everyday practice, the Russian state does not have the unconditional priority in the use of force, the imposition of taxes, and the exercise of justice within the realm of its formal jurisdiction. Instead of a high degree of regulation or a monopoly, in the domains that constitute a modern state there is competition and cooperation among different violence-managing agencies. It therefore seems that, with respect to Russia in the 1990s, we cannot postulate either the existence of the state or its absence. The term that captures this condition best is "state formation."

State formation is one of the central subjects of historically oriented social research. In Europe, this process was especially intense in the early modern period, between the fifteenth and seventeenth centuries. By the nineteenth century, the modern state had acquired its classic form, from which sociologists, notably Max Weber, subsequently distilled the ideal type. The possibility of constructing the ideal type implied that state formation was essentially complete and that all subsequent politics and, accordingly, their analysis, would be conducted within the framework of the modern state. The long and brutal politics of sovereignty that brought about the modern state have given way to a different kind of politics that was no longer preoccupied with the foundations of the state—the monopolies of violence, taxation, and justice—but came to rest on them. That is, once the state as an organizational form making possible the control of violence, the distribution of resources, and effective government was achieved, further struggles, peaceful or otherwise, were redirected toward attaining control over these fundamental capacities. The politics of sovereignty, the effect of which is the formation of a state, and conventional politics, aimed at controlling the state, should therefore be distinguished from the start. Conventional politics are possible and meaningful only when the state formation is complete. This historical sequence also contains a logical relationship. The politics of state formation constitute the condition of possibility for conventional politics. The same logical relationship obtains for studies of both phenomena. Studies of conventional politics as a competition between different groups for the control of the state necessarily posit the existence of the state, however weak, as a presupposition, whereas the analysis of state formation cannot by definition take the state as its point of departure. That is why state formation is naturally conceived as a subject of historical studies, while conventional politics are situated in the present and tend to disregard history.

Students of Russian politics have recently acknowledged the problem of the state's weakness and have inquired as to its primary causes.[1] In doing so, they tend to overlook the distinction between the two types of politics, focusing simultaneously on group struggles within the state and for its levers, as if the state were already in place, and at particular efforts at state building undertaken by the leadership.[2] In these studies, the dimension of practice is rarely considered and the fundamental questions about the nature of current politics are avoided. A bright exception to this trend is the recent work by David Woodruff, which departs from conventional analyses and undertakes a study of the politics of monetary consolidation in Russia, a core aspect of state formation. The mainstream accounts of the post-Soviet transition tend to focus on the failures or successes of the market reform policies the Russian government had to adopt. But to advocate such policies, argues Woodruff,

---

1. Cynthia Roberts and Thomas Sherlock, "Bringing the Russian State Back In: Explanations of the Derailed Transition to Market Democracy," *Comparative Politics* (July 1999): 477–98.
2. For example, Gordon Smith, ed., *State-Building in Russia: The Yeltsin Legacy and the Challenge of the Future* (New York: M. E. Sharpe, 1999).

"is to assume that this government has already gathered to itself the sovereign powers, dominance over money among them, that underpin a market economy of a national scope."[3] He distinguishes between the politics of monetary consolidation, which involves multiple struggles for the definition of the means of payment, and the "politics of the cash register," conflicts over who gets how much from a general till. The first clearly belongs to the politics of state formation, the second to conventional politics. Woodruff's extensive analysis of the intricate barter economy that divided Russia into a multiplicity of closed and nonlegible exchange systems and thus dissolved the state's monopoly on the definition of the means of payment leads him to advocate a change in the conceptual framework used to view current developments. The "monetary consolidation" framework, the proposed substitute for the "market reforms" narrative, stems from the great transformations of the distant past, namely, of the mercantilist period, when states were engaged in creating national markets. Without arguing for any simple parallels between historical periods, Woodruff makes a strong case for the background use of history whereby the retrospective dimension highlights structural similarities and provides interpretive insights that direct the analysis rather than constitute its substance.

Historical parallels are highly conditional, but they carry the potential for estrangement required for sociological research. They are useful epistemologically, since they enable one to see reality differently from how it is imposed on us by the dominant and taken-for-granted discourse of the day. Joel Migdal has noted that states are mistakenly perceived as part of our natural landscape: "What may seem as much a part of the natural order as the rivers and mountains around us is, in fact, an artifact of a small segment of human history."[4] Historical illumination seems particularly useful for unmaking states as reified concepts. An account of the history of state formation also helps to depart from the static essentialist vision of the state and see that the state *is* little more than what the state *does*. State formation, then, is another way of looking at the processes and practices already described here but with a view to their possible, albeit not premeditated, outcomes. The absence of a general organizing will and the lack of certainty with regard to outcomes distinguishes state formation from a related concept, state building, which captures primarily the top-down dimension and has a strong connotation of an intentional plan.

3. David Woodruff, *Money Unmade: Barter and the Fate of Russian Capitalism* (Ithaca: Cornell University Press, 1999), 7.
4. Joel Migdal, *Strong Societies and Weak States: State-Society Relations and State Capabilities in the Third World* (Princeton: Princeton University Press, 1988), 16.

State Formation in Historical Perspective

The Monopoly of Legitimate Violence

Weber's classic definition regards the state as the territorial monopoly of legitimate violence.[5] In practice, the existence of the state is conditional on the capacity of the administrative staff to successfully uphold the claim to the monopoly of force and its legitimacy in the enforcement of its order.[6] Any community that commands superior force and has a durable capacity to control violence within the territory and to protect its boundaries will sooner or later acquire legitimacy. In a brief sketch of the evolution of political community toward becoming a state, Weber mentions three phases: a phase of the competitive and uncontrolled use of violence by groups of warriors engaged in plunder raids; the emergence of territorial monopolies with restricted violence that command increasing legitimacy; and, finally, the phase when the coercive apparatus is transformed into an institution for the protection of rights.[7]

In Weber's approach, state formation is not teleological. He considers the emergence of the state an outcome of the struggles for survival and domination and of organizational solutions that help to build up a superior force. Implicit in this approach is Nietzsche's idea that any significant historical event—and the emergence of a state certainly qualifies—is a reflection of a change in the relationship of forces engaged in permanent struggle, a sign that a superior force has established its dominance. Instead of regarding state formation as an intentional project, as a certain idea achieving its realization, or as a free agreement between parties, a Nietzschean critical inquiry, which Nietzsche named "genealogy," would see state formation as "a succession of the more or less far-reaching, more or less independent processes of overpowering—including also in each case the resistance marshaled against these processes, the changes of form attempted with a view to defense and reaction, and the results of these successful counteractions."[8] According to this view, state formation is a series of organizational innovations in the context of permanent struggle, a process of creating various arrangements and devices for immediate purposes, some of which happen to outlive their creators and change their meaning as they are reappropriated and employed for

5. Max Weber, "Politics as Vocation," in *From Max Weber: Essays in Sociology,* ed. H. Gerth and C. Wright Mills (London: Routledge, 1970), 78.

6. Max Weber, *Economy and Society* (Berkeley: University of California Press, 1978), 1:54.

7. Ibid., 904–8.

8. Friedrich Nietzsche, *On the Genealogy of Morals,* trans. Douglas Smith (Oxford: Oxford University Press, 1996), 58.

different ends. The national tax, *taille royale,* and the regular taxation apparatus, for instance, were clever mid–fifteenth century inventions of the French king to collect the means to finance the first regular military units in Europe, composed of Scottish soldiers of fortune.[9] Only much later was regular taxation recognized as a public institution and turned into an important instrument of macroeconomic regulation.

Elias, one of the first to follow in Weber's footsteps, considered the formation of territorial monopolies of force the law of history. The withering of the Carolingian empire left behind a large number of small, loosely structured kingdoms, lordships, feudal estates, and other territorial units. Their rulers, the former vassals of great princes turned sovereigns in their own right, were engaged in governing their domains, collecting tribute, and waging wars against neighbors to seize booty and new territory. During these wars, many such political units were destroyed or appended to the few victorious ones, providing the victors with new resources for larger wars. Elias reasons that the dynamic of early European states demonstrates that, over time, an ever-increasing number of power chances inevitably tend to accumulate in the hands of an ever-diminishing number of rulers through a series of elimination contests.[10] The monopoly mechanism works, simply because wars have winners and losers: if some of the contenders are victorious, their opportunities multiply; those of the vanquished decrease. Consequently, the power of the victorious ruler increases to the point that he is capable of establishing a monopoly on the use of violence within the territory, which thus becomes his sovereign domain. A theoretical analysis of how an "invisible hand" brings about the emergence of a central agency with a monopoly right of protection and enforcement within the area of its jurisdiction (territory) can be found in the writings of Robert Nozick.[11]

It took a great deal of time before reality began to resemble Weber's ideal-typical definition of the state. The conditions under which different violence-managing agencies competed with or supplemented governments lasted well into the eighteenth century. Relations between governments and private wielders of force, especially in the extraterritorial realm, were long based on temporary alliances rather than full-time service, on tactical considerations rather than legal norms. In times of war, writes Tilly, the managers of full-fledged states often commissioned privateers, sometimes hired bandits to raid their enemies, and encouraged their regular troops to take

9. Perry Anderson, *The Lineage of the Absolutist State* (London: Verso, 1979), 32.

10. Norbert Elias, *The Civilizing Process,* vols. 1 and 2 (Oxford: Basil Blackwell, 1995), 2:345–54.

11. Robert Nozick, *Anarchy, State, and Utopia* (New York: Basic Books, 1974).

booty.[12] The English crown actively employed privateers until the beginning of the nineteenth century. The Sea Dogs contributed to the English victory over Spain throughout the sixteenth century. "Besides plundering Spanish ships and settlements, such Sea Dogs as Drake, Cavendish, Clifford (the third earl of Cumberland), and Raleigh engaged in what might be termed state-sponsored terrorism," asserts Janice Thompson.[13] Drake extorted large ransoms from two Spanish colonial cities by threatening to burn them to the ground, and he destroyed three other cities. Both he and Raleigh shared their loot with the crown and were knighted for their achievements. But later, in 1618, when his depredations in Spanish America ran counter to the crown's foreign policy, Raleigh was executed.

Some Economic Consequences of the Monopoly of Force

Theoretically, it is easy to see that the monopoly of force is a precondition for peaceful economic competition. The classic economic model of free-market exchange implicitly presupposes a condition of equal security for all participants. Such a condition can be created either through individual security measures against equally armed competitors or through the disarmament of all and the abdication of the right to use force in favor of a third party. The first arrangement tends to be unstable and costly (though this depends on the size of the units), and the monopoly mechanism works to bring about the second. This is not to say that the monopoly of force emerges as a result of a contract. Violent competition is able to bring about a progressing distribution of force-wielding capacity in favor of those who tend to win elimination contests. The growing power allows the triumphant violence-managing agency to intensify its efforts to introduce and enforce an increasing number of rules and regulations. The state comes about as a cumulative effect of such efforts. On the other side, a pacified economic space emerges where nonviolent competition and cooperation develop.

Waltz provides a nice illustration of the economic consequences of the monopolization of force which, I believe, pertains equally to any system of relations involving autonomous violence-managing agencies and economic subjects, and not just to international politics. After a shift from a multipolar to a bipolar system of world power had been completed, that is, after the

---

12. Charles Tilly, "War Making and State Making as Organized Crime," in *Bringing the State Back In*, ed. Peter Evans, Dietrich Rueschemeyer, and Theda Skocpol (Cambridge: Cambridge University Press, 1986), 173.

13. Janice Thompson, *Mercenaries, Pirates, and Sovereigns: State-Building and Extraterritorial Violence in Early Modern Europe* (Princeton: Princeton University Press, 1994), 23.

Soviet Union and the United States emerged as nuclear superpowers, cooperation among Western European states increased. Before that, when the European powers were themselves great powers, politics among them tended to be a zero-sum game. Each power viewed the other's loss as its own gain and the other's gain as a threat to its own security. Cooperation took the form solely of strategic alliances among countries against one another. As Europe came to be under the protection of the U.S. superpower and thus to a much greater extent a consumer of security, the economic behavior of European powers became dissociated from immediate military implications. "For the first time in modern history," writes Waltz, "the determinants of war and peace lay outside the arena of European states, and the means of their preservation were provided by others."[14] This new circumstance, which amounted to a structural change in the distribution of violence potential (that is, a great many security concerns were relegated to a superior agency) made possible a much better realization of the common interest. The example shows how a change at the level of structure, in this case, a shift toward a greater monopolization of force, alters the range of expectations of the participating units. Waltz's example can be further extended to account for the continuing efforts of the Western European states to introduce and enforce more homogeneous rules governing the expanding common market in order to capture economic benefits.[15]

Extraction

Although it creates the foundation for all other policies of state formation, the monopolization of force is still only part of the story. The monopoly of force as the prohibition to use violence unless sanctioned by the ruler was closely connected to the fiscal monopoly, the ruler's exclusive right to collect protection tribute and other levies or to control the local economy. The increasing demand for resources to wage war and maintain superiority drove rulers toward organizational innovations that enabled more efficient extraction

According to Joseph Schumpeter, patterns of taxation shaped modern states no less decisively than did warfare.[16] The elementary form of extraction was tribute in kind, but a considerable effort was required to collect and measure it. Another problem for the rulers of emerging states was their de-

---

14. Kenneth Waltz, *Theory of International Politics* (Reading, Mass: Addison-Wesley, 1979), 70–71.
15. A theoretical model of cooperation is advanced in R. Axelrod, *The Evolution of Cooperation* (New York: Basic Books, 1984).
16. Joseph Schumpeter, "The Crisis of the Tax State," in *The Economics and Sociology of Capitalism,* ed. Richard Swedberg (Princeton: Princeton University Press, 1991), 108.

pendency on the loyalty of warriors in wartime. To increase returns from the exercise of power, European rulers had to take measures leading to a monetization of the economy, since only when levies are expressed in a universal medium can the territory be evenly taxed and returns effectively utilized for policy needs. Likewise, the ability to hire mercenary troops and to keep a standing army depended on the availability of a means of payment. The efforts at monetary consolidation, driven by purely strategic considerations, were conducive to the creation of national markets based on the universal means of exchange.

Normally, the king was the largest landowner and his wealth was the product of his domain. Attempts to regularize taxation and extend it to the whole territory met fierce resistance from subjects, often erupting into open rebellion. The common opinion that the king had to live off his own domain just as others did was one of the greatest obstacles to state legitimacy, which had to be overcome by a combination of coercion and persuasion. Tilly summarizes the interdependency between coercion and extraction in the following way:

> Taxation was the chief means by which the builders of states in the sixteenth century and later supported their expanding armies, which were in turn their principal instruments in establishing control of their frontiers, pushing them out, defending them against external incursions, and assuring their own priority in the use of force within those frontiers. Conversely, military needs were in those first centuries the main incentive for the imposition of new taxes and the regularization of the old ones. The need fed itself, furthermore; the overcoming of resistance to taxation required the maintenance of a military force.[17]

The Practices of Control

State formation is by no means limited to the efforts of rulers to consolidate power at the top. It also involves a variety of policies on the micro level, a bottom-up exercise of power of which the state is a summative effect. The state is also a configuration of practices. In his study on the history of manners, for example, Elias shows just how complex was the practical establishment and maintenance of the monopoly of force.[18] He takes credit for brilliantly forging the link between large-scale societal processes and everyday forms of social interaction. Grand military victories and the resulting cen-

17. Charles Tilly, "Reflections on the History of European State-Making," in *The Formation of National States in Western Europe,* ed. Charles Tilly (Princeton: Princeton University Press, 1975), 23.
18. Norbert Elias, *The Civilizing Process,* vol. 1: *The History of Manners* (Oxford: Basil Blackwell, 1993).

tralization of power created structural conditions that allowed the ruler to introduce institutions that molded individual behavior in such a way that violence was effectively controlled. The tight framework of normative regulations of behavior adopted at court, now the site and form of state government, prohibited the use of force unless it was ordered by the ruler. As the victorious prince became the sovereign ruler of the emerging state, former warriors and local strongmen were turned into courtiers. This change of status presupposed that the spontaneous aggression of warriors should give way to civilized manners, which Elias saw as the means for disciplined shaping of individual affects. Turning warriors into courtiers thus became a subtle sociocultural tool for demilitarizing regional power holders. Elias discovered that the moral trajectory from chivalry to civility correlated with the policy of state centralization. The set of policies that in practical terms enabled the territorial control of violence ranged from subtle forms such as refined table manners to explicit prohibitions on settling disputes by force. European monarchs are known to have issued edicts against duels, and Louis XIV introduced regular procedures for resolving disputes and for control over insults.[19] Court society, as the cultural expression of state centralization, imposed an array of constraints on individual affect and thereby gave fresh impulse to the development of the arts and sciences, those essentially peaceful occupations requiring a high degree of self-control.[20] Thus the monopoly of force gave the central power the capacity and the moral right to discipline aggressive drives, a practice that, in the long run, served as the source of civilization and of its discontents.

In the eighteenth century, to enhance the efficiency of government, the state introduced a range of everyday practices of discipline and surveillance that increased the docility of the population—the central concern of Michel Foucault's seminal book.[21] Pierre Proudhon, one of the founders of anarchism in the nineteenth century, was perhaps the first to have catalogued and condemned the modern practices of government. His writings on the subject convey an attitude characteristic of his time toward these fresh and not yet habitual state inventions:

> To be GOVERNED is to be watched, inspected, spied upon, directed, law-driven, numbered, regulated, enrolled, indoctrinated, preached at, controlled, checked, estimated, valued, censured, commanded, by creatures who have neither the right nor the wisdom nor the virtue to do so. To be GOVERNED is

19. Samuel Clark, *State and Status: The Rise of the State and Aristocratic Power in Western Europe* (Montreal: McGill-Queen's University Press, 1995), 168.
20. Norbert Elias, *The Court Society* (Oxford: Basil Blackwell, 1983).
21. Michel Foucault, *Discipline and Punish: The Birth of Prison* (London: Peregrine Books, 1977).

to be at every operation, at every transaction noted, registered, counted, taxed, stamped, measured, numbered, assessed, licensed, authorized, admonished, prevented, forbidden, reformed, corrected, punished. It is, under pretext of public utility, and in the name of the general interest, to be placed under contribution, drilled, fleeced, exploited, monopolized, extorted from, squeezed, hoaxed, robbed; then, at the slightest resistance, the first word of complaint, to be repressed, fined, vilified, harassed, hunted down, abused, clubbed, disarmed, bound, choked, imprisoned, judged, condemned, shot, deported, sacrificed, sold, betrayed; and to crown all, mocked, ridiculed, derided, outraged, dishonored. That is government; that is its justice; that is its morality.[22]

As in the case of the monopoly of force, achieving a strong degree of fiscal monopoly in practice required much more than organizing a particular central apparatus. In his recent book, James Scott has highlighted the domain of everyday practices that led to the rise of the tax state. Innovations as disparate as surnames and urban planning were part of the state strategy aimed at increasing the legibility of the domain, which, in turn, helped to account for and reach every individual taxpayer. The fact that massive popular uprisings against the state have dropped off does not mean the end of resistance, since, as Scott shows, the struggle has been effectively transposed to the level of everyday practice, where grand state projects have often failed.[23]

Legitimacy, Structure, and Boundary Maintenance

The struggle for the legitimation of a regular tax system underlay the transition from "patrimony" to the "state" as public domain.[24] Sooner or later, this transition was completed by all modern states. The private monopoly of force that grants the triumphant ruler the possibility of controlling greater resources also creates the practical problem of managing these resources. The state, then, is initially little more than the organizational response to this

22. Pierre Proudhon, *General Idea of the Revolution in the Nineteenth Century,* trans. J. Robinson (London: Freedom Press, 1923), 293–94. Cited in Robert Nozick, *Anarchy, State, and Utopia,* 11.

23. James Scott, *Seeing Like a State: How Certain Schemes to Improve the Human Condition Have Failed* (New Haven: Yale University Press, 1998).

24. For details, see Rudolf Braun, "Taxation, Sociopolitical Structure, and State-Building: Great Britain and Brandenburg-Prussia," in *The Formation of National States in Western Europe,* ed. Charles Tilly (Princeton: Princeton University Press, 1975), 243–327.

problem. The organ of government, which initially is nothing more than the royal household, tends to grow and become a set of functionally differentiated offices managed by the ruler's agents. As the separation of state government from the ruler's household is completed, and the control over resources becomes the function of interdependent, hierarchically organized apparatus, the state evolves into a separate institutional ("public") realm. Elias calls this a transition from private to public monopoly.

The legitimacy of the state, including the use of violence by its agents, is tied to its claim to serve the public interest, to be an impersonal and public realm. If the military and organizational build-up is the substantive aspect of state formation, the attainment of public status is its structural aspect. To say that a state exists is also to imply the maintenance of boundaries such as those between public and private, formal and informal, impersonal and personal, and so on. These are structural, that is, purely relational categories. Unlike territorial boundaries that mark out objective space, structural boundaries are constituted through the behavior and attitudes of participants, both state officials and citizens. With regard to state formation, the distinction between public and private has to do with economic interests, that between formal and informal with the system of laws and rules, and that between impersonal and personal with the mode of their application. The state is legitimate, that is, its orders are willingly obeyed and its principles followed, when the state manages to maintain these boundaries in the most efficient way, and when, as a consequence, it is regarded as a public, formal, and impersonal domain. Mechanisms of boundary maintenance are also part of the state. They range from methods of socializing and training state officials for the purpose of creating an ethos of state service, to engaging in purges and extremely brutal forms of persecution against employees who fail to observe the boundaries. Failures and disruptions—indeed, all forms of imperfect boundary maintenance—are normally called "corruption."

Historically, it took a long time for these structural boundaries to emerge and for boundary maintenance to assume efficient forms. The historical steps taken to introduce these boundaries and the day-to-day efforts at boundary maintenance also need to be distinguished. History (the diachronic perspective) shows how states and their particular structures took shape and how they differed from moment to moment. The daily maintenance of these structures (the synchronic perspective) highlights the state's dependence for its everyday reproduction on people's behavior and attitudes and gives an idea how a state can cease to exist structurally if the boundaries become blurred—even though its substantive elements remain. The ethos and tradition of state service save a large proportion of the resources and efforts spent on boundary maintenance. The erosion of tradition and the draining of resources, which has as its corollary massive opportunistic behavior on the part of state functionaries, leads to the structural decline of the state.[25] A structural crisis can hit virtually any aspect of the state, but its most serious form, of course, occurs in the constitutive elements of the state—its capacity to control violence, collect taxes, and exercise justice. It is thus possible to conceive how the public monopoly of force—whose public character is also the source of its legitimacy—can disintegrate into a multiplicity of private monopolies. Then a similar fate awaits the other two monopolies.

Now we can further dissociate the structural aspect of state formation from the substantive one and see the state in purely configurational terms. The substantive aspect involves the creation of various organizations and other attributes of states, including those enhancing its protective and coercive potential. This is the state hardware as it were. The structural aspect of the state is the relations of forces and the boundaries that follow from them. Even though the monopolization of force involves the substantive growth of the military, policing, and administrative apparatus, their mere existence does not bring the state into being (though it may create a powerful illusion thereof). The monopolization of force is a redrawing of boundaries between violence-managing agencies, which at every moment defines which entities use actual or potential violence against one another. In one configuration, it is individuals and groups that are engaged in relations of force; then, as the boundaries are redrawn, it is larger organizations, like city-states or principalities. Whatever their size and name, such entities maintain a relatively secure and orderly environment within their boundaries and compete violently outside them. A new relationship of forces produces a new condition, where boundaries are redrawn and the subjects of politics assume a different shape. They become nation-states in the international arena, for example. The same process can take the opposite direction and lead to an almost unlimited fragmentation of larger monopolies and the rise of a multitude of other configurations of forces. This happened many times when empires or large states broke up. From the standpoint of configurational change, the notion of territory is secondary and derivative; it simply expresses the boundaries of more stable monopolies. The units of these configurations vary in size and reappear under different names, from protection racket gangs to empires. As historical sociologists have established, states tend to be the most stable of these because of their stronger legitimacy and economic productivity.

25. For a detailed study of the opportunistic behavior of state functionaries, see Steven Solnick, *Stealing the State: Control and Collapse in Soviet Institutions* (Cambridge: Harvard University Press, 1998).

The Withering Away of the State

Now we are better equipped to understand the dynamics of the Russian state in 1987–2000. In view of the distinction between the substantive and the structural aspects of the state (and of state formation), the condition in which the hardware of the state remains yet the state is absent should be easier to imagine. The withering away of the state began before the breakup of the Soviet Union. Likewise, the legal establishment of a new Russian statehood did not reverse the process of the structural decay of the state for at least five to seven years. By exploring the emergence, interaction, and evolution of various violence-managing agencies and their economic functions, I have highlighted the structural decay of the state. It should be clear that "structural decay" or "withering away" of the state does not necessarily imply a territorial breakup into a number of smaller political units as in the former Yugoslavia, though the emergence of the warlord regime in Chechnya gives an idea of how this might have happened. A monopoly of force may dissolve in a latent way, without immediate territorial consequences.

The state as a monopoly of force is in the first place an analytical category and an ideal type. No state can claim a full monopoly, of course. It is more important that the state be an organization seeking a fair degree of monopolization over violence and that it constantly take measures to that end. It differs from other competing force wielders in that its use of violence is seen as legitimate, since it rests on the claim that it is pursuing the public interest. The propositions I have made about the state of nature and the withering away of the state are more analytical or epistemological than empirical, though the failure to contain violence and the loss of state capacity in many areas was evident in Russia throughout the 1990s.

A major symptom of the structural decay of the Russian state was the advance of violent entrepreneurship on the everyday level. Earlier I focused more on criminal groups and private protection companies than on the protective arrangements closely associated with or formally belonging to the state. State officials with access to the state's coercive capacity, from heads of local militia subdivisions to members of the government, were also active players in violent entrepreneurship in their respective fields. They were to large state-oriented enterprises and the oligarchs what criminal groups were to small and medium-sized private companies.

The Informal State "Roof"

Earlier I classified violence-managing agencies as private and illegal (criminal groups), private and legal (private protection companies), and public and illegal (state employees acting as private entrepreneurs). A similar typology can be applied to "roofs." "Roof" *(krysha)* is a colloquial term for a private protection arrangement or "enforcement partnership"; it denotes the service provided by violence-managing agencies. Accordingly, a "roof" may be provided by a criminal group, a PPC or PSS, or by state employees, normally high-ranking bureaucrats in conjunction with state security or law enforcement officers. The fourth type of "roof" (and of violence-managing agency) is obviously both public and legal, that is, the ideal state. It should be evident that a structural change expressed as a strengthening of the fourth type and a weakening of the three other types is what, in this case, constitutes state formation.

It is virtually impossible to name all conceivable combinations of state officials and organizations that may be involved in episodic or permanent "roof" businesses. Still, access to state coercive capacity is vital for this arrangement, irrespective of whether it is managed by high-ranking security and law enforcement officers or by civic state officials at various levels. The informal state "roof" (see figure 5 below) is an extremely flexible arrangement by virtue of its simultaneous access to several instruments of coercion: bare force, administrative capacity, and legal action. Someone who has a special task police force, tax and fire inspection, and the judiciary at his disposal can solve any question at the appropriate level (local, regional, or central) and is virtually unbeatable. Large segments of medium-sized and big businesses operate under this type of protection.

Essentially, this type of enforcement partnership rests on the selective use of state coercive capacity—on a commercial basis and for private interests. It is therefore not that the state is entirely feeble or inefficient. The informal state "roof" is the flip side of the state's lack of regularity, its weakness as a state, which does not exclude the episodic efficiency of its particular segments. It is an expression of the structural weakness that, as was suggested earlier, is compatible with substantive strength. Furthermore, the informal state "roof" represents a specific type of corruption, the selective use of public violence and coercion. Under conditions where the ethos of state service is weak and salaries low, the threat of legal sanctions and competition are the only instruments that keep this "roof" arrangement in check. However, the case for corruption becomes much weaker, as it does in many other cases, when all state officials do is efficiently perform their formal duties from time to time. What makes this protection arrangement efficacious is the fact that, under the conditions of incomplete state formation (or weak institutions), selective application of formal rules often becomes a form of punishment. Thus, an investigation by the anticrime police or an audit by a tax inspection agency may often be part of resolving a private dispute between enterprises, one of which has special access to the state's coer-

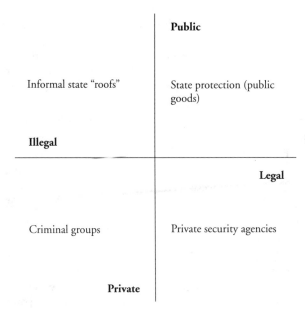

Fig 5. A typology of "roofs"

cive capacity, for which it then pays in some way. In such cases, when private benefits and exchange relations involved in "roofing" are carefully disguised, it becomes virtually invincible when legal actions are taken against it. A study of charitable donations by Petersburg private businesses, for example, uncovered that the regional MVD organs are, after the disabled, the second largest receiver of charity from local business companies: 35 percent of companies represented in the survey admitted making such donations (the disabled figured in 45 percent of cases).[26] Private sponsorship has become largely an institutionalized and legitimate form of private protection payments.

Purely criminal arrangements lack long-term stability. After their heyday in 1991–95, criminal "roofs" began to dwindle away or evolve under the triple pressures of capitalization, competition, and law enforcement. According to expert estimates, in 1998 in Petersburg only 10 percent of all "roofs" were purely criminal.[27] A respondent who, at some stage in his career, had been involved in private protection as a member of an organized criminal group in Novosibirsk pointed out that purely criminal "roofs" were

26. *Pchela* 12 (1998): 7.
27. Andrei Konstantinov, *Banditskii Peterburg 98* (St. Petersburg: Folio Press, 1999), 279.

being driven out of legal business and superseded by informal police protection (6).

Another outcome of the continuous interaction between pure types of "roofs," as it were, was the emergence of the so-called combined roofs. This is an institutional arrangement whereby parts of violence-managing agencies of different types, that is, criminal groups, private security agencies, and state employees cooperate to resolve particular problems. This creates more enduring interaction patterns and a new kind of informal organization. The result is high efficiency and versatility: such a conglomerate can use thugs for intimidation, PPC official resources and image for civilized protection, and bureaucratic and legal connections for higher-level protection and patronage for itself and its clients.

In the mid-1990s, when organized force was an especially valuable market resource, various semiautonomous armed organizations were active players in the economy and in politics.[28] The most powerful of them, until the summer of 1996, was the Presidential Security Service (*Sluzhba bezopasnosti prezidenta*, SBP), headed by General Alexander Korzhakov, Yeltsin's personal bodyguard since 1985. The SBP was created in November 1993 from the Chief Guard Directorate (the former Ninth Chief Directorate of the KGB responsible for the protection of the Party leadership). The SBP quickly became an elite and well-paid security service of more than 750 officers. In June 1995 it upgraded its status by becoming a subdivision of the Administration of the President, which gave Korzhakov the rank of minister. The new security organization also acquired the formal right to use FSB surveillance and information resources and was informally backed by the FSB through Korzhakov's close personal connection to its chief, Alexander Barsukov.

From the memoirs of Korzhakov and those of his deputy, former MVD colonel Valerii Streletsky, we learn of the enormous political influence that the SBP exerted as a result of its close connection to the Russian president, its formidable and highly mobile armed corps, and its unprecedented tapping and surveillance opportunities.[29] Corruption in the government was widespread; as a result, compromising information became a kind of political currency. Both Korzhakov and Streletsky claim to have filed tons of corruption cases, some of which actually resulted in formal investigations and

---

28. For example, in 1993, the Russian Union of Cossacks, which has its own paramilitary units, began providing protection at one of the largest Moscow city markets, Danilovskii. "Soyuz kazakov vzial Danilovskii rynok" (The Union of Cossacks has taken over Danilovskii market), *Izvestiya*, 20 July 1993.

29. Alexander Korzhakov, *Boris Yeltsin: Ot rassveta do zakata* (Boris Yeltsin: From dawn to dusk) (Moscow: Interbook, 1997); Valerii Streletsky, *Mrakobesie* (Moscow: Detektiv-Press, 1999).

Two entrepreneurs of violence: Ruslan Koliak ("Lupatiy"), *avtoritet* of the Tambovskaya criminal group, and Alexander Korzhakov, former chief of the president's security service. By permission of the Agency for Journalistic Investigations, St. Petersburg.

court hearings. There was also a less well-known aspect of the activities of the SBP: it was a supplier of private protection. It took control of distributing oil export quotas to private companies and, unsurprisingly, established one of its own, Rostoplivo. In addition, the SBP brought the state precious metal–exporting organization Roskomdragmet fully under its own supervision—officially, to prevent illegal exports of precious state resources; in practice, simply to establish SBP's monopoly over this business. According to some sources, it was also heavily involved in arms exports.[30] Needless to say, these activities were not part of the formal duties of the SBP.

When violence-managing agencies are numerous, they see any increase in another agency's power as a threat to their interests and, accordingly, are prone to use their violence potential to limit the power of opponents. Experts offered no coherent alternative to Korzhakov's own version of the notorious showdown on 2 December 1994 between the SBP and the PSS of the Most financial group, backed by the Moscow regional FSB (then FSK). In his memoirs, the president's bodyguard mentions Yeltsin's informal order to put pressure on Gusinsky, the head of the Most group, to "create an at-

30. Alexei Mukhin, *Informatsionnaya voina v Rossii: Uchastniki, tseli, tekhnologii* (Information war in Russia: Participants, goals, techniques) (Moscow: Tsentr politicheskoi informatsii), 65.

mosphere around him as if the earth were burning under his feet."[31] Korzhakov suggests it was an intrigue by another tycoon, Boris Berezovsky, who was competing for political influence, that triggered such a harsh order. At the same time, he does not hide his own irritation with Gusinsky. What actually caused the growing irritation of the president and the SBP (also echoed in Streletsky's memoirs) was the public demonstration of force by the PSS Most, as the tycoon used to cruise around Moscow with an escort of armored cars stuffed with armed guards. The fifteen hundred–strong PSS Most was known to be one of the largest private security agencies. An informal security division of Most was set up already in 1989 but it did not turn into a capable organization until 1993, after Philip Bobkov, the former KGB deputy chief and creator of the "antidissident" Fifth Chief Directorate in charge of ideological control, became its head. David Remnick quotes Gusinsky on this dubious choice: "We'd be ready to hire the devil himself if he could give us security."[32] In addition to the standard security and enforcement functions, the PSS was also involved in political and business intelligence, that is, in collecting compromising information. The office of Most was located at the time at the headquarters of the Moscow mayor; "it was as if Citibank were inside Gracie Mansion," notes Remnick.[33]

The security service was only one of the financial group's subdivisions, and, theoretically, pressure could have been applied elsewhere. The fact that the SBP chose the security subdivision of Most as its primary target testifies to the centrality of force-wielding capacity for private economic subjects and reflects a broader structure of business relations. (Later, in 1999, during Evgenii Primakov's term as prime minister, state security would target the security service of Berezovsky, the PPC Atoll). Adequately armed, Korzhakov's men closely followed Gusinsky and his escort from his dacha to headquarters and then performed a typical *naezd*. Gusinsky's bodyguards were beaten right outside the building in the center of Moscow by "unknown men" in ski masks who also searched the premises of Most. The bodyguards were thrown face down in the snow and kept there for two hours. Scared to death, Gusinsky first called the Moscow RUBOP and reported a criminal assault. A special RUBOP team arrived, checked the "unknown men's" identification and, not surprisingly, left quietly. After observing all this through the office windows, Gusinsky called his crony, the head of the Moscow FSB, Evgenii Savostyanov. Korzhakov cites the radio interception of the call: "Zhenya, help out, some bandits are after me! The cops came at my emergency call,

31. Korzhakov, *Boris Yeltsin*, 285.

32. David Remnick, *Resurrection: The Struggle for a New Russia* (New York: Random House, 1997), 186.

33. Ibid.

but they did not do anything and left. You're my only hope."[34] Savostyanov immediately rushed into action, and another special team arrived on the scene and started shooting into the air. It was reported that a few bullets hit the car of Korzhakov's men. Luckily, one member of the FSB team recognized his former colleague among the SBP men, just as they were about to shoot back. More of Korzhakov's heavily armed men arrived after the gunfire to arrest the opponents and confiscate their weapons. The next day all the newspapers reported a mysterious shootout in the center of the capital.

As a result of this miniwar, Gusinsky fled abroad, Savostyanov was ousted, and the SBP demonstrated its preeminence over other security organizations. The power of the competing oligarchy was temporarily cut back. This event was unusual because of the media coverage and the status of the organizations involved. But its scenario did not differ very much from many other similar conflicts featuring local force-wielding organizations formally belonging to the state but used by local power holders to protect affiliated economic subjects or pursue their interests at the expense of various competitors.[35] The Moscow incident attested not to the strength of the state but rather to its weakness. It demonstrated that a private security company with its office in the Kremlin was at that moment stronger than the company affiliated with the Moscow mayor's residence at Novyi Arbat.

The Competition for the Taxpayer

The economic system of state socialism functioned by extracting in advance the surplus that resulted from state ownership of major productive assets rather than on taxation. Mancur Olson once called it "implicit taxation."[36] Formally, taxes did exist, but in the administrative economy their nature was different from the conventional understanding of taxation. It was as if an individual put money from one of his pockets into another pocket, then into another, placing in various small and large pockets different amounts of money—and called this taxation! In this case, money is moved between pockets without changing owner. Conventional taxation can be understood as one individual taking money from another who is the owner of the money and who regularly gives a fixed share to the collecting individual. This implies a distinction between the taxing authority (the state) and the entity taxed (the private economy) and, accordingly, a system of exchange

34. Korzhakov, *Boris Yeltsin*, 286.

35. The press also mentioned a conflict in which the Moscow FSB warded off the RUBOP, which tried to conduct a search in the head office of Logovaz, Boris Berezovsky's main company. *Izvestiya*, 14 April 1995, 4.

36. Mancur Olson, "Why the Transition from Communism Is So Difficult," *Eastern Economic Journal* 21, 4 (fall 1995): 460.

between them. A transition to full state ownership, then, amounts to the removal of the distinction and the replacement of exchange with distribution. In this case, the two individuals become one, as it were, which in reality is achieved by turning everyone into state employees. All the surplus of socialist enterprises belongs to the state before it is even produced, and the subsequent "taxation" is nothing but its redistribution according to the plans of economic and social development. Wages of state employees, whether of managers or workers, are also determined by the socialist state, that is, individual incomes also belong to the state before they are even earned, and only those that are returned in the form of salary are taxed in the conventional sense, at the fixed rate (which, again, is simply withheld from the salary when it is calculated). In understanding this confiscatory system, let us nevertheless keep in mind that, in Russia, a great deal of enterprise profits and personal income were returned to employees through the powerful welfare system, which included free and high-quality education, art programs, health care services, sports and leisure, and so on, which helped to legitimate the administrative system.

The principal difference between the state socialist system, where no taxation in the conventional sense ever existed, and the capitalist model of state-economy relations highlights the scope and depth of the changes required to achieve the goals of "market reform" declared by the Russian authorities. A transition to the conventional model of taxation requires a fundamental remaking of relations between the state and the economy, both on the macro level and on the micro level, which is more difficult. The latter change presupposes a massive modification of the behavior and attitudes of a substantial part of the population, while changes in the macro level entail a fundamental redefinition of the role of the state. The transfer of state assets to private ownership and the development of new private enterprises put the creation of new taxation agencies and the definition of rules and rates of taxation on the reform agenda. The law of 27 December 1991 set the terms of the new system and established the State Tax Service; the creation of the Federal Tax Police followed in March 1992.[37] The tax code, however, was not adopted until the year 2000 (its first part was adopted separately in 1998), which allowed central and regional governments to set and change tax rules and negotiate their application.

It is usually assumed that an imperfect and predatory tax system is respon-

37. See Alexander Morozov, "Tax Administration in Russia," *East European Constitutional Review* (spring/summer 1996); Daniel Treisman, "Russia's Taxing Problem," *Foreign Policy* (fall 1998): 55–65; Frank Gregory and Gerald Brooke, "Policing Economic Transition and Increasing Revenue: A Case Study of the Federal Tax Police of the Russian Federation, 1992–1998," *Europe-Asia Studies* 52, 3 (May 2000): 433–55.

sible for the growth of the shadow economy. While generally plausible, this assertion needs to be qualified somewhat. For several years, the formal tax status and procedures related to new cooperative and private enterprises was indeed undefined, and state tax authorities made little effort to tackle the problem. The proliferating racketeering gangs, on the contrary, were very efficient in collecting protection money based on simple ad hoc calculations. The situation did not change very much in the 1990s: the state's intricate and predatory taxation system was no match for the simple methods of defining and collecting tribute by alternative tax authorities. Assertions that the total of all local and federal levies, if properly paid, would approach 100 percent are cited in most studies of Russia's entrepreneurs.[38] The conventional explanation, to which I subscribed in previous chapters, is that, because the state tax rate is high and arbitrary and payment cumbersome, a large proportion of private businesses chose to operate outside the legal framework, giving rise to alternative protection and justice services. Now that explanation needs to be reexamined, since it rests on a gross simplification, which becomes apparent once the following questions are asked: Why and how did those enterprises that remain in the alleged "100 percent tax" zone survive? How do criminal groups and other private protection agencies manage to operate in the legal business sector, that is, in the domain of another tax authority? What keeps the tax rate in the shadow sector significantly lower than that in the legitimate sector? The concept of shadow economy is often regarded as implying its "other," the legitimate economy as a homogeneous realm with fairly distinct boundaries. Enterprises, then, are either in one sector or the other. The pervasiveness of tax evasion and the difficulties with state tax collection in Russia are widely known. At the same time, it is assumed, and to a large extent rightfully so, that shadow tax authorities are very efficient in accounting for their clients' income and collecting their dues. It is, then, not very clear why economic subjects have to rush to the shadow sphere if they can enjoy more fiscal freedom in the legal domain.

One of the corrective explanations I have proposed has to do with the use of coercion and other strategies by private violence-managing agencies to achieve control over private economic activity. In a large number of cases, especially in the earlier period of reforms, the strategies of violence-managing agencies had supremacy over the choices of economic subjects. The latter

---

38. According to estimates by Tatiana Dolgopiatova, in order to pay employees 1 ruble of salary, an enterprise had to pay 99 kopeks of tax to the state, while profit tax withheld 67–69 percent of the profit. Tatiana Dolgopiatova, ed., *Neformal'nyi sektor v rossiiskoi ekonomike* (The informal sector in the Russian economy) (Moscow: ISARP, 1998), 43, 44. For evidence about predatory taxation provided through interviews, see Eva Busse, "The Embeddedness of Tax Evasion in Russia," in *Economic Crime in Russia*, ed. Alena Ledeneva and Marina Kurkchiyan (London: Kluwer, 2000), 132–33.

were forced to pay whatever tax was imposed on them if an alternative protective solution was unavailable. This is how a substantial segment of the tax base was initially appropriated by informal or overtly criminal violence-managing agencies. In comparison to shadow tax authorities, the state behaved much less aggressively.

A study of fiscal behavior of both collectors and taxpayers has revealed another set of important details that suggest that "competition for the taxpayer" may be a more adequate definition of the phenomenon in question than the "shadow economy."[39] Theoretically, the difference between tax-evading and taxpaying enterprises and that between state and private (illegal) tax authorities can be easily understood, but in the actual practice of taxation, where real transactions take place, such differences rarely obtain. In practice, several different agencies compete for the taxpayer and adjust their tax rates to the latter's actual payment capacity. In small businesses, which are less visible than large stationary enterprises, escaping a predatory tax authority and transferring payments to another is relatively easy. In bigger businesses, this leads to complex negotiations aimed at redistributing taxable income among several tax authorities in a manner that paradoxically reduces the total amount of levies. One and the same enterprise may pay to a criminal group and to a state tax inspectorate, and the two may even be aware of this fiscal situation. In such a case, the formal tax would be reduced to a minimal level, while protection and enforcement would be provided by the criminal group for the regular 20–30 percent. Taxpayers (in small, medium-sized, and large businesses alike) tend to adjust the amount of payment to the practical levying capacity of tax authorities and to negotiate reductions by maneuvering among different authorities. According to a study of everyday fiscal behavior based on interviews and participant observation, state tax inspectors tend to collect as much tax as they are able but not as much as prescribed by federal and local regulations. Likewise, economic subjects pay only the amount of tax they cannot refuse to pay and not the amount required by these formal regulations. The consistent application of formal rates and procedures would indeed be very damaging to economic subjects and rarely occurs—when it does, it is usually a form of punishment—since it effectively damages and sometimes even bankrupts the business. Hence the formal tax rules and the audits aimed at enforcing them remain largely an instrument of coercion and punishment available to state authorities at any time and against virtually any company. Businessmen, then, have to learn not to "show" too much of their revenue, since that would naturally lead to higher levies, and not to "show" too little, which may invite a puni-

39. Vadim Volkov, ed., *Konkurentsiya za nalogoplatel'shchika: Issledovaniya po fiskal'noi sotsiologii* (Competition for the taxpayer: Studies in fiscal sociology) (Moscow: MONF, 2000).

tive audit and result in enormous fines. The result of multiple adjustments and competition, as the study asserts, is the establishment of a relatively efficient actual tax rate of 10–30 percent, comparable to that in the shadow sector.[40]

In the mid-1990s, the practice of negotiated taxation permeated all levels of the economy. Negotiations involved not only rates but also means of payment. Woodruff's discussion traces how "more and more of Russia's state-owned or newly private enterprises dropped out of the officially visible money economy" and engaged in barter exchange.[41] Tax authorities, in turn, oscillated between accepting payments in kind and demanding cash. In October 1996, the state created a new organ, the Emergency Tax Commission (otherwise known as "VeCheKa," like Lenin's secret police) to coerce every large tax debtor to pay and in cash. The assault on large debtors, such as the automobile plants VAZ and Kamaz and the natural gas monopoly Gazprom, resulted in a considerable, 61 percent increase in tax debt collection in 1997 and reestablished the priority of Moscow over regional tax authorities. However, it scarcely contributed to the reconstruction of the state as a public entity, but on the contrary reinforced the practice of personal negotiations. Moreover, as Woodruff notes, the coercive solution of tax difficulties may well have resulted in a transfer of assets to power Moscow financial groups rather than the central government, since the transfer of ownership resulting from the enforcement of debts was handled by the banks controlled by the oligarchs.[42]

The competition for the taxpayer occurred on many levels. At the level of large enterprises, the federal tax authorities competed with regional and local governments, the latter lobbying in Moscow for a redistribution of the tax burden and endorsing barter locally, which made local economies nonlegible and therefore less taxable from the center. Central efforts at tax collection were selective and irregular; they represented the emergency solutions of a powerful group to fill its coffers to the extent needed for survival. On the level of medium-sized and small business, regional and local tax inspectorates, backed by the tax police, competed with private violence-managing agencies. The competition was indirect; its outcome was expressed in the amount of income declared by enterprises for official tax purposes. (Police operations against organized crime may be viewed as direct competition.)

40. Ella Paneyakh, "Izderzhki legal'noi ekonomicheskoi deyatel'nosti i nalogovoe povedenie rossiiskikh predprinimatelei" (Costs of the legal economic activity and tax behavior of Russian entrepreneurs), in *Konkurentsiya za nalogoplatel'shchika: Issledovaniya po fiskal'noi sotsiologii* (Competition for the taxpayer: Studies in fiscal sociology), ed. Vadim Volkov (Moscow: MONF, 2000), 31.
41. Woodruff, *Money Unmade*, 143.
42. Ibid., 190.

The hidden part of the income, then, became the object of various informal levies. A criminal leader boasted in an interview with a Moscow journal: "If tax inspectors had learned to work with businessmen as we do, the state would have no problem collecting taxes. Have you ever heard, for example, of someone offering a bribe to our auditor?"[43] This frank statement naturally points to a potential difficulty that will have to be resolved should the state tax authorities indeed attempt to consolidate their efforts. So far, the combination of intolerable tax rates, their practical adjustment, and the lack of regularity in the work of state tax authorities has provided profitable opportunities for subsidizing alternative institutions of protection and enforcement. To the extent that a consistent politics of state formation requires a monopoly on taxation, it will involve, in practice, efforts at outcompeting, by all available means, the rival tax authorities.

Transactional Strategies and Dispute Settlement

Sociological studies of different methods and strategies used by businessmen to settle disputes and resolve transactional problems tend to yield different results depending on the structure of the sample. Throughout the 1990s, the economy remained highly segmented and heterogeneous, reflecting a transition to postsocialist forms of property and management.[44] A more accurate picture of the behavior of managers can therefore be obtained by juxtaposing the results of the few existing studies and the segments of the economy examined by each. Most systematic are two independent surveys conducted in the same year (1997) by Russian scholars directed by Vadim Radaev and by U.S. scholars Kathryn Hendley, Peter Murrell, and Randi Ryterman.[45] Although the problematic of Radaev's study is wider, touching on the structure of transaction costs and the business ethic of the emerging markets, the two studies both focus on patterns of problem solving in a highly erratic business environment. Both draw on substantial samples of private enterprises, but whereas in Radaev's survey the majority of enterprises were created after 1989 by new private entrepreneurs, the conclusions drawn by Hendley et al. are derived from the study of formerly Soviet state

43. Alexander Ryklin, "Bratva na nervakh," *Itogi*, 8 December 1998, 15–16.

44. See David Stark and Laslo Bruszt, *Post-Socialist Pathways: Transforming Politics and Property in East Central Europe* (Cambridge: Cambridge University Press, 1998).

45. Vadim Radaev, *Formirovanie novykh rossiiskikh rynkov: Transaktsionnye izderzhki, formy kontrolia i delovaya etika* (Moscow: Tsentr politicheskikh tecknologii, 1998); idem, "Corruption and Violence in Russian Business in the Late 1990s," in *Economic Crime in Russia*, ed. Alena Ledeneva and Marina Kurkchiyan (London: Kluwer, 2000); Kathryn Hendley, Peter Murrell, and Randi Ryterman, "Law, Relationships and Private Enforcement: Transactional Strategies of Russian Enterprises," *Europe-Asia Studies* 52, 4 (2000): 627–56.

enterprises that were in operation before the reforms. While the former sample includes primarily small and medium-sized, relatively well-off businesses, up to 70 percent of enterprises included in the latter sample suffered from serious liquidity problems, operating far below capacity. Radaev's survey differentiated among enterprises by a number of variables (time in operation, size, level of protection costs, etc.) that turned out to affect the entrepreneurs' inclination to appeal to state law or to alternative mechanisms and their propensity to use violence as the method of dispute resolution. Regrettably, the other study did not relate the managers' choices of problem-solving methods and evaluations of their efficiency to any independent variables, treating the managers sampled and their enterprises as a homogeneous group. Still, the two studies may be viewed as largely complementary, and their conclusions are related to the segments of the economy that they have studied.

Drawing on data from these and other studies of similar issues, I will now reconstruct in a very general narrative form the evolution of dispute settlement and enforcement in Russian business in the 1990s. The existing social relations (kinship, friendship, shared work experience, etc.) were used as the primary resource for forging new economic ties in the postsocialist economy. They were central to maintaining and governing business relations independently of the form of property, specialization, age, and so on. Informal "peaceful" settlement remained the most important mechanism of tension management in business relations, but it remains unclear who participated and what the substance of the settlement was. No study so far has managed to explicate what this seemingly obvious method involves, except that it is semantically opposite to external coercive interference. Throughout the 1990s, former Soviet business managers and new entrepreneurs made extensive use of networks to enforce contractual obligations and of informal negotiations to settle disputes, trying hard to avoid appeals to external agencies so as to preserve network solidarity. But when negotiations failed, managers of former state enterprises were inclined to appeal privately to local government officials or initiate lawsuits in arbitration courts. In 1997, while formal and informal meetings remained the preferred method for solving transactional problems, the incidence of the use of arbitration courts by medium-sized and large former state enterprises was significant (25.46 percent of enterprises), higher than the use of other external agencies, such as local governments (10.43 percent) or private enforcers (2.76 percent).[46] Conservatism, a long history of working together, cash shortages, the high technological complexity of enterprises, and close relations with state organs, traits typical of former Soviet enterprises, are the factors most likely to determine

46. Hendley et al., "Law, Relationships and Private Enforcement," 636.

transactional strategies. When confronted with threats or violence, this group demonstrates a consistent inclination to appeal to state militia for protection.[47]

In the segment of newly created private enterprises with a greater share of young entrepreneurs, the picture is similar where the reliance on business networks is concerned but different when it comes to third-party enforcement. The earlier in time entrepreneurs started their businesses, the more frequently they use protection by criminal groups and the higher the incidence of violence. Enterprises set up for rapid capital accumulation in 1989–93, that is, those with low investment needs, low technological complexity, and, most important, rapid cash turnover, were heavily dependent on criminal arbitration at least until 1997. The later a given enterprise emerged in the 1990s, the more choice was available to it with regard to adjudication and enforcement. Reformed arbitration courts began working in 1992, but a significant increase in cases occurred only in 1996. In general, new entrepreneurs were not satisfied with the efficiency of state arbitration, though by 1997 24 percent claimed to prefer *arbitrazh* courts in case of a dispute. Only 11 percent openly admitted a readiness to use force; and 55 percent were in favor of "informal negotiations," whatever that may mean.[48] Among entrepreneurs who preferred state arbitration, those with a low level of protection costs prevailed. Those who evaluated their protection expenditure as high were also more inclined toward informal settlements and the use of force. Throughout the 1990s the protection costs borne by newly emerging entrepreneurs grew, but some felt more secure and some less. A sizable proportion of entrepreneurs (up to 30 percent) paid substantial protection money; they were inclined to use the services of criminal groups more than others and continued to confront with violence in personal experience. Another group (over 40 percent) got better value for its protection money, felt less threatened, rarely used criminal enforcers, and preferred informal settlements. Such entrepreneurs either internalized protection or managed to secure a more efficient informal state "roof." Their interest in using the law remained relatively low. Overall, surveys indicate that the degree of penetration of criminal protective arrangements and the reliance on criminal adjudication were more modest than generally assumed. High criminalization was a feature of the late 1980s and early 1990s and pertained only to particular segments of the economy. The rate of criminalization had dropped by the late 1990s, when the state system of justice began to recover. At the same time, the justice system seemed highly fragmented: different groups of economic subjects used different systems of justice, so that the

47. Radaev, *Formirovanie novykh rossiiskikh rynkov,* 190.
48. Ibid., 128.

general tendency is hard to uncover. It is clear, however, that the majority of managers and entrepreneurs prefer to remain somewhere between the two systems, try to avoid both, and instead rely on interpersonal relations. All that should be seen against the background of the low level of trust among the population toward the state justice system, as indicated in public opinion surveys. Throughout the 1990s, the procuracy, courts, and the public defenders remained among the least trusted institutions, only slightly more credible than trade unions and political parties.[49]

Putin's Dilemma

Thus far I have considered the dynamic of the state largely autonomous in relation to the policy decisions of its leaders and have focused primarily on everyday interactions. I have understood the withering away of the state in the 1990s as an erosion of the state monopoly of force, taxation, and justice not immediately visible on the macro level, with the exception of tax federalism and the problem of Chechnya.[50] In the aftermath of the August 1998 crisis and the change in government, however, conditions for a reassertion of the state began to emerge. Popular attitudes shifted to favor a strong state; demands for law and order became more pronounced and supplanted the earlier calls for freedom and individualism. On the one hand, this was a reaction to the decline of welfare programs caused by the shrinking of the state budget, a consequence of the state's inability to raise enough tax revenue.[51] On the other hand, private entrepreneurs, the primary beneficiaries of freedom and individualism, increasingly felt that the arbitrariness of authorities and, consequently, the low predictability of economic activity threatened their business. A consensus regarding the need for a more orderly business environment has emerged.[52] Furthermore, the competition and growing involvement in capital accumulation have produced a consolidation of protection enterprises. The emerging balance (or stalemate) of forces, combined with the increasing stakes in the economy, have made negotia-

49. Lev Gudkov, "Otnoshenie k pravovym institutam v Rossii" (Attitudes toward institutions of law in Russia), *Monitoring obshchestvennogo mneniya* 3 (May–June 2000): 30–39.

50. Daniel Triesman, however, has argued that the policy of asymmetrical fiscal federalism prevented Russia from disintegrating in 1992–95. Daniel Triesman, *After the Deluge: Regional Crises and Political Consolidation of Russia* (Ann Arbor: University of Michigan Press, 1999).

51. David Mason and Svetlana Sidorenko-Stephenson, "Changing Public Perceptions and the Crisis of Confidence in the State," in *State-Building in Russia: The Yeltsin Legacy and the Challenge of the Future,* ed. Gordon Smith (New York: M. E. Sharpe, 1999), 162–73.

52. Caroline Humphrey, "Dirty Business, 'Normal Life,' and the Dream of Law," in *Economic Crime in Russia,* 177–90.

tions more desirable than conflict between protection enterprises; conflict with state law enforcement has become even less desirable. For those violent entrepreneurs who successfully transferred their activities to the legal economy, predictable relations with the state have become a new priority. By the end of the 1990s an imperfect but working system of rules and shared expectations was created through ongoing interaction between violence-managing agencies of all kinds and economic subjects. Without a decisive top-down effort, however, the consolidation of governing institutions and the homogenization of rules could go on for an indeterminate time. At a certain point, various developments and policies of state formation, which had only a loose sense of common direction, were articulated and transformed into a conscious intention of state building on the part of politicians. This is essentially what happened when Vladimir Putin rose to power in 1999–2000.

As a matter of fact, the need to strengthen the state was already voiced by Yeltsin in his September 1997 address to the Council of Federation. On that occasion, talk of a strong state, not itself novel for the president, was actually backed up by some concrete policy measures: a strengthening in the enforcement of juridical decisions, tax reform measures, and the regulation of large, newly privatized enterprises.[53] As deputy chief of the Administration of the President, Putin may have participated in the realization of this new policy in 1997–98. Once he became prime minister in the summer of 1999, he indicated his readiness to go much further in implementing the state-building project. As if replaying the "classic" state-building scenario, he began, or was forced to begin, by war-making. The subsequent support for the armed forces and state security, though still largely symbolic because of the scarcity of state finances, seemed to indicate that the strengthening of state hardware would be his top priority.

Putin's presidential address to the legislature on 8 July 2000, however, demonstrated that he understands the state's weakness as structural rather than purely substantive, and that measures for strengthening the state will also be structural. He declared that he was totally convinced that "an ineffectual state is the main cause of the lengthy and profound economic crisis" and gave a fairly accurate diagnosis of the nature of the state's ineffectiveness:

> We have created islands, separate little islands of authority with no bridges between them. . . . The center and the territorial, regional, and local authorities still compete among themselves—compete for powers. These frequently destructive tussles are watched by those who benefit from such disorder, from such arbitrariness, those who turn the lack of an effective state to their own advantage. . . . This vacuum of authority has led to state functions being ap-

53. Russell Bova, "Democratization and the Crisis of the Russian State," in *State-Building in Russia*, 17–40.

propriated by private corporations and clans. They have surrounded themselves by their own shadowy groups, lobbying groups, and dubious security
services using illegal means to obtain information. At the same time, state
functions and state institutions are different from entrepreneurship ones in
that they must not be bought or sold, privatized or handed over to be used or
leased. Professionals for whom the sole working criterion is the law are needed
in state service. Otherwise the state opens up a route to corruption and the
time may come when it will simply degenerate and cease to be democratic.[54]

The diagnosis, referred to as the "degeneration" of the state, was behind the
measures proposed to achieve economic growth. In short, Putin stressed the
need to ensure the protection of ownership rights and of fair competition, to
liberate business from administrative dictatorship and to ease the tax burden. The declared politics of state formation à la Putin is in fact very close to
mainstream liberal thinking about the role of the state. To be sure, the new
president did balance it with calls to consider Russian geography and traditions in defining the degree and level of state regulation. But the core principles of dissociating state power from entrepreneurship and creating an impersonal rule-governed space for private economic competition (from which
"dubious security services" must be excluded) have so far been supported by
most of his other major statements. The "dictatorship of the law" has since
become Putin's chief slogan.

Economic Effects of the Rule of Law

The obvious challenges that Putin, like any state builder, faces, in the
form of open and covert resistance by competing power holders, are not the
only factor that may doom his program to remain nothing more than a slogan. There is a more dangerous set of underlying tensions and contradictions that need to be resolved if the declared aims are to be achieved. The
rule of law is regarded by Putin's team as the essential instrument for achieving economic growth. Efficient and consistent enforcement of the universal
rules of the game is seen as the major precondition for increasing investments. Those committed to enforcing the rule of law will naturally have to
see that those who do not obey the law are dispossessed and punished. The
state, then, would have to define who is and who is not a criminal. The
names (and nicknames) of local violent entrepreneurs turned powerful businessmen are known to almost everyone there, not least because of previous
efforts by law enforcement agencies. Many of these powerful businessmen
own or manage substantial assets, displaying some degree of economic suc-

54. Address by Russian President Vladimir Putin to Russian Federal Assembly in Moscow
on 8 July 2000. RTR TV, 08:00 GMT, trans. FBIS.

cess. Persecuting them for their criminal careers during which they accumulated these assets would entail a redistribution of their property, another round of ruthless struggle and, inevitably, yet another period of economic disruption. The cost of the unconditional "dictatorship of law" may thus be economic decline, not growth. On the other hand, continued lenience by the authorities toward criminal leaders would hollow out the policy of strengthening the rule of law and, consequently, could discredit the new president, as it did his predecessor. Theoretically, then, the formula "more rule of law—more economic growth" sounds plausible. In practice, and especially in the Russian political-economic context of 2000, it is a dubious policy. At best, the concrete application of the rule of law will determine the outcome, not the principle itself. What is certain, therefore, is that during his presidential term Putin will have to adopt a policy consisting largely of attempts to resolve the dilemma of accommodation versus persecution and to boost economic growth without overly compromising the rule of law.

One obvious solution to Putin's dilemma is to abstain from the retroactive enforcement of laws. Essentially, this means a politics of amnesty combined with a newly set "zero-point" after which all infringements of the law are subject to punishment. This means the state will be responsible for rendering the rules more transparent and their enforcement impersonal and efficient, which would, understandably, require some time to achieve. The legitimacy of such a decision from the standpoint of the entrepreneurial class is likely to be higher than the legitimacy of state authorities setting out to sort out "criminals" from "honest businessmen" on the basis of vague criteria and with reference to a varying set of past and present laws. The interest key business groups have in stable rules should be greater now that the initial accumulation of capital has been accomplished than when the process was still under way, in the mid-1990s. Uncertainties about the application of rules is one of the major factors that may cause resistance to the rule of law. Thus, to be successful, the "dictatorship of law" should be future-oriented.

The presidential address cited above contains a message to that effect. At the very beginning, after declaring the centrality of the rule of law, Putin suggests that past state policies strongly contributed to the expansion of the shadow economy, corruption, and capital flight. Then he goes on to stress the importance of looking forward rather than backward and emphasizes a common responsibility on the part of "entrepreneurs, the power-wielding structures, and all citizens" for the fate of the country. At the conclusion of this part of the speech, Putin announces a "new social contract," whose substance, however, remains undefined. Another remarkable feature of the presidential address is what is absent from it. Unlike Yeltsin, who used to make strong statements about organized crime and promised to take appropriate police measures, Putin mentions crime only once, in the context of his criticism of the state's incapacity to protect entrepreneurs in a regular and competent manner. But he does not urge an intensification in police activity, turning instead to a discussion of how to strengthen institutions.

However important a clear position (so far understated) articulated by the central authority may be on this extremely delicate and important issue, much depends on how the game is played out on the regional and local levels. We have seen through the analysis of the careers of violent entrepreneurs that solutions have already been found locally. Regional and local authorities have already concluded informal pacts with certain financial-industrial groups despite their criminal origin. Formal recognition and informal guarantees against legal persecution on the basis of past acts were offered in exchange for investments and a higher degree of obedience to the law. The central authorities have thus far tended to refrain from interfering too much. Yet in some regions where the elected authority failed to reach a compromise with the local strongman, the coercive power of central authorities was effectively mobilized to remove the rival through a criminal investigation. Thus, soon after General Lebed was elected governor, he clashed with the aluminum baron Anatolii Bykov, the informal *khozyain* of the region. Lebed managed to mobilize the General Procuracy and solicit a special team to investigate Bykov's past, when the racketeering gang leader was transforming himself into the regional tycoon. For over a year now, following his arrest by Interpol in Hungary and his extradition to Russia, Bykov has been under investigation. The future of the giant Krasnoyarsk aluminum and energy holding company TANAKO will be unclear until the fate of its owner is decided.[55] Possible disruptions caused by the dispossession of local strongmen could be minimized only if a mechanism for a smooth change of ownership is devised and enforced by the state authorities. So far, transfers of ownership and management in Russia have frequently been rife with conflict, with each side using special police units, private security services, and thugs (the differences being minor) to enforce or resist the transfer.[56]

A public declaration of financial amnesty or the open approval of local informal pacts by the central authorities is unlikely, since this could have a damaging moral effect. But a case-by-case policy of accommodation of eco-

---

55. In summer 2001, under arrest and facing trial, Anatolii Bykov was reportedly still clinging to his remaining 28 percent share in Krasnoyarskii Aliuminievyi Zavod (KrAZ), with the rest of the company owned by the world's second largest aluminum holding company, Russkii Aliuminii (RusAl). *Kommersant,* 7 August 2001, 4.

56. Among the most violent and dramatic management conflicts in 2000 were those in Petersburg at the Vyborg Paper Factory and the Lomonosov Porcelain Factory; in Moscow at the major vodka distilleries Krystall and Smirnoff; and in the Urals at the Kachkanar Mining Plant.

nomically successful violent entrepreneurs on the basis of their economic efficiency and their contribution to the public good, as happened in many Western countries during the early capitalist phase, is likely.

Policies for Reconstructing the State

The policy of the state toward violent entrepreneurs has not yet been defined, but some aspects of it are already discernible. The range of policies leading to the consolidation of the monopoly of violence is in fact limited. Competing agencies and their personnel can either be coercively neutralized through legal prosecution; integrated into the state by direct appointment; or pacified by reducing them to the status of economic enterprises without any coercive capacity. There is evidence that by the year 2000 the politics of state formation in Russia had come to combine all three policies: neutralization, integration, and pacification. The Procuracy and the anti–organized crime agencies of both the FSB and the MVD have visibly intensified their law enforcement activity while at the same time practicing a differentiated approach. The latter consists of targeting those persons and groups where the incidence of law-breaking or confrontation with state authorities has been particularly high, thereby sending disciplining signals to the others. Throughout 2000, this policy was applied to large oligarchic and to smaller criminal groups. Parallel to the well-publicized legal pressure on, and tough negotiations with, the oligarchs during the summer, there were also a number of significant arrests of thieves-in-law in Moscow and of two large criminal groups in Petersburg. The groups had the usual structure consisting of the leadership, brigadeers, several legally registered private security agencies, and affiliated businesses. According to expert sources, they were distinguished by their greater brutality, the frequent use of violence, and involvement in purely criminal affairs. They belonged to the unreformed breed, and when the time came they were eliminated.[57]

The current state policy toward legal private security agencies consists of tightening regulations, increasing the number of inspections, and sorting out criminalized agencies. Business associations have similar filtering effects. Closer cooperation between private security agencies and the state's legal system in settling disputes and protecting property rights can be taken as an indication of the growing significance of the state's legal institutions at the expense of private enforcers. Another round of struggle between MVD officials and the private security sector with its powerful lobby is likely when

---

57. In January 2000 law enforcement officials arrested all members of Sasha-Akula's group and closed its security company, Falkon-95; in July 2000 it arrested the members of Andrei "Malen'kii"'s group. Information provided by the Agency for Journalistic Investigations.

the State Duma resumes discussions of the new version of the law on private protection and detective activity. To restore public control over the use of force and dispute settlement, however, the government does not necessarily need to ban private security agencies, but rather to establish and enforce a clear division of competence, limiting the activities of these agencies to physical and informational security while strengthening state arbitration and justice (a structural rather than repressive measure). The "disarmament" of economic enterprises, combined with more efficient state protection, is the obvious path toward reconstructing the state. In one of its major aspects, then, state formation coincides with divergent trajectories of violence-managing agencies: some are integrated into the market economy, transformed into business firms, and stripped of political functions; others become isolated, subjected to central control, or co-opted by the state.

One of the most controversial, though not unimaginable, policies is for the state to co-opt violent entrepreneurs or delegate some state functions to them. Some examples can be cited. In summer 1999, the government acquired a new minister. As Boris Ivaniuzhenkov intimated in an interview, it took him four days to accept the offer by then prime minister Sergei Stepashin (former head of the MVD and then of the FSB) that he become minister of sports. In police files, Ivaniuzhenkov is known as "Rotan," the right-hand man of Sergei Lalakin ("Lutchok"), the leader of the Podol'skaya criminal group. Born in the suburban town of Podol'sk near Moscow, Ivaniuzhenkov embarked on a dual career, achieving the title of master of sports in wrestling and a leading position in the local racketeering group. Podol'sk, he claims, "is the only town were there were never ever any feuds. The situation was always stable."[58] In other respects, *podol'skie* went through the same evolution as many other similar organizations. They took control of the local market, trades, and businesses, consolidating power in the locale and expanding beyond it. The ability to maintain order and to give generously to charity (the *khoziain* attitude) brought the violent entrepreneurs popular support: Lalakin "Lutchok" was made an honorary citizen of Podol'sk, and Ivaniuzhenkov ("Rotan") was elected to the Moscow *oblast'* legislature in 1997. In 1999 Ivaniuzhenkov recalled being appointed to the ministry: "So they summoned me and made the offer. They asked: Are you able to? I say: No question. I want the country to remember it has sportsmen."[59]

Another sign of the government's pragmatic orientation came during the December 1999 election campaign. The new electoral bloc Edinstvo (unity), otherwise known as "Medved" (bear), created on the eve of the elections and closely associated with Putin, co-opted the Greco-Roman wrestler

58. Dmitrii Pavlov, "Novaya vlast'" (The new power), *Vlast'*, 31 August 1999, 8.
59. Ibid., 7.

and three-time Olympic champion Alexander Karelin. He was made the number two man on the party list. The impressive image of the 130–kilo wrestler appeared on every party poster. In the course of the election campaign Karelin assumed two incarnations: the authoritative heavyweight athlete and the colonel of the Federal Tax Police. Initially, he became a cult figure in the Novosibirsk region. There he was prominent not only because he was the world's top heavyweight wrestler, "the strongest man in the world," as he was often called. In the beginning of the 1990s, he also turned to active fund-raising, securing large donations by local private businessmen for the development of sports. In 1993, he joined Otari Kvantrishvili, a wrestling coach and leading Moscow criminal authority, in his effort to create the political party "Sportsmen of Russia." Karelin became one of three cochairmen of the athletes' party. There is no evidence that Karelin was in some way involved in Kvantrishvili's protection rackets. It is more likely that he believed in some of the party's slogans and in corporate solidarity and the need to promote a healthy drug-free lifestyle, as he said in one of his early interviews. At the same time, he was aware that "sports is politics, it is big money, and therefore economics."[60] When the Moscow boss was assassinated, the newly born party of athletes was dissolved. In Novosibirsk Karelin set up a charity foundation in his name. According to press publications and interview sources, the wrestler became a leading figure in regional business relations, providing informal protection to local businessmen from criminal elements in exchange for charity donations to the Karelin Foundation.[61] That foundation gained popular approval for its charitable activities supporting sports schools and churches, while its director headed for his third Olympic gold medal in Atlanta and world celebrity. As a member of the Dynamo club, traditionally associated with the "power ministries," Karelin had a formal rank in the militia.[62] In 1997 he transferred to the Federal Tax Police and received the rank of colonel, and in 1998 became Yeltsin's adviser on sports, which gave him direct access to the Kremlin. The invitation to join the "party of power" was thus a logical next move. It also proved quite successful: the appearance of the formal and informal tax officer and wrestling champion among the leadership of the "party of power" helped the party achieve an impressive electoral victory in December 1999 (in Sydney 2000 Karelin only came in second).

For the new government, the policy of reconstructing the state is a war on

60. Interview with Alexander Karelin conducted by Alexander Skliarenko, *Novosibirskie novosti*, 22–29 January 1994, 16.

61. Liza Brichkina, "Samyi sil'nyi chelovek Kremlia" (The strongest man in the Kremlin), *Profil'* 28 (1998): 76.

62. Dmitrii Pisarev and Dmitrii Novikov, "Moi obshchestvennyi ves 130 kg" (My public weight is 130 kg.), interview with Alexander Karelin, *Novaya Sibir'*, 30 October 1998, 1.

many fronts. Reform of federative relations and tax reform have so far been its two main battles. In July–August 2000 the new tax code defining rules and taxation rates became law. The previous measures of tax reform yielded some positive fiscal results in 1999–2000. According to the reports of the Ministry of Taxation and Levies, tax collection has improved dramatically after 1998 (see table 4). The overall amount of tax revenue provided by the ministry (consolidated budget) increased by 70 percent in 1999 and by 62 percent in 2000. The federal budget grew by 47 percent in 1999 and 75 percent in 2000. If in 1998 growth can be largely attributed to the devaluation of ruble and the increase in prices (the reports do not specify the amount of tax in real terms), the year 2000 growth remains impressive even if the 21 percent inflation for that year is taken into account.

The same tendency, claimed the ministry, continued in January–September 2001 as the total tax revenue for this period transferred to the federal budget reached 670.59 billion rubles, a 57 percent increase in comparison with the same period of 2000. During the first half of 2000, the federal tax police initiated 16,500 criminal cases for tax evasion, more than for 1999 as a whole.[63] After the adoption of the tax code and the new revolutionary 13 percent general income tax (in effect as of 1 January 2001), the government hopes to have less need for intimidation. Vice Minister of Finance Sergei Shatalov, reportedly the author of the new code, expects 40 percent growth in tax revenue within two to three years. He points to the reduction of the tax burden in the United States in the 1920s, from 75 to 25 percent, which, according to Shatalov, led to a 60 percent increase in the taxes collected.[64] A no less radical move has been made to standardize and decrease the profit tax: an unprecedented 23 percent profit tax was introduced along with the abolition of the intricate system of tax exemptions.[65]

Thus far, the regular use of special paramilitary units to back up the financial audits of private companies has been continuously perceived as private conflict resolution by means of force, a *naezd*, an act of extortion rather than a manifestation of the rule of law. The number of financial audits backed by armed tax police increased in summer 2000. Spectacular actions to retrieve the financial documentation of large private companies were conducted in twenty-six regions, including at Media-Most, AvtoVAZ, and LukOil.[66] Even the July visit of tax inspectors to the offices of Sibneft, the oil giant controlled by the oligarch Roman Abramovich, was called a *naezd*,

---

63. Statistics section of http://www.nalog.ru, official site of the Ministry for Taxes and Levies of the Russian Federation, accessed 7 November 2001.

64. *Vechernyaia Moskva,* 2 July 2000, 2.

65. *Vlast',* 3 June 2001, 9–14.

66. http://www.gazeta.ru, accessed 11 January 2001.

Table 4. Tax and Levies Transferred to the Budgets of the Russian Federation, 1998–2000 (billion rubles)

Type of budget	1998	1999	2000
Consolidated budget	524,8	891,4	1442,5
Territorial budgets	331,4	527,7	805,0
Federal budget	193,5	363,6	637,6

Source: http://www.nalog.ru, the official website of the Ministry of Taxation and Levies of the Russian Federation.

an act of intimidation, in media reports, despite the absence, in this case, of the usual backup forces of armed men in camouflage and masks.[67] After the police action against ORT Channel One in December 2000, which involved a demonstration of force, the procurator general made a public statement condemning the use of special forces as part of financial audits: "We will no longer tolerate the use of force in civil organizations, in such cases [as ORT] the use of psychological pressure on people is unjustified. Force wielders should only be used . . . against criminal strongholds or in the case of direct obstruction." He reportedly began work on a special regulation concerning the use of special forces in law enforcement.[68] On 11 January 2001 the Procuracy announced that the regulation had been adopted and the use of paramilitary force would be limited to a set of specified cases. The first half of 2001 also witnessed further legislative initiatives by the government and the Duma aimed at reducing the bureaucratic burden imposed on the economy.

In his second address to the legislature, on 3 April 2001, Putin announced that the disintegration of the state had been stopped, but admitted that the state was still largely inefficient in serving the interests of legitimate property owners and "protecting citizens from racketeers, bandits, and bribe takers." The president outlined a set of structural measures aimed at increasing the efficiency of the state, which he defined as determined "not so much by the amount of [state-controlled] property but by the efficaciousness of political, legal, and administrative mechanisms for ensuring public interests in the country." It thus took Russian policy makers ten years to arrive at the understanding of what the state, created by decrees in 1991, should look like in practice and to define its place in relation to the economic market.

This conceptual achievement and the political will to implement the new model of the state distinguish the current phase of post-Soviet politics from the previous one. The shift coincided with the change in political leadership

67. See *Vlast'*, 15 July 2000, 16.
68. http://www.gazeta.ru, accessed 8 December 2000, with reference to RIA Novosti information agency.

but was also determined by a more fundamental dynamics. State builders arrived on the scene after a brutal decade of violent entrepreneurship on whose outcomes they depended in a vital albeit not immediately apparent way. Violent entrepreneurs did much of the preliminary dirty work, each capitalizing on the decay of the state and further worsening it, yet producing, in the long run, a range of consequences that few of them intended but which made them change their patterns of action. In building up their violence potential to extort money from new private businessmen, they had to work out a set of rules that made it possible to limit and regulate violence; with little more than outright extortion in mind, they were compelled to protect and even nurture their past victims to withstand fierce competition; in devising a set of tricks that allowed them to embezzle huge amounts of cash, they were led to work out a system of guarantees that secured the transactions of their clients; after showing their utter contempt for the law, accounting, and public opinion, they eventually found themselves hiring lawyers, accountants, PR professionals, and even state police units to protect and manage their assets.

Initially, violence-managing agencies were set up to establish, preserve, and expand monopolies of force over certain business domains, however small, in order to turn them into sources of permanent revenue. Such domains included clusters of enterprises in certain trades and industries, or "territories" linked by various formal and informal ties to and through the core "political" groups that possessed resources of coercion and, consequently, the capacity to protect and govern (to "solve questions"). If economic exchange between such domains was to take place, some kind of common secure space had to be created. With varying degrees of awareness and success, all the protection agencies, from purely criminal to officially state-controlled but virtually autonomous in practice, were involved in creating such a space. Throughout the 1990s that space was decentralized and economically burdensome, since it was maintained through interaction among thousands of independent agencies called "roofs." Key to the late 1990s was the consolidation of protection agencies; of them, the so-called state roofs, organized primarily around regional power holders, proved more powerful than the others. It is therefore hardly surprising that they were the first targets of the central power's effort to reconstruct the Russian state. From below, the consolidation of protection agencies was and continues to be driven by the "invisible hand" of competition and capital accumulation; from above, it is quite visibly being shaped by actors who distinguish themselves from *bandity* and other violent entrepreneurs by calling themselves *gosudarstvenniki,* state builders.

Key to Interviews

Interviews were conducted from March 1998 to August 2000.

Name	Occupation	Status	Organization	City
1 "Amir"	Enforcer	Unknown	The Chechen diaspora	Petersburg
2 Badyrov, Pavel	Enforcer	Director	Skat PPC	Petersburg
3 Denis	Enforcer	Brigadir	Criminal group	Petersburg
4 Evgenii	Expert	Captain (former)	Anticrime police	Petersburg
5 "Gennadii"	Enforcer	Adviser	Criminal group	Petersburg
6 Ivan	Enforcer	Unknown	Criminal group	Novosibirsk
7 Konstantinov, Andrei	Expert	Director	Agency for Journalistic Investigations	Petersburg
8 Krasiuk, Dmitrii	Expert	Press secretary	OPS Uralmash	Ekaterinburg
9 Lebedev, Roman	Expert	Captain (former)	Anticrime police	Kazan'
10 Markarov, Boris	Enforcer	Director	Alex PPC	Petersburg
11 Metelev, Kirill	Expert	Editor	Operativnoe prikrytie	Petersburg
12 Moshkov, Dmitrii	Enforcer	Codirector	Avanpost PPC	Petersburg
13 "Roman"	Enforcer	Brigadir	Criminal group	Petersburg
14 Sasha	Businessman	Director	A building company	Moscow
15 Senya	Enforcer	Brigadir	Criminal group	Petersburg
16 Strigalov, Boris	Expert	Major	Regional MVD Directorate	Petersburg
17 Tiutiaev, Dmitrii	Enforcer	Codirector	Avanpost PPC	Petersburg
18 Tsepov, Roman	Enforcer	Director	Baltik-Escort PPC	Petersburg
18 Vadim	Businessman	Director	Chain of pharmacies	Petersburg
20 Vadim "the Korean"	Enforcer	Brigadir	Criminal group	Petersburg
21 Veronika	Businessman	Director	Multimedia company	Petersburg-Moscow
22 Viktor	Expert	Major	RUBOP	Petersburg
23 Vitalii	Enforcer	Leader	Criminal group	Petersburg

Name	Occupation	Status	Organization	City
24 Vladimir	Businessman	Director	Silicon production company	Moscow
25 Yurii Mikhailovitch	Security director	Chief	Grand Hotel Evropa	Petersburg
26 Yurii Viktorovitch	Expert	Major	Regional MVD Directorate	Petersburg

Glossary of Russian Words and Phrases

avtoritet   "authority," a leader of a criminal group

bandit, bandity (pl.)   bandit(s), member(s) of criminal group specializing in the use of violence

baryga   a businessman, a trader

bespredel   unjustified use of violence

brigada   a brigade, the operational unit of a criminal group

brigadir   brigade leader

chastnik   private entrepreneur

gosarbitrazh   state arbitration court

gosudarstvennik   state builder

gruppirovka   a criminal group, a group of racketeers

khozyain   owner and manager of a territory or enterprise

kidok   a cheat, a dupe

kommersant   a businessman

krysha   a form of private protection

naezd   an assault, harassment

obschak   a criminal group's communal fund

OPG   organized criminal group

OPS   organized criminal society

poluchat'   to collect protection money

probivka   a probing, information gathering

razborka   a showdown, a shootout

razvodka   a dupe, a form of soft and friendly extortion
reketir   a racketeer
RUBOP   Regional Anti–Organized Crime Directorate
sinie   "the blue ones," heavily tattooed criminals
skhodka   a criminal gathering
sozdat' problemu   to create a problem or set-up
sportsmeny   sportsmen, athletes
strelka   a meeting of criminal groups to settle a dispute
tema   a business opportunity
ugolovniki   criminal elements
voroskoi mir   the traditional underworld
vor v zakone, zakonnik   a thief-in-law, a member of the traditional criminal elite
zona   places of confinement

Index

The Archaeological Landscape of Bute

George Geddes and Alex Hale

Royal
Commission on the
Ancient and
Historical
Monuments of
Scotland

British Library cataloguing in Publication Data: A CIP catalogue record for this book is available on request from the British Library.

The maps are based on Ordnance Survey material with the permission of the Ordnance Survey on behalf of Her Majesty's Stationery Office © Crown Copyright. All rights reserved, OS Licence Number OS 1000 25406. Unauthorised reproduction infringes Crown Copyright and may lead to prosecution or civil proceedings. Except where otherwise stated, all the illustrations and images in this publication are Crown Copyright RCAHMS.

Crown Copyright © RCAHMS 2010
ISBN: 978 1 902419 74 9

Book layout by Mitch Cosgrove
Printed by Allander, Edinburgh

Front cover: An oblique aerial view of the vitrified fort of Dunagoil (at right, 40291) and the fort of Little Dunagoil (at left, 40280). See page 22. DP062659

Front cover inset: St Colmac cross, standing stone with later inscribed cross (40317). See page 15. SC408104

Back cover: A detailed plan from 1780 of Dunagoil vitrified fort (40280) and its surrounding landscape. See page 4. DP075180 © Bute Archive at Mount Stuart

Page iv: A view from Glencallum bay at the SE corner of Bute towards the Dunagoil archaeological complex in the distance. Much of the dramatic intervening landscape was cultivated until the 18th century, when the south of the island became a sheep farm. DP062664

Published in 2010 by The Royal Commission on the Ancient and Historical Monuments of Scotland.

The Royal Commission on the Ancient and Historical Monuments of Scotland (RCAHMS)
John Sinclair House
16 Bernard Terrace
Edinburgh EH8 9NX
tel 0131 662 1456
fax 0131 247 4163
www.rcahms.gov.uk
Registered Charity SC010240

For over 100 years, the Royal Commission on the Ancient and Historical Monuments of Scotland has been collecting, recording and interpreting information on the archaeological, architectural, industrial and maritime heritage of the nation, creating a unique archive that offers a remarkable insight into the special nature of Scotland's places. Many millions of items, including photographs, maps, drawings and documents are made widely available to the public via the web, through exhibitions and publications, and at the RCAHMS search room in Edinburgh.

Contents

Foreword

The partnership between the Discover Bute Landscape Partnership Scheme (DBLPS) and the Royal Commission on the Ancient and Historical Monuments of Scotland (RCAHMS), from which this volume emanates, has been a truly rewarding example of successful partnership working between Scottish Government agencies and local people. With the assistance of funding from the Heritage Lottery Fund, the long wished for reassessment of the archaeological record of Bute and the enhancement of that record into a modern, easily accessible resource has become a reality. As significant, the symbiotic knowledge transfer between the RCAHMS Survey and Recording staff and the local Bute residents has been a process that has been educational, inspirational and, most importantly, a whole lot of fun! We are delighted that this volume will stand as a long term legacy for the project, and one that will encourage involvement in, learning about and enthusiasm for the archaeology of Bute for generations to come.

Paul Duffy
Deputy Project Manager (Archaeology)
Discover Bute Landscape Partnership Scheme
September 2010

Acknowledgements

This booklet was written by G Geddes and A Hale and edited by J Sherriff, JB Stevenson, R Bailey and R Turner. The maps and the survey drawings have been prepared by G Brown and I Parker and the aerial photographs were taken by R Adam and D Cowley and other members of the RCAHMS aerial survey team. Additional photography was provided by D Smart, S Wallace and by RCAHMS field investigators. In addition to those noted above, fieldwork was undertaken principally by P Dixon, A Dutton, A Gannon, L Fisher, J Hepher, A Leith, L McCafferty, P McKeague and M Middleton. Thanks also to O Brookes, M Sutherland and W Toole for production, proof reading and indexing.

The Commission is grateful to many individuals who provided assistance throughout the project. Those to be thanked at the Discover Bute Landscape Partnership Scheme (DBLPS) include B Paterson (Scheme Co-ordinator), and the members of the Archaeology Research Project, including P Duffy. Of the members of the local community who participated in the fieldwork (too many to individually mention here), special thanks are extended to A Hannah and J Herriot. Thanks also to S Hothersall from the Association of Certificated Field Archaeologists (ACFA), S MacDonald (Administrator), I McArthur (Buteshire Natural History Society), A Speirs (Curator, Bute Museum), A McLean, archivist at Mount Stuart, and J Turner, who facilitated access to Inchmarnock. For providing other specialist advice, thanks are due to T Cowie and A Sheridan (both National Museums of Scotland) and N Finlay (Dept of Archaeology, University of Glasgow). RCAHMS is also especially grateful to all the landowners, including the Marquess of Bute, Lord Attenborough and Sir Robert Smith, and to all the tenants who willingly allowed access to the sites.

Site References and More Information

Sites and monuments are consistently labelled throughout this publication with their RCAHMS number. This is a unique identifier that will allow the reader to make the connection between sites which are mentioned in the main text or in captions, and sites which are highlighted on maps. The number will also enable readers to obtain further information about a particular site, including bibliographic and archive details, by accessing the RCAHMS sites and monuments database Canmore. This can be found at rcahms.gov.uk. Within the advanced search page, the reader should enter the number in the box marked 'Canmore ID' and click on the search button.

Readers can also discover more information about sites and monuments on Bute by searching the ScotlandsPlaces website: scotlandsplaces.gov.uk. This offers an alternative way of accessing the site-records held within the RCAHMS database as well as other source material.

Each illustration in this publication has a caption which includes, when appropriate, the name of the site, its main classification and its number. Further, a code number at the end of each caption identifies the digital file held in the RCAHMS archive and this should be cited if the illustration is required for reproduction.

Plan Conventions

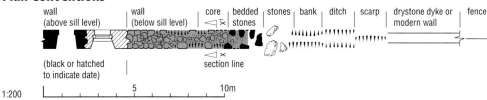

wall (above sill level) | wall (below sill level) | core | bedded stones | stones | bank | ditch | scarp | drystone dyke or modern wall | fence

(black or hatched to indicate date) | section line

1:200 5 10m

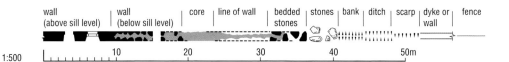

wall (above sill level) | wall (below sill level) | core | line of wall | bedded stones | stones | bank | ditch | scarp | dyke or wall | fence

1:500 10 20 30 40 50m

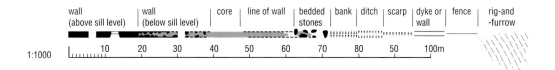

wall (above sill level) | wall (below sill level) | core | line of wall | bedded stones | bank | ditch | scarp | dyke or wall | fence | rig-and -furrow

1:1000 10 20 30 40 50 60 70 80 50 100m

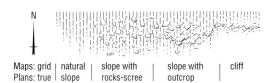

N

Maps: grid | natural | slope with | slope with | cliff
Plans: true | slope | rocks-scree | outcrop

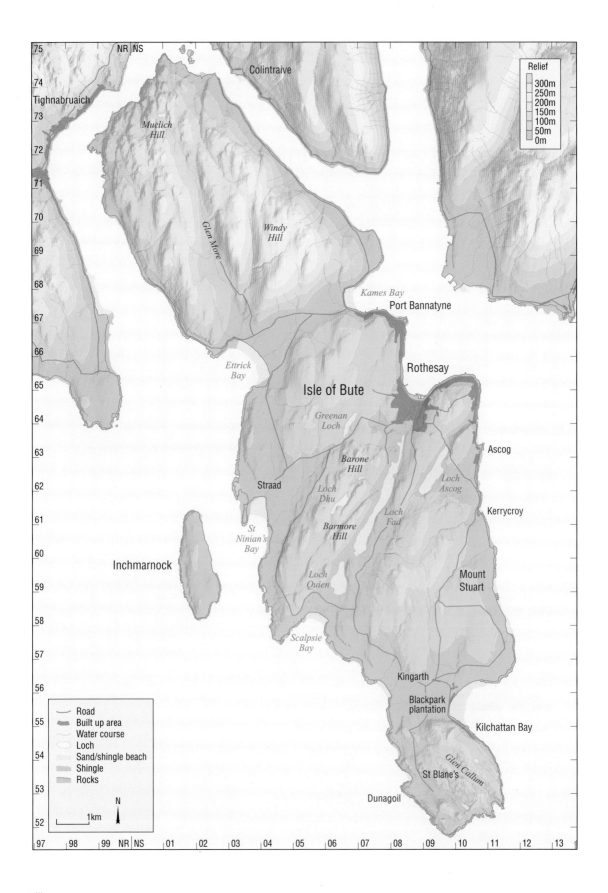

NR NS

75
74
73
72
71
70
69
68
67
66
65
64
63
62
61
60
59
58
57
56
55
54
53
52

Colintraive

Tighnabruaich

Muelich Hill

Glen More

Windy Hill

Kames Bay
Port Bannatyne

Ettrick Bay

Rothesay

Isle of Bute

Greenan Loch

Ascog

Barone Hill

Loch Ascog

Straad

Loch Dhu

Loch Fad

Kerrycroy

Inchmarnock

St Ninian's Bay

Barmore Hill

Loch Quien

Mount Stuart

Scalpsie Bay

Kingarth

Blackpark plantation

Kilchattan Bay

Glen Callum

St Blane's

Dunagoil

Relief
300m
250m
200m
150m
100m
50m
0m

Road
Built up area
Water course
Loch
Sand/shingle beach
Shingle
Rocks

N

1km

97 98 99 NR NS 01 02 03 04 05 06 07 08 09 10 11 12 13

Introduction

This booklet is a result of a partnership project undertaken in 2008–10 between the Royal Commission on the Ancient and Historical Monuments of Scotland (RCAHMS) and the Discover Bute Landscape Partnership Scheme (DBLPS), the co-ordinators of a four-year programme of improvements to Bute's rural landscape funded largely, but not solely, by the Heritage Lottery Fund. The short-term aims of the project were to revise the existing RCAHMS archaeological records for Bute, working closely with the local community, and to produce a booklet that summarises the archaeology of Bute. The principal long-term aim is to provide the local community with the information that will allow them to determine priorities and make decisions about the archaeological work they are likely to initiate in the future.

This volume contains a commentary on the character of the archaeology of the island, one that has been informed principally by the evidence contained within the revised archaeological record. Although there has never been a systematic archaeological survey of Bute a great deal of work has been undertaken. In recent times the locations of several early prehistoric sites have been identified through the discovery of surface scatters of stone artefacts; documentary research has provided clues regarding pre-Improvement period landscapes; fieldwork has resulted in many previously unrecorded upstanding monuments being reported; and, since 1977, aerial survey has yielded evidence

The Isle of Bute, showing Rothesay, other settlements and geographical features. GV004571

RCAHMS staff and local volunteers discuss the archaeological landscape of Scalpsie Bay, where prehistoric forts, burial cairns, an improvement farmstead and what may be a medieval building lie in close proximity. DP084694

of a broad range of cropmarks. Nevertheless, comparatively large areas of the island still have secrets to reveal, and further work in all these disciplines, plus others, such as geophysical survey and excavation, will undoubtedly reveal more evidence in the years to come.

The revision of the Bute archaeology records has made some use of documentary evidence. First, second and third editions of the Ordnance Survey 6-inch-to-a-mile map, respectively published in

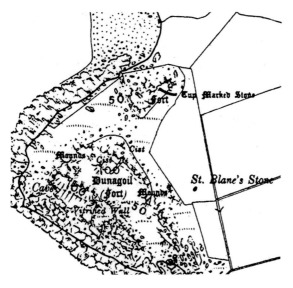

Extract from the 3rd edition of the 6-inch Ordnance Survey map showing Dunagoil (Buteshire 1924, Sheet CCCXXVII). This depiction of the landscape, which was clearly influenced by Dr J N Marshall's contemporary survey and excavation, includes a number of archaeological sites that had not been previously shown, some of which have subsequently been lost or reclassified. In contrast, there are only two sites depicted on the earliest edition of the survey of Bute (published in 1869) where their interpretation has been subsequently doubted – forts at Achamor Wood (40393) and Suidhe Chatain (40286). SC1208177

1869, 1897 and 1924, have been referred to, but two 18th century estate surveys, now held within the Bute Archive at Mount Stuart, have been particularly useful. One, by John Foulis in about 1758–9, is roughly contemporary with Roy's Military Map of 1747–55, but it provides a more accurate and detailed record. The other, compiled about 1780–2 by Peter May, the Bute Estate factor, records precise details of the land-use within the estate, including the location of farmsteads, smallholdings and single buildings, with notes on acreages and tenancies. It is supported by a ledger that contains an astonishing amount of detail.

Scope of survey

The partnership agreement between RCAHMS and DBLPS required the archaeological site records for Bute to be thoroughly revised, with the necessary fieldwork providing opportunities for local volunteers to become involved. The evaluation of the record started as a desk-based exercise late in 2008, and a programme of field survey, which was undertaken in the spring and summer of 2009, incorporated the informal

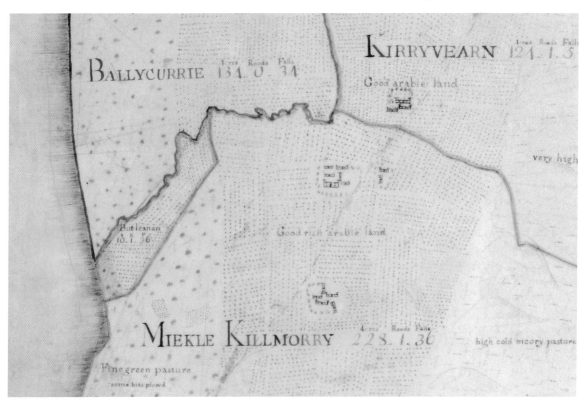

training of members of the local community in archaeological survey techniques. The overall contribution made by the volunteers was invaluable, not only saving RCAHMS staff a considerable amount of time in an unfamiliar landscape by identifying the locations of sites that would have otherwise proved difficult to find, but in making RCAHMS aware of a significant number of sites that had not previously been reported.

Although prospective fieldwork – proactively searching for previously unreported monuments – did not constitute a formal part of the project, the simple act of visiting known sites with local people who had already undertaken a considerable amount of fieldwork resulted in about 120 'new' sites being recorded. This was in addition to the 525 previously recorded Bute archaeological records in the RCAHMS database that were revised and the 260 or so other records that have been created through the accessioning of recent work.

One aspect of the existing RCAHMS database that the revision did not cover was the broad range of artefacts that have been found; these form a significant proportion of the archaeological record. However, this topic is currently being addressed by another project within the Landscape Partnership Scheme.

Although the project specification stipulated the revision of the archaeological records for Bute, it should be recognised that the distinction between archaeology and architecture, especially when ruined buildings are concerned, can be a fine one. A number of relatively recently abandoned farmsteads were visited – not because of any intrinsic architectural merit (though this may be present), but because map or documentary evidence suggested that earlier remains might have been evident. As in the case of those working farmsteadings that were either visited on the ground or photographed during aerial survey, a note about the place was recorded for the RCAHMS database.

Extract from the Survey of the Isle of Bute undertaken in 1758–9 by John Foulis. His survey, which is accompanied by brief texts, recorded both the position and orientation of each building, and the size and land-use of each farm. DP077260 © Bute Archive at Mount Stuart

John Patrick Crichton-Stuart, the 3rd Marquess of Bute (1847–1900). Along with his predecessors and descendants, the 3rd Marquess sponsored a number of archaeological projects and funded the restoration of buildings that included St Blane's church. © Mount Stuart Archive

Previous work

The present archaeological record owes much to the Earls of Bute, who, since the late 18th century, have either initiated work or readily given permission for others to do so. Perhaps the earliest noted archaeological investigation on Bute was that undertaken at Dunagoil, planned in 1780, where several cairns (40070) were 'excavated' soon after by John Norton, chief gardener at Mount Stuart, under the direction of John Blain. The 19th century saw several small excavations being documented and probably a lot more not, and culminated with the publication in the 1890s of *The Isle of Bute in the Olden Time* by James Hewison, Church of Scotland minister of Rothesay parish. Although Hewison's volumes reproduced a lot of the rather vague information that appeared in earlier publications, including the *Statistical Account*, they provide an excellent summary of the archaeology of Bute at that time, some of their illustrations containing information that is now lost.

The leading figure in Bute archaeology in the early part of the 20th century was Dr John Marshall, a founder member of the Buteshire Natural History Society (BNHS) and of the Bute Museum. Dr Marshall excavated at Dunagoil from

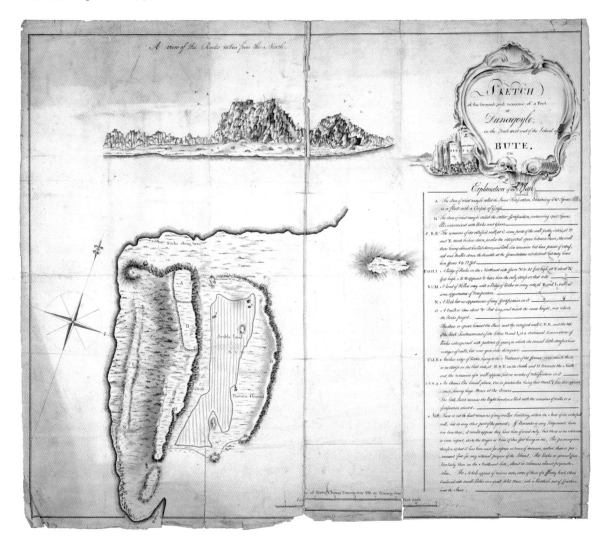

A detailed plan and sketch section of Dunagoil vitrified fort (40291) and its surrounding landscape. The plan, dated 1780, and probably produced by either Peter or Alexander May, depicts and describes archaeological features at Dunagoil. It is a remarkable symbol of the early interest and investment of the 3rd Earl and 1st Marquess of Bute in aspects of the island's heritage. DP075180 © Bute Archive at Mount Stuart

1913, first in the cave (40278) and then in the fort (40291), and undertook what would be called today a watching brief at Townhead gravel quarry (40377), where he recorded details of a Neolithic settlement site.

Dr Marshall's contribution to Bute archaeology was eventually eclipsed by his youngest daughter, Dorothy, who studied under Sir Mortimer Wheeler at the Institute of Archaeology in London and, after her mother's

death in 1949, gained considerable experience working on excavations both at home and abroad. Much of what is now understood about the archaeology of Bute is a consequence of work that she instigated, work that has been warmly appraised by Jack Scott (1992). Dorothy Marshall's legacy, however, is not just the records of the important excavations she undertook or her reorganisation of Bute Museum, it is also the enthusiasm she engendered among the local community. That passion has persisted since her death in 1992 and to this day others have continued to investigate aspects of Bute's heritage through research, excavation and survey.

Initially encouraged by Dorothy Marshall, and more recently led by Edwina Proudfoot, members of the Society have been recording rural

Hawk's Nib, cave and midden (40675). A group of volunteers accompanied by RCAHMS staff ascend to explore this cave site. Excavators in the 1930s discovered midden material and evidence for hearths, but no categorical dating evidence. DP073220

Excavations at Eilean Buidhe island dun (40458) in August 1936. One of a number of important archive photographs held by Bute Museum, this image shows Dr J N Marshall (1860– 1945) in the trench flanked by his daughter Dorothy (1900–1992) and J Harrison Maxwell, who directed the excavations. The photograph was taken from the south-west showing one of the trenches cut through the rampart; the building in the background is the boat house at Caol Ruadh School. SC1210134 © Bute Museum

settlement remains for many years. Since 1991, the Bute Settlement Survey project has systematically added to the corpus of information through desk-based research, walk-over surveys and detailed recording. As a result, the local community has made and continues to make a very valuable contribution to Scottish rural settlement studies. At the start of the revision of the RCAHMS records for Bute a large proportion (about 200 out of 525) of the archaeological records related to settlement sites, mainly farmsteads, which had been reported by members of the Society.

The abundant legacy outlined here has been built upon by the partnership project between RCAHMS and DBLPS, which has seen such a significant involvement by the local community, and by the RCAHMS Scotland's Rural Past project. The revision of the archaeological records will provide a solid platform on which to base future research, and the fieldwork undertaken by the local community in tandem with RCAHMS in 2009–10 will better equip them to undertake that work. The authors of this volume hope that it may help in directing and encouraging their efforts.

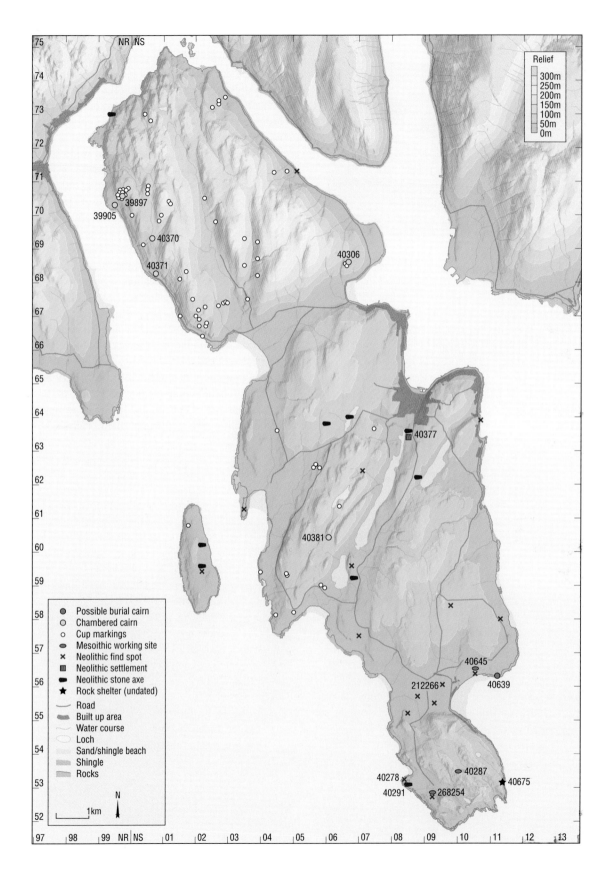

Relief
300m
250m
200m
150m
100m
50m
0m

NR NS

39897
39905
40370
40371
40306

40377

40381

40645
212266
40639

40287
40278
40291 268254 40675

Possible burial cairn
Chambered cairn
Cup markings
Mesoithic working site
Neolithic find spot
Neolithic settlement
Neolithic stone axe
Rock shelter (undated)
Road
Built up area
Water course
Loch
Sand/shingle beach
Shingle
Rocks

N

1km

The Mesolithic and Neolithic

c12,000BC – c2200BC

Mesolithic c12,000BC – c4500BC

Evidence from Howburn Farm in South Lanarkshire has recently demonstrated that Scotland was visited as early as 14,000 years ago. To date, no evidence for such early settlement has been found on Bute, where, as far as is known, the first visitors were itinerant Mesolithic foragers (fisher-hunter-gatherers) who populated the west coast of Scotland between the end of the last ice age (about 11,000 years ago) and the beginning of the Neolithic period.

Three locations on Bute, all close to the south end of the island, have so far yielded Mesolithic artefacts. In the early 1970s an assemblage of agate tools and waste material was discovered on Plan Farm (40287). Most of the material is of Neolithic or later date, but the collection includes two earlier very small worked blades – microliths. A larger assemblage of about 200 flints (40645) from a raised beach at the north end of Kilchattan Bay also contained microliths as well as late Mesolithic cores and waste. Again, most of this material is of later date. In 2003 fieldwalking on Garrochty Farm, just 1km south-west of the source of the agate-working site, resulted in the discovery of another flint and pitchstone assemblage (268254) with a small Mesolithic component, this time including two platform cores and a core rejuvenation blade.

Distribution of Mesolithic and Neolithic sites and artefacts. This map probably reflects to a large degree an original bias in the overall distribution of rock carvings and chambered tombs in the northern third of the island. However, that distribution has certainly been affected by other factors, including intensive agriculture since the medieval period, which may have resulted in the removal of even the most substantial monuments. GV004572

A shell-midden below the chambered cairn at Glecknabae (40371) was partly examined when the tomb was excavated at the beginning of the 20th century. No artefacts were found at that time, but a suggestion that the midden was Mesolithic has not necessarily been disproved by the identification of the flint core found more recently in the eroding edge of the midden as probably Neolithic.

The small number of Mesolithic sites so far identified on Bute precludes any in-depth comment on their distribution. However, there is considerable potential for identifying further sites of this date on the island, as fieldwalking exercises in other areas of Scotland have demonstrated that Mesolithic material will invariably be found on prolonged and extensive searches of cultivated ground. The fact that the fieldwalking at Black Park Plantation (123472, 123473) at the south end of Bute yielded only material of Neolithic and Bronze Age date need only be a reflection of the comparatively small area examined.

Although arable fields provide the most obvious targets for fieldwalking, other locations on Bute ought to be considered, and work elsewhere in Scotland has shown the potential of examining moorland landscapes. However, the best opportunity for locating relatively undisturbed Mesolithic evidence on Bute and Inchmarnock may be in the numerous caves and rock-shelters that have been identified. Several of these were looked at by Dorothy Marshall, who found no evidence of human activity in most of them, the one exception being at Hawk's Nib (40675) at the south end of Bute, which contained an undated shell-midden. Evidence for the more recent use of caves and

View of Dolmen at Bicker's Houses.

Bicker's Houses, chambered cairn (40381). Sketch of the chambered long cairn viewed from the south by J K Hewison (1893, 65). In addition to the main burial chamber at the north (far) end of the cairn, this sketch shows what may have been a cist that is no longer visible inserted in the southern part of the mound. The 'fort' in the background is probably Barone Hill (40424). SC1163929

rock shelters has been found close by at Dunagoil (40278, 40279) and on Inchmarnock (300171, 300178) see page 20.

Neolithic c4500BC – c2200BC

Our understanding of how and where the first groups of farmers on Bute lived and worked is hampered by the dearth of identified and accurately dated settlement sites. Consequently, the information gained from the distribution of

Kilchattan Bay. Excavations at the quarry in the distance uncovered evidence for a Neolithic settlement (212266). The nearby hamlet once included a thriving brick and tile works (158613) and a parish church (81886), while prehistoric burial cairns stood sentinel on the bay's edge (40639). The pattern of rectangular fields, established in the Improvement period, rolls over the edge of the old shoreline cliffs. DP057287

funerary, ceremonial and ritual sites, rock art (which cannot easily be included in any of those categories) and a thin scatter of diagnostic artefacts, paints an incomplete picture of events that were spread over at least two millennia.

Between 1914 and 1919, and again in 1929, the working of a gravel-pit at Townhead (40377) on the southern edge of Rothesay revealed a range of artefacts, including a polished stone axe and pottery, which indicated the presence of some form of Neolithic settlement. However, little detail is known of this settlement and there is scant evidence of any structure that might have existed here in association with the artefacts and what was probably a hearth. A number of shallow trenches that were revealed in the surface of the gravel were interpreted as probable 'sleeper beams', but they are more likely to have been field drains or the bottoms of cultivation furrows. A radiocarbon date for a burnt shell of a hazelnut from the probable hearth produced a date around the middle of the 4th millennium BC.

More recently, excavation at another gravel quarry – at Kingarth (212266) towards the south end of Bute – revealed what may be a round-ended

Michael's Grave, chambered cairn (39905). The position of even the most significant monuments has been carefully checked with survey grade GPS. This particular cairn was excavated by T H Bryce in 1903, and the burial chamber now sits proud of the surrounding field, divorced from its protective round cairn which has been heavily robbed and largely ploughed out. DP082856

Neolithic building. This structure has been compared to broadly similar buildings elsewhere, particularly in Argyll and Ireland, but it yielded no absolute dating evidence and could not be shown to have had any direct association with any of the other excavated features or with the scatter of flint, quartz and pitchstone artefacts recovered in the vicinity.

If the paucity of identified habitation sites limits discussion about the character of Neolithic settlement on Bute, then the situation is significantly improved with regard to the funerary, ritual and ceremonial sites, and, of course, the rock art. There are six chambered cairns on Bute, five in the northern third of the island and one, Bicker's Houses (40381), in the central part, some 4km south-west of Rothesay. A chambered cairn is a large mound of stones that contains a stone burial chamber which could be opened whenever the

remains of the dead needed to be interred. All of the known chambered cairns on Bute have either been 'explored' by antiquaries or excavated in more recent times, and they have been thoroughly discussed elsewhere. Audrey Henshall's work makes it clear that each cairn probably had a long and complex history, in some cases extending into the Early Bronze Age. Three of the chambered cairns, Glecknabae (40371), Hilton (40306) and Michael's Grave (39905), appear to have been built as round cairns and remained that way throughout their use. In its final form, Glenvoidean (39897) is a trapezoidal cairn that covers two earlier round cairns, and Bicker's Houses and Carnbaan (40370) are long mounds that may well have developed from earlier round cairns. There is only one radiocarbon assessment for any of the Bute tombs, a burnt deposit from beneath one of the side-slabs of the chamber at Glenvoidean producing a date around the middle of the 4th millennium BC.

The bias in the distribution of the tombs in the northern third of the island probably reflects their original range even allowing for the undocumented destruction of some tombs and the possibility that previously unrecorded examples will be identified in the future. The most recently recognised chambered cairn is situated at Hilton, overlooking Kames Bay. First reported in the early 1970s, it exhibited no evidence of its Neolithic origin until it was excavated. Similar monuments could easily have been swept away in the tide of agricultural improvements; others may yet be recognised.

There is also the possibility that other forms of Neolithic burial may also be present on Bute. For instance, there may be tombs in which the mortuary chambers were constructed in timber rather than stone. If this is the case, their identification can only be confirmed by excavation. In this context, mention should be made of a number of apparently man-made mounds that have been examined without yielding any evidence of burial. Investigation of two such mounds (40639), which formerly stood about 40m apart at Kerrytonlia on the north side of Kilchattan Bay, established that each comprised a boulder cairn under a cover of beach sand. A thin layer of charcoal was detected under the cairn within the western mound, but no artefacts were recovered. Whether these cairns represented an episode of early prehistory that the excavators simply failed to recognise will now never be known since both mounds have been destroyed.

The most ubiquitous, yet least understood, manifestation of Neolithic settlement is rock art – the carving of symbols on bedrock and on stones ranging in size from small portable boulders to large glacial erratics. There are over 80 recorded examples of rock art on Bute, all of them comprising either simple cups or cups within rings. What stands out about this corpus is that it contains only simple carvings. None is elaborate or complex, and this contrasts markedly with neighbouring Argyll.

Although widespread throughout Bute, the distribution of the rock art appears to favour the west side of the island and the main concentration is

Scarrel, cup-marked rock (40326). Typical of the rock art on Bute, this example is located in improved pasture, and bears a number of cup marks, highlighted by recent rain. The island of Inchmarnock is visible in the background. DP066517

found in the north. This distribution is probably in part influenced by the likelihood that this category of monument will survive (and be detected) in unimproved land, but it may not be a coincidence that this is also where most of the chambered cairns are found. On this note, none of the Neolithic monuments should be considered in isolation, with each forming an integral part of the wider landscape. The pottery and artefacts that were deposited with the dead in the chambered cairns were the same wares and tools that were being used on the settlements.

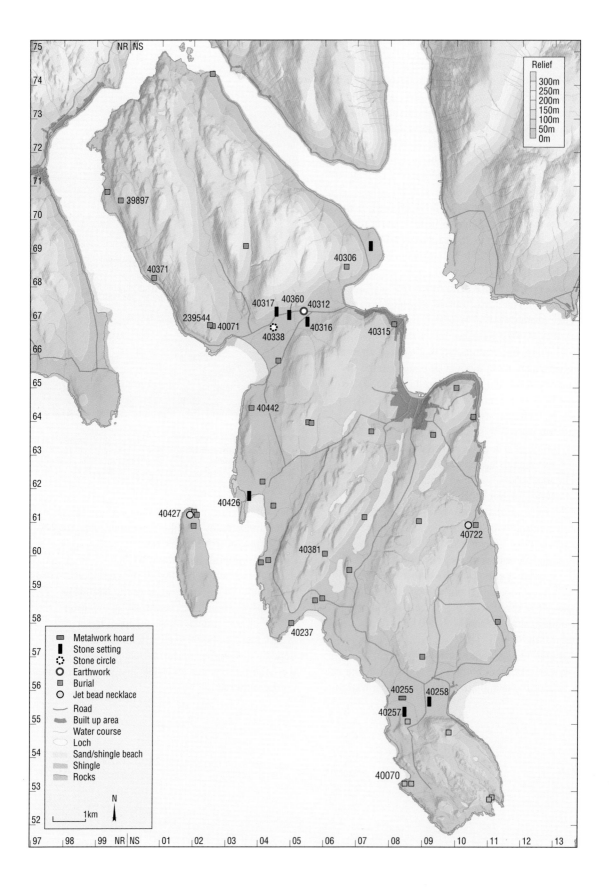

The Early and Middle Bronze Age

c2200BC – c1000BC

Three general features that mark the transition from the Neolithic to the Early Bronze Age are the introduction of bronze metalwork, the adoption of different ceramic forms, and the move away from the use of megalithic chambered cairns that were essentially charnel houses used over a long period of time. New rites included the inhumation and cremation of single and multiple burials in pits, cists and pottery vessels, often under specially constructed mounds (cairns and barrows), but also sometimes within earlier monuments such as the chambered cairns, or under conspicuous natural knolls. No doubt some burials were interred without anything to mark the grave and there may well have been other methods of disposing of the dead that have left no trace in the archaeological record. It ought to be emphasised that no Bronze Age houses have been positively identified on Bute and that any discussion of the pattern of settlement is dependent on what is known about other contemporary monuments, burials and artefacts.

Excluding for the moment those features directly associated with funerary practices, other monuments within the Bronze Age landscape of Bute include stone circles, stone settings and standing stones. The stone circle at St Colmac Cottages (40338) – the only surviving stone circle on the island – originally comprised nine stones, of which four still stand erect, three survive as stumps and an outlier stands close-by to the south-

The distribution of Early Bronze Age sites and artefacts demonstrates that activity was widespread across the whole of Bute at this time. However, the main foci of monuments such as standing stones and stone circles appear to have been in the two low-lying and narrowest points of the island. GV004573

N

5   10m   1:200

St Colmac Cottages, stone circle (40338). This stone circle is one of two that once stood in what is now a cultivated field. The other, which was situated 25m to the west, is depicted on an early 19th century plan of Kames Estate (RHP 14262), but it was removed before 1814, some of the stones having to be blown up by gunpowder first. This circle survives because by that time it had already been enclosed within a small plantation. GV004721

west. The circle appears to have stood adjacent to another about 25m to the west, of which nothing is now visible. However, it was described by Aiton

St Colmac Cottages, stone circle. A number of monuments in the valley between Kames and Ettrick Bay can be seen to represent an early prehistoric ritual landscape. The most significant of these, this circle of eight stones, was set within a protective plantation bank around 1800, though very few of the trees now survive. DP064299

in 1816 as *'a circle of stones, of great size and height; but they are all thrown down and most of them removed. Some of them were so large as to require to be blown with powder'*. A late 18th or early 19th century estate plan appears to show an arc of five stones on the west side of the current circle.

One of the most interesting features of the site is its position within the local topography. Overlooking Ettrick Bay to the south-west, the surviving stone circle stands within a natural amphitheatre in which there are also three standing stones (40316, 40317, 40360), one of them (40317) bearing a later early Christian cross. Also, the stone circle is overlooked by what is likely to be the roughly contemporary Watch Hill

burial cairn (40442) at the south-east end of the bay and a possible cist cemetery (40071, 239544) above Kildavannan at the north-west end. Even if the Bronze Age ritual landscape here has been reduced to a series of individual monuments isolated from each other within modern farmland, the range and density of those sites provides enough evidence to suggest that this location was somehow special, apparently more so than anywhere else on Bute. Further, these monuments appear to represent a major change in focus in ceremony, ritual and burial activity away from what are today the marginal lands in the northern third of the island favoured by the Neolithic tomb builders, to a much more fertile farming landscape only a relatively short distance to the south-east.

An earthwork, Cnoc an Rath (40312), which stands on the watershed on the north-east edge of the amphitheatre, has been proposed as a henge. If this is the case then the monument may have served as the main focus for ritual, ceremony and funerary practices throughout the Late

St Colmac cross, standing stone with later inscribed cross (40317). Standing near the site of Colmac's chapel (40349), now removed, this stone may have originally formed part of a Bronze Age ritual landscape. Recorded in the 1990s as part of a long running RCAHMS survey of medieval carved stones, it forms part of an important corpus from Bute, much of which is now housed in Bute Museum. SC408104

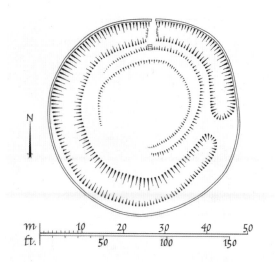

Cnoc an Rath, earthwork (40312). This site, situated on the watershed between the bays of Ettrick and Kames, is defined by a ditch and an inner bank, with a causewayed entrance on the east-south-east. First surveyed by RCAHMS in 1982, the date and function of the monument remains elusive. SC1208314

Neolithic and Early Bronze Age. However, there is no dating evidence from the site, which others have suggested is an Iron Age fort, a medieval ringwork, and, most recently, a Norse 'ting' site.

Elsewhere on the island there is a scatter of standing stones and stone settings which are presumed to be of Early Bronze Age date. Of the latter, the three-stone alignment at Largizean (40257) at the south end of the island is similar to many other examples elsewhere in Britain, and it may be significant that the stones stand only about 350m south-east of the find spot of a hoard of bronze halberds found in the 19th century (see below). Another stone setting, at Blackpark Plantation (40258), stands just 850m east of the hoard site. First referred to as *'the remains of one of the circles of the Druids'*, the evidence provided by various descriptions of the site is at best ambiguous, and there is little compelling evidence to show whether the stones belong to a circle that once comprised more than the three stones that are visible today or some other form of setting. There must also be some doubt about a setting of two stones at St Ninian's Bay (40426). Measuring only up to 1.4m in height and 1.3m apart, the stones are slighter than might be expected of a Bronze Age monument.

There are at least 30 Early Bronze Age burial sites on Bute that have produced evidence of either single burials or cemeteries. There are also seven cairns, the characteristics of which suggest they are probably also of this date. The whole corpus of Bronze Age burials cannot be reported here in detail, but a few sites deserve particular mention. At four sites graves have been inserted into earlier, Neolithic, cairns. At Glecknabae (40371) one of the two chambers contained sherds of a Beaker, possibly indicating re-use of the tomb in the Late Neolithic/Early Bronze Age. Later still, a cist containing an inhumation was inserted into the west edge of the cairn. A vessel that was described as *'looking like a flowerpot'*, which was found and then lost before excavations in the early 20th century, was probably another secondary burial. At Glenvoidean (39897), an Enlarged Food Vessel and a cremation were found in an unusual two-tiered cist, and at Hilton (40306) Marshall found an apparently empty cist that had been sunk into the body of the chambered cairn but which had, in turn, been covered by its own discrete mound. At Bicker's Houses (40381), the possible cist inserted into the mound close to its south end, which was noted as *'rifled'* by Hewison, can no longer be seen.

Fine spacer-plate necklaces of jet or jet-like material have been found accompanying inhumations in cists at Kerrycroy (40722) and at Northpark on Inchmarnock (40427). As high prestige artefacts with a broad distribution across northern and western Britain, they provide striking evidence of how rich some sections of the Early Bronze Age population on Bute were. The Kerrycroy example was found along with a Food Vessel and a corroded bronze object in 1887; the Northpark necklace, which comprised 139 beads

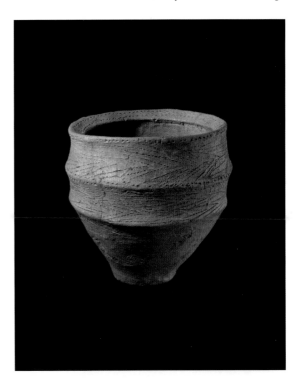

recycled from at least four other necklaces, was found in one of three cists discovered in 1960 and originally excavated by Marshall. One of the other cists yielded an old and worn spacer plate from another jet necklace.

Recent research has seen the re-excavation of the cist that contained the necklace. A sample of bone yielded a radiocarbon date around 2000BC, in the middle of the Early Bronze Age. Bone isotope analysis, undertaken as part of the Beaker People Project, revealed that the bones were those of a woman who was almost certainly local and who did not eat fish – a surprise considering that she was buried (and therefore presumably lived) on a comparatively small island.

In addition to the Northpark cist, only one other, at Cnoc-na-mhanan (239544), has been scientifically dated. Here, one of what may be a cemetery of cists contained a miniature Food Vessel and a cremation that has been dated to between 2000 and 1700BC. Another cemetery, which comprised no less than

eighteen cists and was found beneath a cairn at Ardbeg (40315), provides a striking contrast to the single burials or those in small groups. It was dug into before 1840 and again in 1858, but nothing now survives either of the cairn itself or of the several *'sepulchral urns'* that were found in the graves.

Edwina Proudfoot has recently reviewed the evidence for Early Bronze Age burials on Bute and, notwithstanding those sites (mainly noted

by antiquaries) from which the evidence is either dubious or, at best, ambiguous, the picture presented suggests that probably the whole of the island (and Inchmarnock) was exploited by a farming population whose material culture was no different to that on the mainland to the east and Argyll to the north and west. This distribution is heavily influenced by the discovery of burials mainly through the agencies of arable cultivation, quarrying and construction, but it should be recognised that

A group of three cists were found in 1960 by a farmer at Northpark Inchmarnock (40427). One of the cists contained the remains of a single woman, accompanied by a flint knife and a spacer plate necklace of 139 jet beads, re-strung and photographed by Alison Sheridan, NMS. Re-excavation in 2006 formed part of a significant re-assessment of the discovery by Bute Museum and NMS Archaeology Department. © Trustees of the National Museums of Scotland.

activities such as these occur in the very areas that are likely to have most attracted early farming populations. In mitigation, though, an additional pointer to the use of the landscape at this time is provided by those Bronze Age burials in Neolithic cairns that are situated on or just outwith the limit of recent intense arable cultivation.

A full consideration of the Bronze Age pottery from Bute is beyond the scope of this booklet and commentary is restricted here to noting that there is a paucity of Beaker pottery – especially outwith the chambered tombs, there is only one confirmed discovery of a cinerary urn (40237), but Food Vessels are comparatively common, with no fewer than eight examples being found.

In addition to the badly corroded metal object found in the Kerrycroy cist noted above, there has been only one recorded discovery of Early Bronze Age metalwork on Bute – that of five halberds (40255) found in the 19th century when the farmer at Langalbuinoch was digging a drain. A halberd comprises a long, axe-like, blade attached at right-angles to a wooden or metal shaft. While medieval versions were designed and used as

weapons, the precise function of those of Early Bronze Age date is not known. The circumstances surrounding the deposition of the hoard are also unknown, but the find-spot is located in an area of poor natural drainage and it is possible that the halberds were a votive offering within an originally wetland location.

Five Bronze Age halberds (40255) were found in the mid 19th century by a farmer digging a drain on Langalbuinoch farm. Three survive in the National Museum of Scotland, where they have been dated stylistically to between 2300BC and 2000BC. © Trustees of the National Museums of Scotland. Licensor www.scran.ac.uk. 000-190-004-241-R

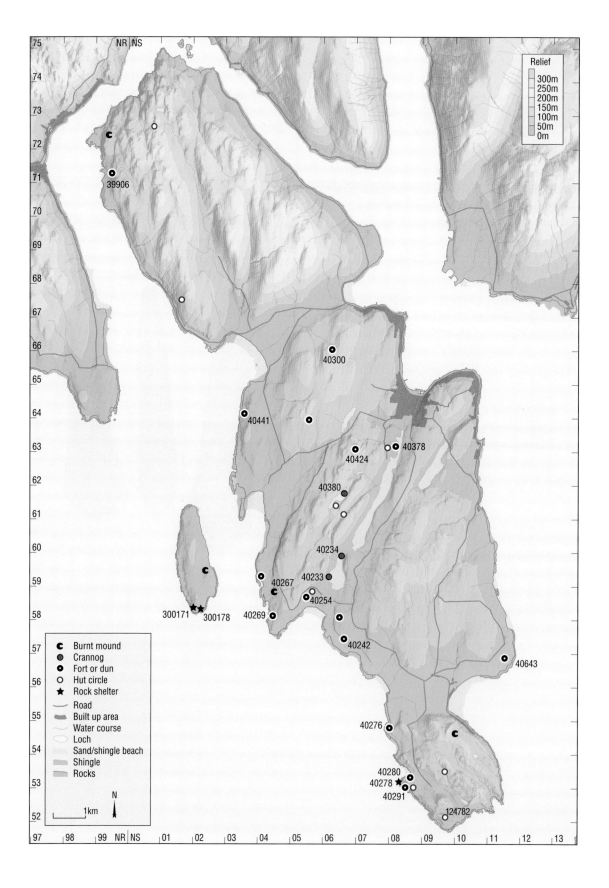

Relief
- 300m
- 250m
- 200m
- 150m
- 100m
- 50m
- 0m

NR NS

39906

40300

40441

40378

40424

40380

40234

40267

40233

40254

300171   300178

40269

40242

40643

40276

40280

40278

40291

124782

Burnt mound
Crannog
Fort or dun
Hut circle
Rock shelter
Road
Built up area
Water course
Loch
Sand/shingle beach
Shingle
Rocks

N

1km

NR NS

20

The Late Bronze Age and Iron Age

c1000BC – cAD600

If the Early Bronze Age on Bute is categorised by a lack of settlement sites in favour of ceremonial, ritual and funerary monuments and the Middle Bronze Age is marked by a total dearth of identified monuments of any description and no artefacts, then the Late Bronze Age (c1000BC – 700BC) at least offers some tangible evidence for settlement. Any of the prehistoric round-houses or burnt mounds so far recorded could date from this time and there is also evidence for metalworking in this period.

Prehistoric round-houses take two forms on Bute: hut-circles, where the building is preserved as a low, roughly circular stony bank, and platforms, where all that is now visible of the structure is the artificial terrace, dug into a hillside, on which it was built. Perhaps the best example of one of these platforms is that built within the earthworks at Dun Scalpsie (40254). It is impossible to date a prehistoric round-house from visible evidence alone and any of them could date to a period spanning over a thousand years. None of the ten examples so far recorded on Bute has been excavated.

A burnt mound is a large pile of fire-shattered stones, charcoal and soil that is thought to have accumulated as a result of an open-air cooking process. Three burnt mounds have been recorded on Bute and there is one possible example on Inchmarnock. The burnt mound at Mecknock

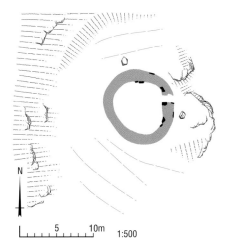

Barr Hill, hut-circle and cultivation remains (124782). This hut circle, with its thick stone wall and east-facing entrance, is typical of the small prehistoric round-houses found all over Scotland. The cultivation adjacent to it is probably medieval or later in date. GV004729

(40267), up to 10m across and 1.4m in height, has been excavated but has not been dated. Elsewhere in Britain and Ireland, while similar mounds have generally been found to date to the Middle and Late Bronze Age, others have been found to be Early Historic or even medieval in date.

The Late Bronze Age and the first part of the Iron Age – the centuries spanning the end of the 2nd millennium BC and the beginning of the 1st millennium BC – was a period of great transition across Scotland. It was a time of social upheaval, which saw the widespread abandonment of permanent occupation in upland locations affected by increased rainfall, cooler temperatures and the

Distribution of sites and artefacts of the Late Bronze Age and the Iron Age. Many of the settlements identified here could have been built and/or occupied within a period lasting up to 1,800 years. The bias in the distribution of forts and duns on the west coast may reflect contemporary politics, though the small fort at Kerrytonlia (40643), visible today as a cropmark, indicates that similar sites existed on the east coast. GV004574

An oblique aerial view of the vitrified fort of Dunagoil (at centre right, 40291) and the fort of Little Dunagoil (at centre left, 40280), taken from the north-west. There is no evidence of fortification on the intervening ridge, but the landscape between the two forts is dotted with the remains of burial cairns, clearance cairns and cultivation remains. DP062659

formation of peat. The resulting pressure on the most fertile and productive land is thought to be one of the reasons why forts and other forms of defensive enclosure began to be constructed.

However, whilst there are a comparatively large number of sites that can fairly confidently be assigned to the 1st millennium BC, the settlement pattern on Bute at this time is not at all well understood. None of these sites has produced good dating evidence from reliable contexts and it is likely that the picture is complicated by several sites being re-used in the Early Historic or medieval periods.

The vitrified fort on Dunagoil (40291), at the south end of Bute, and the fort on the summit of Barone Hill (40424), overlooking Rothesay, are the

only two large forts on the island. Barone Hill is undated, but the partial excavation of Dunagoil nearly a hundred years ago recovered artefacts dating from the Neolithic to the Iron Age, and included evidence for bronze working. A vitrified fort is one that had a high and thick stone wall, internally braced by timbers, which has been burnt to such a high temperature that large portions of its rubble core have been fused into a solid mass. As a technique, the use of timber-lacing cannot be used to date forts, but those which have been dated by other means have been shown to lie within a long period spanning the first millennium BC and the first millennium AD.

The excavation account of Dunagoil is vague about the exact nature of the metalworking, but given the close proximity of the site to Little Dunagoil (40280), where socketed axes were being produced in the Late Bronze Age, it seems fair to infer that it, too, was probably occupied in some form at that time. Most of the artefacts found during the excavation of Dunagoil are undiagnostic

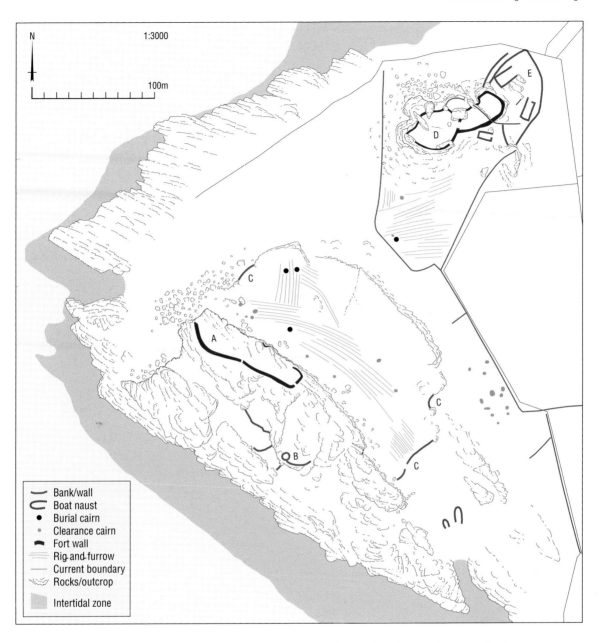

Map of the archaeological landscape at Dunagoil, including: (A) the vitrified fort (40291); (B) a probable round-house platform; (C) the lengths of wall that partly define the enclosure north-east of and below the fort; (D) the fort on Little Dunagoil (40280); (E) the later buildings and building-platforms (90299), and burial cairns (40070). GV004726

in terms of date, but they include a brooch (dating to the 3rd century BC) that probably provides some indication of when the actual fort was occupied. The results of the excavation at Little Dunagoil fort were inconclusive.

Dunagoil and its environs, including the fort on Little Dunagoil, have recently been reconsidered by D Harding of Edinburgh University. His conclusion – that the excavations and artefacts demonstrate that the Dunagoil 'complex' attracted settlement from the Neolithic to the Early Historic periods is sound enough, but he has also radically reinterpreted the fort and its relationship to the immediate topography and other features within the landscape. Foremost in this reinterpretation is his proposal that adjacent to and contemporary with the timber-laced fort was what he calls a 'bailey'. This comprised a terrace immediately north-east of and below the fort that was defined largely by topographical features,

Little Kilchattan, cropmark enclosure (40644). The transcription of oblique aerial photography has allowed cropmarks across Bute to be accurately mapped and their features measured. In the case of this enclosure, which was first recorded in 1977, its purpose is unknown, but its 4m broad ditch suggests that it may have been for something more significant than stock control. SC1203299

which offered excellent natural protection, linked by lengths of timber-laced wall (C on the plan on page 23). The claim that this enclosure was contemporary with the summit fort is based on an observation that there is in situ vitrified bedrock visible in one of these lengths of wall at the north-west end.

The presence of vitrified material, wall core rather than bedrock, was confirmed in the present survey. However, the function and date of this wall has yet to be established, and it is difficult to see

how a 'bailey' may have worked: there is a gap of some 100m between the south-east 'bailey' wall and the summit fort, a gap that would have allowed relatively unimpeded access to the lower enclosure from the south.

Whether these large forts were built as tribal centres, community gathering places or simply for the purpose of making ostentatious political statements may never be known, but, whatever the reason, large forts probably served a very different purpose to smaller sites, which were most likely built by small farming communities as a response to some perceived threat. The majority of these sites on Bute are relatively small, thick-walled enclosures that have variously been classified as forts and duns. However, the distinction between the two is sometimes a fine one and the classification used by RCAHMS in its recent revision of the Bute archaeological records is based on a definition of forts and duns used in the first Argyll Inventory. This simply states that the internal area of forts was large enough to serve the needs of a small community while duns were capable of accommodating only a single family.

This fairly loose definition is almost certainly an over-simplification, but using it means that the enclosures at Kerrytonlia (40643), Little Dunagoil (40280), Clachan Ard (40269) and probably Ardnahoe (40242) – the smallest fort with an internal area measuring 25m by 23m – have been added to the list of forts. The enclosure at Balilone (40378), with an internal area of only 24m by 19m, is on the cusp between fort and dun. Previously described as a fort, the enclosure at Aultmore Burn (39906), which has an internal area of only 19m by 16m, has been reclassified as a dun and takes its place with four others – Dunstrone (40276), Dun Scalpsie (40254), Dun Burgidale (40300) and Castle Cree (40441). The last mentioned site, however, is unusually narrow and rectangular and it may actually be medieval.

Few of the forts or duns display any notable architectural features, despite several of them having been investigated by excavation. Exceptions are Dun Scalpsie, where a door-check is still visible within the entrance passage, and Dun Burgidale, where there are almost certainly passages between the walls.

As far as the distribution of the forts and duns is concerned, there appears to be a definite

The cropmark fort at Kerrytonlia (40643) is one of a number of archaeological sites that were first noted during an aerial sortie undertaken by RCAHMS on 7 July 1977. SC1203301

emphasis on the west coast, though some allowance should be made for sites that have either been destroyed or have yet to be recognised. Late 18th and 19th century local historians made unsupported references to all manner of archaeological monuments, including forts which had already been destroyed. In part, that lost record has been retrieved by aerial survey, which, since 1977, has revealed the cropmarks of a number of sites, in particular broad-ditched enclosures that may represent the earthwork equivalent of the stone-built sites.

One of these sites is at Kerrytonlia (40643), on the north side of Kilchattan Bay. Here, a promontory extending from the old sea-cliff has been defended by two broad arcing ditches drawn across its neck, the inner one accompanied by a narrow palisade trench along its inner edge. Whether this last feature was an integral part of a system of defence with the ditches or represents an independent period of enclosure is not known. Its presence, however, is a useful reminder that, irrespective of how well preserved a site may appear on the surface, more ephemeral features will seldom be seen and the visible remains will only tell a fraction of the full story of any particular site.

That some sites enjoyed extended periods of use has already been noted at Dunagoil, but the same is also true at Little Dunagoil (40280) and probably also at Dun Scalpsie (40254). Little Dunagoil is noted in the next chapter, but Dun Scalpsie, which occupies the summit of a rocky knoll on the north side of Scalpsie Bay, is of considerable interest because it is one of the few sites on Bute where more than one phase of construction can be demonstrated from the visible evidence alone. Until recently, the site was thought to comprise simply a dun with a narrow entrance in its north-west side (A on plan). However, survey by RCAHMS in 2010 has demonstrated the presence of a very substantial stone wall (B) lower down the slope on the south and east. This wall follows the

Dun Scalpsie was partly excavated in the 1950s (40254). This plan shows the dun (A) that sits on the summit; the wall of the possible fort (B) below; the timber round-house (C), and the fox-hole type shelters (D) that were probably constructed by local defence volunteers (LDV), later the Home Guard, during the Second World War. GV004725

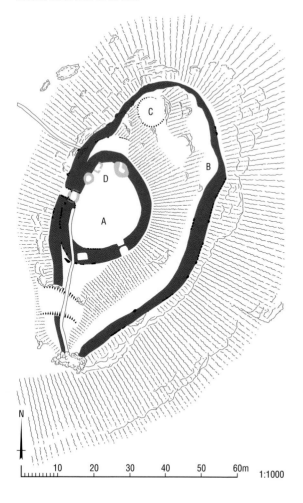

N

| 10 | 20 | 30 | 40 | 50 | 60m |
1:1000

crest of a steep slope on the north-east and appears to underlie the wall of the dun on the north. On the west flank there is little trace of the wall, but it may have been destroyed by a ditch that was dug to protect the later dun. The visible evidence is ambiguous and it is not possible to state whether the outer wall represents a fort that occupied the rocky knoll before the dun was placed on the summit or is a contemporary outwork of the dun, providing additional defence on its vulnerable flanks. The results of a trench dug inside the dun in 1959, which revealed two periods of occupation, is not helpful in this respect. Also unhelpful is the disturbance to the summit area caused by the construction during the Second World War of several dug-outs (D).

Of particular interest at Dun Scalpsie, however, is the recognition of a stance for a timber round-house (C) immediately outside the wall of the dun and within the area of the outer enclosure. The exact context of this building, which is one of only a small number of timber round-houses recorded on the island, is not known. It may be contemporary with either the earliest or later enclosures on the knoll; equally it may represent a period of settlement that has no association with either phase of enclosure.

Something similar may be said of what is probably the stance for a round-house on the south-west-facing flank of Dunagoil, some 50m south of the fort (B on plan on page 23). Measuring little more than 5m in overall diameter, the undated structure sits on a very steep, craggy area of ground characterised by short lengths of wall, some incorporating blocks of vitrified stone, which define a series of discrete enclosures.

Other forms of settlement that deserve mention are crannogs, and caves or rock-shelters. A crannog is an artificial island built to support a building, usually of timber. There are three crannogs on Bute: one in Dhu Loch (40380) and two in Loch Quien (40233, 40234), all undated. The crannog in Dhu Loch was discovered in 1812, when the water level was low enough for a plan to be drawn of the remains, which included horizontal timber beams and numerous piles. Subsequently the water level in the loch was raised and the site now lies completely submerged. The two crannogs in Loch Quien, which are visible today as wooded islets close to the shore, were both surveyed in 2003.

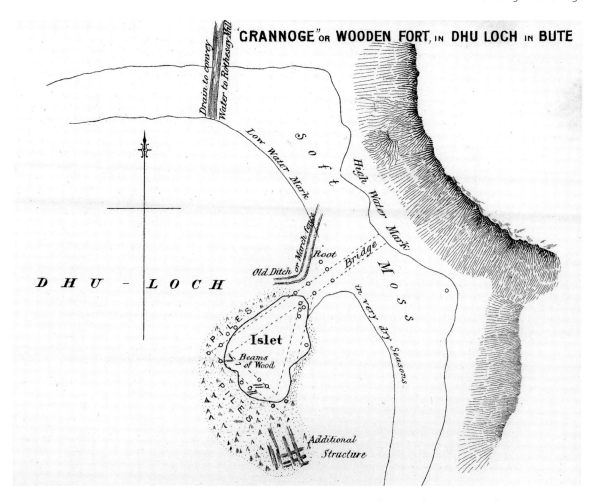

Dhu Loch, crannog (40380). First surveyed in the early 19th century, this crannog was subsequently completely submerged when the loch became a reservoir for Rothesay's water supply. There are three crannogs on Bute, and a survey in 2003 resulted in the discovery of a rotary quern stone at Quien north (40234), now at Bute Museum. SC1163938

Caves and rock-shelters (shallow cave-like openings at the base of a cliff, often with a wall built across the mouth), have been used in a variety of ways by humans from earliest prehistory to recent times. Two rock-shelters at the south end of Inchmarnock (300171, 300178) have been shown to contain evidence of some form of use in the second half of the 1st millennium BC. Dorothy Marshall considered the cave in the cliff below the fort on Dunagoil (40278) to have been used in the Iron Age as well as the Neolithic. As noted above, several caves and rock-shelters contain no obvious evidence for any human activity, but only a relatively small number on Bute have been examined. With more sites of this type yet to be recorded, caves and rock-shelters may represent one of the best opportunities for recording in situ later prehistoric deposits.

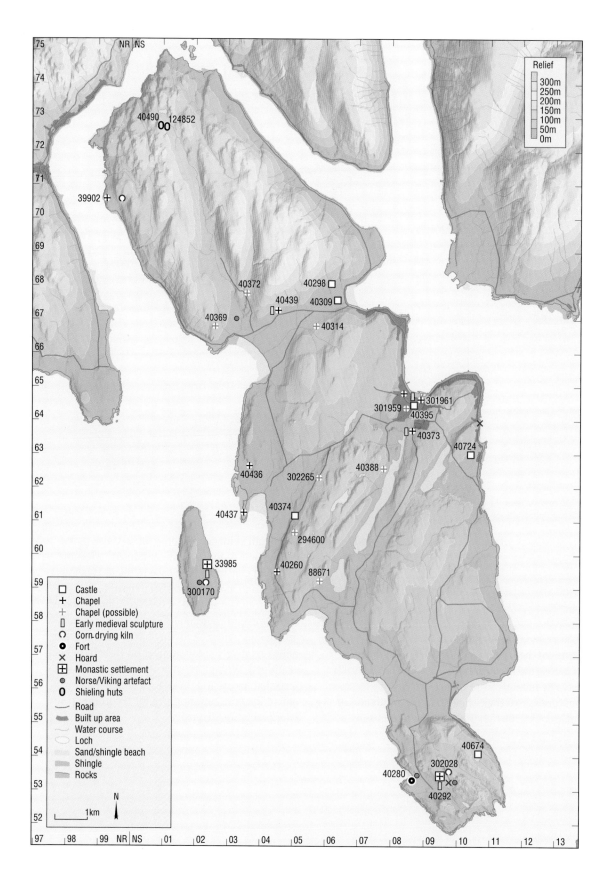

Relief
300m
250m
200m
150m
100m
50m
0m

NR NS

75
74
73
72
71
70
69
68
67
66
65
64
63
62
61
60
59
58
57
56
55
54
53
52

40490 124852

39902

40372   40298
        40439 40309
40369   40314

                    301959 301961
                    40395
                    40373
                            40724

40436   302265   40388
40437 40374
       294600
        40260 88671
33985
300170

Castle
Chapel
Chapel (possible)
Early medieval sculpture
Corn-drying kiln
Fort
Hoard
Monastic settlement
Norse/Viking artefact
Shieling huts
Road
Built up area
Water course
Loch
Sand/shingle beach
Shingle
Rocks

N

1km

                                    40674
                            302028
                    40280
                            40292

97 98 99 NR NS 01 02 03 04 05 06 07 08 09 10 11 12 13

The Early Historic and Medieval Periods

cAD600 – cAD1600

For Bute, it is convenient to consider the Iron Age as ending at the start of the Early Historic period, which for the purposes of this text has been assumed to commence about the beginning of the 7th century AD and end around the 10th century. Vikings are only briefly referred to below, and actual Norse settlement in the 11th to 13th centuries is considered to be medieval, a period accepted here as running to the end of the 16th century.

In the Early Historic period Bute found itself sandwiched between the power-bases of Dal Riata in Argyll to the west and Strathclyde to the east. In what must have been extremely turbulent times, a dynamic landscape was first disturbed by the Viking incursions in the 7th and 8th centuries and later, during the 12th century in particular, became heavily influenced by the Kingdom of Man and the Isles. Finally, it was included in the Stewart kingdom.

Currently, our level of knowledge about the archaeology of this time is limited by a paucity of securely dated sites and a comparatively modest amount of documentary evidence. Consequently, almost nothing is known of the settlement pattern at this period and the little knowledge available is necessarily biased towards three major sites – the monastic settlements at 'Cenn Garah' (Kingarth; 40292), at the south end of Bute, and that dedicated to St Ernan on Inchmarnock (40268), both probably established around the beginning of the 7th century AD, and at Little Dunagoil (40280), where Dorothy Marshall's excavations in the late 1950s and early

Distribution of Early Historic and Medieval sites and artefacts. As with the preceding periods, the record is dominated by high status religious and secular establishments. GV004575

St Blane's Church (40292). An oblique aerial view of the 12th century church and graveyard, taken from the north-west. The upper and lower burial-grounds, both to the right of the church, are reputed to have been reserved for men and women respectively. What may be a medieval chapel is visible in the lower graveyard. DP066101

1960s yielded artefacts indicating activity in the second half of the 1st millennium AD.

The evidence from the excavation of the monastery on Inchmarnock has yielded a wealth of information, detailed in an excellent book (Lowe 2008), but little is known about contemporary secular settlement there. At Kingarth we know the names of two of the 7th century bishops but, despite the late 19th century exploration there at the request of the 3rd Marquess of Bute, we know very little about that establishment's relationship with either its lay neighbours or the wider landscape.

The documentary evidence for the Early Historic period in the upper Firth of Clyde implies that Bute contained a flourishing population, the spiritual

St Blane's Church (40292). This early photograph, taken around 1895, of the medieval church shows the nave prior to its restoration, which was undertaken by the architect RW Schulz, and sponsored by the 3rd Marquess of Bute. The photograph was presented to the National Buildings Record (now part of RCAHMS) by Mr A Curtis, whose given address at 14 Grays Inn Square, London, was the former office of Schultz. SC1161664

needs of which were serviced through a network of chapels. The existence of these chapels is not documented, although their presence can surely be assumed to coincide with the occurrence of cross-slabs at Kilmachalmaig (St Colmac), where the carved stone (40317) still stands; at St Mary's Church, Rothesay (40373); and at an unidentified site near Rothesay Castle (301961), where a broken slab (now in Bute Museum) was found in the early 19th century. The MacAlister Stone (40406), also

now in Bute Museum, probably also came from a chapel, the site of which is not known. Apart from St Ninian's Chapel (40437), which has been excavated, there is little evidence that any of the other surviving chapels date earlier than about the 12th century AD.

The assumption must be that there was a relatively thriving population that could sustain the infrastructure implied by the presence of a network of religious establishments. Elsewhere in the north and west of Scotland there is evidence that some duns were reoccupied in the Early Historic period and in this context we can note that at least one Norse place-name, Dunburgidale, may be linked to a specific structure of earlier date. However, the majority of Bute place-names are later, many being derived from Scottish Gaelic, and the best evidence for a continuity of settlement is provided by the fort on Little Dunagoil (40280) and its immediate environs.

Rothesay High Kirk, cross (40406). This cross-shaft, known as 'MacAlister's Stone', was re-erected in 1886 after lying recumbent for many years on a burial-plot belonging to a family of that name. Tradition associated it with the Ascog area, about 2km south-east of Rothesay, but there were conflicting accounts of its earlier provenance. Hewison tentatively identified it with a stone which formerly stood at Kilwhinleck (NS c.0580 6230). The stone was removed to Bute Museum in 1996. SC403494

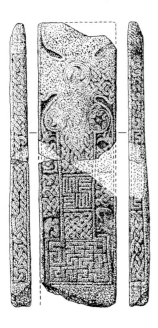

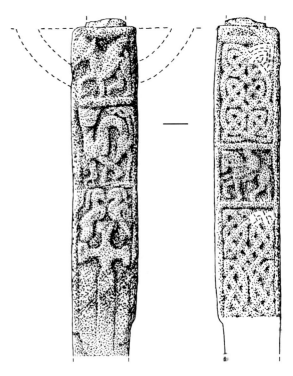

Rothesay Castle, cross-slab (301961). This rectangular cross-slab of sandstone was found in Rothesay Castle in 1816, re-used in two fragments at the foot of the stair in the north-west tower. It remained there until some time after 1903 when it was moved to Bute Museum. SC403493

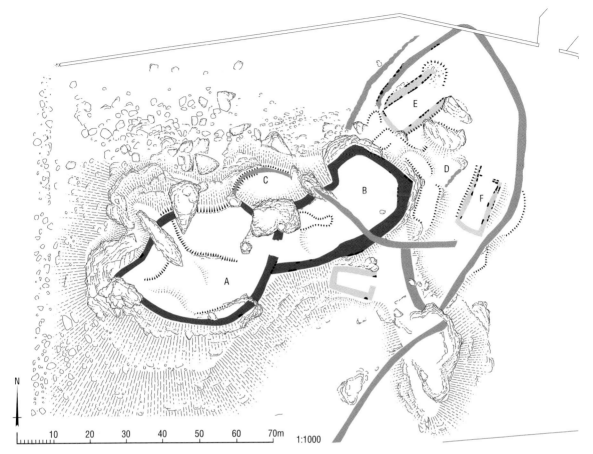

N

10 20 30 40 50 60 70m

1:1000

The fort (40280) and farmstead (90299) on Little Dunagoil, showing the location of: (A) the summit fort; (B) the later addition to its east side; (C) the additional wall on the north side; (D) the cluster of subrectangular building platforms, and (E, F) the buildings (farmstead) partly excavated by Dorothy Marshall around 1960. GV004724

Excavations demonstrated that the fort had a long history stretching from prehistory through into the Early Historic period. However, while the excavations demonstrated the depth of chronology of the site in general, it failed to reach an adequate understanding of the defences and the structural remains within the fort. The resurvey of the site in 1994, part of a reassessment of the Dunagoil complex, had a fresh look at the earthworks without radically altering the previous interpretation of the remains.

The most recent survey, undertaken by RCAHMS in 2010, shows that the small thick-walled enclosure on the summit of the rocky knoll (A on plan) was added to on the east by another enclosure (B) that effectively doubled the size of the defendable area. It was probably at this time that a short length of additional wall (C) was added on the north. Perhaps more important is the recognition of a group of subrectangular building platforms (D), which lie below the east end of the fort. These platforms are very different in character from the large 12th/13th century buildings (E, F) previously investigated and are demonstrably earlier than those buildings (90299).

The significance of these platforms cannot be overstated as they represent part of the Early Historic occupation of the hill that probably dates to a period after the fort went out of use but before the 12th or 13th century buildings were constructed. This small group of platforms therefore represents the most tangible link between the monastic settlement of Kingarth, if it survived into the 9th and 10th centuries, and its nearest secular neighbour. That link may have continued into the late Norse period in the form of the two large hall-like structures which are quite unlike any other buildings so far recorded on Bute.

The hall-like buildings at Little Dunagoil excepted, the only structures of the medieval period (13th to 16th centuries) that are readily identifiable in the landscape are churches, chapels and castles. The churches and chapels are predominantly found on the west coast, perhaps an indication of the direction from which the inspiration for their foundation derived. At Kingarth, a parish church (St Blane's) succeeded the monastic settlement (40292) and there was also a parish church (St Mary's) in Rothesay (40373). Inchmarnock may have had medieval parish status, but it is more likely that Rothesay and Kingarth continued as the only parishes until the creation of North Bute in the 19th century.

St Michael's Chapel and Burial Ground (39902). This aerial view taken from the north-east shows the ruinous medieval chapel set within its circular burial-ground. DP067130

Kilchousland Chapel (40436), which lies within an enclosure formed by a thick bank on the south-west and the face of a relic shoreline cliff on the north-east. The original entrance to the enclosure, which may have served as a burial ground, was probably situated in the broad gap in the wall on the south. GV004723

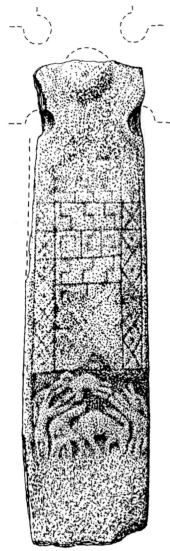

St Blane's, cross no. 10 (301996). Free-standing cross of white sandstone, re-used as a grave slab south of the nave of the church. SC403036

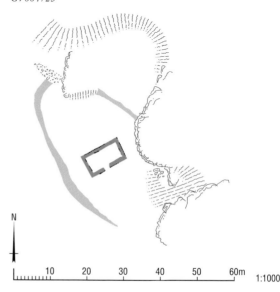

N

10 20 30 40 50 60m   1:1000

In addition to the medieval parish churches there was a network of chapels, one in Rothesay Castle (301959) and a series of others – St Michael's (39902), St Ninian's (40437), Kilchousland (40436), Kilmory (40260) and East St Colmac (40349) – dotted at fairly regular intervals along the western seaboard. A chapel may also have existed at Chapelton (40388), where an alleged font was

Rothesay Castle (40395) is the most powerful symbol of Bute's medieval period. Sitting in a prominent location that dominates the town, it is surrounded by a moat that was redesigned as a garden in the late 18th century. SC800098

once seen, and the possible locations of others, including Acholter (40314), Cnoc-na-Mhanan (40369), Kilwhinleck (302265), Kilbride (40372) and Kilmory Hill (294600), are hinted at either in tradition or in place-name.

Medieval castles existed at Rothesay (40395), Kames (40309) and possibly also at Kelspoke (40674), Ascog (40724) and Wester Kames (40298). Buildings associated with the Stewart dynasty include Meikle Kilmory (40374), where there is evidence for what may have been the house of the 'Sheriff Crowner' of Bute in the 16th century. In contrast to the majority of the churches and chapels,

Kames Castle (40309). This tower, one of only a handful of medieval strongholds on Bute, is surrounded by a suite of 19th century buildings, and set within extensive later gardens. DP010303

these secular foci are usually found on the east side of the island, and this may be an indication that by that time the people of Bute were focusing more on the Scottish mainland than anywhere else.

Other than castles, towers and religious buildings, evidence for rural settlement on Bute in the medieval period is mainly restricted to the mention of farms and estates in documents. With the exception of two excavated kilns (see below), no rural farm buildings earlier than 18th century in date have been identified on Bute, though recent excavation at Quien (88671) may have uncovered a small medieval building and enclosure. It is clear, however, from the detailed histories published in the 19th century that the majority of the modern farms on Bute have roots in land-holdings that were already in existence in the late medieval period. Exchequer rolls from 1450 include references to many names that are still in use today, but it is difficult to tie these references to

particular locations and impossible to link them to specific structures.

Nevertheless, there are several locations where there are groups of rectangular buildings, albeit surviving only as grassed-over wall-footings, which are not depicted on detailed estate maps of the mid to late 18th century, the inference being that they were already abandoned by that time and as such could belong to a much earlier period. The problem here, though, is a 13th century building that has been reduced to footings will probably look very similar to one dating to the 15th, 16th or 17th century. These potentially early sites have been recognised in the north of the island in particular – including on the lower flanks of Fly Hill (124772, 124773, 302308) and Edinbeg Hill (124763) and around Split Craig Hill (139140, 294622) in the comparatively remote north-west corner. One of them (124793), which is tucked into a corner of a pasture field well above Stuck farmsteading, comprises two buildings beside a stream. It is often difficult to establish from field evidence alone what the function of buildings that have been reduced to footings has been. Here, however, it is possible to state with some confidence that the building which has a drain running out of it is a byre and that the other structure was a dwelling.

That medieval buildings can and do survive within a heavily modified landscape has been demonstrated at St Blane's (302028) and more recently on Inchmarnock (300170), where corn-drying kilns have been excavated. However, medieval kilns take much the same form as 18th century examples, which are relatively common, and excavation is required to differentiate them.

One solution to the problem of identifying possible medieval farmsteads and other rural buildings may be through their association with contemporary field-systems, including those containing rig-and-furrow. Much of the 450ha of pre-Improvement period cultivation that survives on Bute is relatively late in date, representing the last arable use of the land before it was put under sheep in the 18th or 19th century. However, parts of it, in particular those containing broad, reverse S-shaped rigs, may have been abandoned at a much earlier period. A useful topic of future research would be the exploration of the relationships that might exist between this potentially early cultivation and farmsteads, buildings or other structures.

To the debate on the pattern of medieval settlement must be added a number of relatively isolated individual and groups of structures, most little more than huts, any of which could be of medieval date, though most are probably later. They

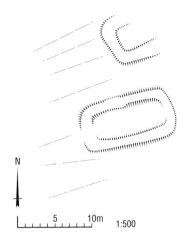

The date that this farmstead (124773) on Ardmaleish farm was abandoned is not known but the adjacent rig-and-furrow that appears to encroach upon it is no later than mid 18th century: an estate plan prepared by John Foulis in 1758–9 records the area as 'moory pasture' and does not depict the buildings. GV004722

most likely fulfilled a broad range of roles. Some of the structures, particularly two small groups on Muclich Hill (40490, 124852), probably represent shieling activity, and the presence of structures within prominent mounds at one of the sites (40490) indicates that this took place over a considerable length of time. It remains the case, however, that the majority of the small oval or subrectangular structures that are found in rural settings have yet to be fully understood.

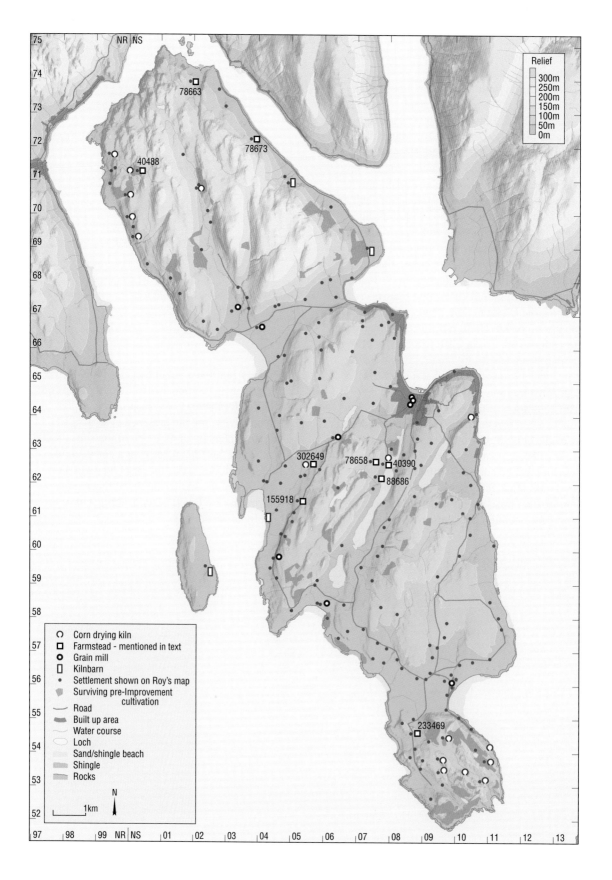

The Pre-Improvement Period

17th and 18th Centuries

The archaeological record of the 17th and 18th centuries on Bute is dominated by abandoned rural settlements and the remains of cultivation – relics of an agricultural landscape that owes much to the medieval period and one that was to a great extent removed during the period of vigorous improvements that so drastically altered the Scottish landscape. Early interest in the archaeology of this period on Bute was limited to a handful of small-scale excavations, but in more recent times study of this period has been the principal focus of attention of the BNHS.

In addition, there is a rich cartographic record for mid and late 18th century Bute, which provides a valuable source of evidence for numerous sites that are no longer visible. The estate maps compiled by Foulis and May have already been mentioned, but another rich font of information is Roy's Military Map, for which the survey of Bute was undertaken between 1752 and 1755. It provides a good indicator of the character of the pre-Improvement period landscape, depicting about 178 named or annotated features on a background of cultivated land and rough grazing. Of these, about 156 were farms and smallholdings (locally referred to as 'butts') and

Distribution of pre-Improvement activity that comprises an outline of the surviving areas of pre-Improvement cultivation derived from Historic Landscape Assessment data combined with the settlement pattern in the mid18th century obtained from Roy's Military Map (1747–55). Many of the settlements recorded by Roy are depicted on contemporary estate maps and noted in documents of that period. Some, which have not developed into modern steadings or been destroyed, survive as archaeological sites. GV004576

about 81 of these were rebuilt in the 19th century as Improvement farmsteads.

The landscape of Bute prior to the introduction of the agricultural improvements was dominated by long-established farms working a mixed economy of cereal production (barley, bere and oats) coupled with the rearing of black cattle and sheep. Many of the farms had two tenants, and the division of the land into two main parts is often reflected in the common place-name elements mor/beg, upper/lower, and meikle/little. Some farms were further subdivided to include several butts and it was common for a farm to contain up to five separate settlement foci.

Present knowledge suggests that only a few 18th century rural buildings have survived relatively intact. These include freestanding cottages, such as that at Kerryfearn (155918), and a few buildings that have been incorporated into ranges within 19th century farmsteadings, one at Lubas (233469) being a good example. Roofed rural buildings did not form part of the recent RCAHMS archaeological record revision project, but there can be little doubt that a detailed study of these would yield significant results.

Very few pre-Improvement period farmsteads are visible today. The majority were demolished or modified between 1810 and 1870, and attrition has continued into recent times with forestry effectively destroying sites at Glenchromag (88686), Chapelton (40390) and Bullochreg (78673), and road building causing the removal of Achmore (78658). Those that do survive as upstanding archaeological remains are mainly situated at the south and north ends of the island

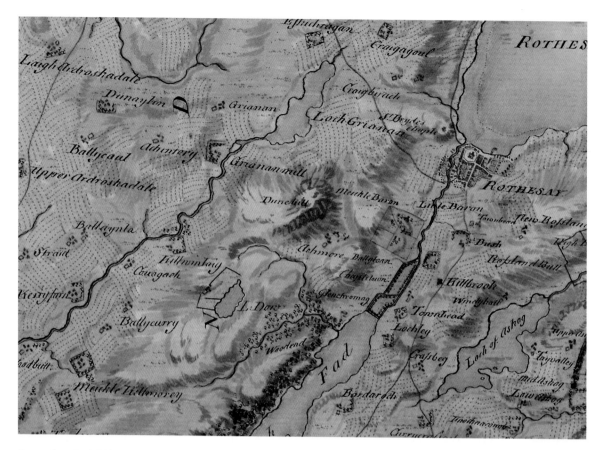

Extract from Roy's Military Map (1747–55) showing the central area of the island. The surveyors, who sketched the area using sighting compasses and measuring chains, depicted roads, streams, settlements and areas of cultivation. Though the 178 settlements and features are shown schematically, as seen in this example, areas such as the gardens of Mount Stuart and the town of Rothesay are depicted in more detail. © The British Library Board (C.9.b 13/5b)

Extract from May's estate plan of Glenchromag (88686) dated 1781. The plan, orientated with top to west, shows two buildings and what is probably a corn-drying kiln within a patchwork of arable fields and grazing. DP075159 © Bute Archive at Mount Stuart

– areas that were given over to sheep in the late 18th and early 19th century respectively. Complete farmsteads are uncommon and it is more likely that a steading will be represented by only a single surviving structure, for example a corn-drying kiln at Kilwhinleck (302649). Sometimes, what was once a thriving complex of buildings and farm activity is marked now only by a few mature trees growing on the banks of former enclosures and yards. Where buildings do survive, they are often little more than grassed over wall-footings and display little or no architectural detail.

An exceptional site, however, is Ardnagave (40488), where the entire farmstead is visible in moorland. Typical of buildings of this period, the

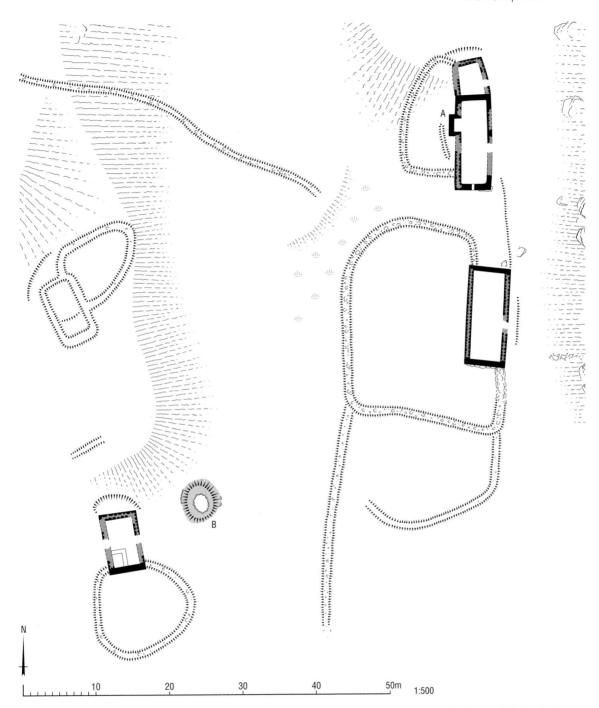

Ardnagave, farmstead (40488). This is a typical 18th century upland farmsteading which was probably abandoned around 1830–40. The byre-house (A), which incorporates a bed-nook (a rare survival) in its west wall, originally extended as far as the end of the outshot. The building immediately to the south was another byre-house and the small building on the south-west, adjacent to the corn-drying kiln (B), may have been a winnowing barn. The building and enclosure on the north-west appear to be earlier in date than the other buildings. GV004728

two long byre-houses are built on slightly sloping ground to allow free drainage. Less typical is the projecting bed nook that has been incorporated into one of the side-walls. At another farmstead, Balnakailly (78663), cruck-slots, a feature that was probably once common throughout the island, are visible in the side-walls.

39

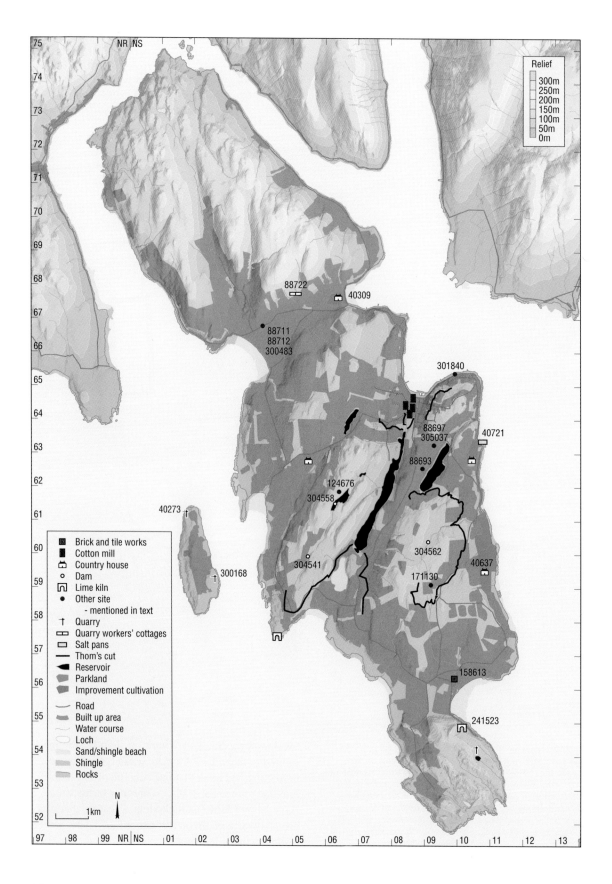

Relief
300m
250m
200m
150m
100m
50m
0m

NR NS

88722
40309

88711
88712
300483

301840

88697
305037   40721

88693

124676
304558

40273 †

300168 †

304562

304541   304541

171130   40637

Brick and tile works
Cotton mill
Country house
Dam
Lime kiln
Other site
  – mentioned in text
Quarry
Quarry workers' cottages
Salt pans
Thom's cut
Reservoir
Parkland
Improvement cultivation
Road
Built up area
Water course
Loch
Sand/shingle beach
Shingle
Rocks

158613

241523

N

1km

The Improvement Period

Late 18th and 19th Centuries

The transformation of the Bute landscape started around the middle of the 1700s as technological, ideological and economic factors combined to create a climate ripe for change. The thirst for productivity and profitability resulted in a decrease in the area under arable cultivation but an increase in the intensity that the land was worked. There were major changes in the settlement pattern of the island, which saw a significant proportion of the rural agricultural population move towards service and industry in Rothesay, to mainland Scotland, or emigrate abroad. The patchwork of small cultivated plots interspersed with irregular settlements that characterised the earlier landscape was steadily replaced by an ordered network of large, more regularly shaped fields drained by modern methods and enclosed by hedges and walls. The turf, stone and thatch buildings were gradually torn down and replaced with more substantial stone buildings that were lime-mortared, roofed in slate and designed according to contemporary best practice.

Despite its national scope, Improvement in all its forms was driven by individuals. Successive Earls of Bute, Lord Bannatyne of Kames, Peter May and John Blain – whose role as farmer, factor, historian and magistrate gave him a unique insight – instituted and provided incentives for reform. Roy's Military Map depicts one aspect of the changes that were happening in the landscape by mapping large

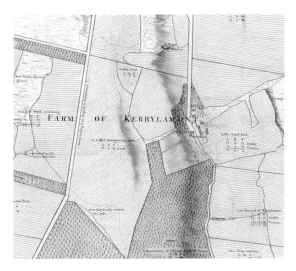

May's plan of Kerrylamont farm (142610), undated but probably contemporary with a number of plans dating from 1780–2. A regular network of squared fields, plantations and roads had been laid out by this time, though some aspects of the informal pre-Improvement field system remained, and the farmstead itself had yet to be remodelled. DP075177 © Bute Archive at Mount Stuart

The Improvement period landscape, derived from Historic Land-use Assessment data, is clearly overlain by significant features such as country houses and industrial sites. The latter include Rothesay's cotton mills, which were water-powered by an extensive system of reservoirs and lades designed by Robert Thom and known locally as Thom's Cuts. GV004577

enclosures at Loch Dhu (124676), High Bogany, Ascog, Barone Park and around Kames Castle (40309); these stand out in a landscape otherwise characterised by relatively small patches of unenclosed rig. John Foulis' survey (1758–9) adds further detail to the transformations that had already happened, depicting the policies of the estates at Ascog, Kames and Mount Stuart. The same vigour had been applied to tenanted farms as early as 1748, by which time the Earl of Bute had introduced to his estate farmers from parts of the country *'where agriculture was supposed to be better understood'.*

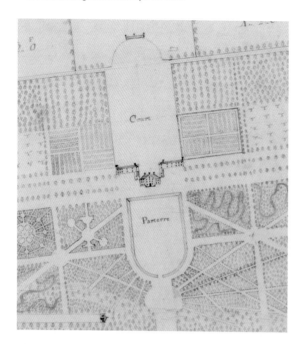

This extract of a plan of Mount Stuart house and gardens (40637), undertaken by John Foulis and dating to 1758–9, shows the accuracy and detail that could be applied to the most significant subjects. DP077240 © Bute Archive at Mount Stuart

Foulis' survey also depicts the major changes that had been made to the landscape around Mount Stuart (40637), not only in the plantations and gardens, but also in the establishment of the New Farm (171130). It was about this time that the Mount Stuart estate introduced fixed-term leases and removed their stake in crops (payment in kind), instead demanding a cash rent – tactics designed to promote Improvement. In addition, they began to pay cash incentives for the best bulls, cheese and butter, and for waste land that was *'brought into culture'*. Good practice in the use of fertiliser, flax-spinning and fishing was also encouraged.

The enhancement of Bute's farmsteads lagged somewhat behind investment in the land. As late as 1780, repairs and modifications were still being made to pre-Improvement period farmsteads in which the majority of the buildings were certainly unsophisticated. Even at that time, many tenants still inhabited byre-houses, though the use of lime harl provides some evidence for changing standards in the repair of old buildings (May *et al* 1782–1827, 132). The same inventory notes a house at Laigh Bogany (301840), now demolished,

that contained two rooms, a cellar, a kitchen and a lobby, demonstrating that some buildings were being built to higher standards than previously.

During the first decades of the 19th century, many more of the old farmsteads were rebuilt in stone and lime, with slated roofs and regular courtyard plans, often according to similar designs, and most equipped with horse engines or water wheels. Windyhall (305037), which is still a working farmsteading, was rebuilt about 1811 after an amalgamation of three smaller holdings – Windyhall itself, Bishop's Butt (88697) and Townhead Butt (88693). The new steading had two separate ranges housing a stable, barn and byre as well as a 'mill house', probably for a thresher driven by a horse engine. The house itself had a parlour, kitchen, bedroom and dining room.

Nevertheless, despite widespread improvements to land and buildings, there was clearly some way to go, prompting Blain to comment around this time that *'improving tenants cannot be expected to find accommodation for themselves and their stock in the present buildings'* (Ross 1880, 286).

Agriculture may have been the mainstay of the Bute economy in the 18th and 19th centuries, but industry, too, played its part and has left its impact on the landscape. Research has already been undertaken on some aspects of Bute's industrial past, with the results often published in the *Transactions of the Buteshire Natural History Society*.

Perhaps the most obvious indication of Bute's industrial past is the system of roads and tracks that provided the framework which linked together the population centres, farms, mills, quarries, piers, etc. The development of the road system on Bute and the maintenance of its infrastructure (bridges, culverts, milestones, quarries) is a subject that has never been fully explored, but it is surely one that would pay rich dividends.

Quarries are ubiquitous on Bute and they will be found anywhere there are buildings, roads or walls. They come in all shapes and sizes; most cannot be accurately dated, but there is one above Kilchattan, now flooded as a reservoir, which was opened around 1750 to supply limestone to the nearby kiln (241523). The kiln provided fertiliser for the 3rd Earl of Bute's estate. The remains of other industrial-scale workings can be seen on

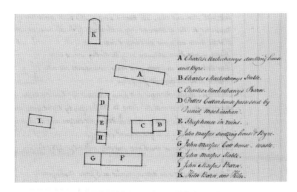

Sketch of Kilbride farmstead (301014) included in May's inventory and valuation dated 1782. This document, which describes many of the farmsteads of Bute, catalogues the details of each building, including their dimensions and the character of the construction materials. DP075519 © Bute Archive at Mount Stuart

Glenmore, farmstead (203566). This courtyard steading was constructed in the mid 19th century when the earlier farmsteads of Upper Glenmore (88733) and Lower Glenmore (88732) were combined. DP067141

Inchmarnock, the quarries there (40273, 300168) producing roofing-slate for export long before the Improvement period, but going out of use before the middle of the 19th century. On an even larger scale were the slate quarries on the hillside north of Kames Castle, which also went out of use at about that time. Another tangible legacy of this industry can be seen at North St Colmac, where the grassed-over footings of the quarry-workers' cottages (88722) are still visible.

Bute's best known historic industry is cotton, which once employed over 400 people. A description of the surviving mills, lades, workers' cottages, etc, lies outwith the scope of this publication, but mention should be made here of the extensive system of reservoirs (eg 304541, 304558, 304562) and lades (Thom's Cuts) constructed in the early 19th century to supply water to power the Rothesay mills. The system, which was built under the direction of Robert

Bute, general (183832). In the course of aerial sorties, RCAHMS staff take oblique photographs of cropmarks, upstanding archaeological sites and buildings. General shots are also taken, which record both the context of individual monuments and the character of the landscape as a whole. This image, taken from Scalpsie Bay, looks past Loch Quien and Loch Fad towards Rothesay DP066201

Thom, also included a supporting infrastructure of sluices, bridges and culverts, and features, such as catch-drains, which appear to have received little previous attention but which are significant features in the landscape. There is also clear evidence that the system was developed over a considerable length of time and it is likely that at least some of the features still visible today belong to a water supply system that pre-dates Thom's work.

Water was not always the most convenient method of fuelling industry in the late 18th and early 19th centuries, when a cheap and constant source of power was demanded. Contemporary industries elsewhere, particularly those relatively close-by on the Scottish mainland, had a huge advantage over Bute by having access to cheap coal.

Despite a number of attempts to find this fuel on Bute for both domestic and industrial use, no ready supply was located.

One of the small-scale industries that would have used coal had it been readily available was the processing of salt from sea water. This industry could only ever have been of modest scale as only one site is known, at Ascog (40721), with two salt pan houses, and even here there is some doubt whether salt production actually ever started. Another relatively small-scale industry was brick and tile production, which was undertaken at Kilchattan Bay (158613). These works, now largely removed, are likely to have supplied much of the needs of the island and, although some research has already been carried out, further work may reveal the full range of products made and what sort of market they satisfied.

Similarly, further research may elucidate the date of what are commonly referred to as charcoal burning platforms, which may have supplied one of the raw ingredients to the Kames Gunpowder Works (76430), or, less likely, fuel for the blast furnaces at the iron works at Loch Fyne (23401) or Bonawe (23521). An obvious avenue of future research is the Bute Archive, which may well have records concerning the management of timber resources on the Mount Stuart estate.

Although the town of Rothesay was outwith the scope of this project, it is worth noting that the majority of the villages of Bute, and Rothesay itself, assumed their present form in the last 250 years, and the way they developed owed much to the wealth created by agricultural improvement, industrial investment and tourism. By all accounts, Rothesay was in a state of decline in the mid 18th century, a process that was halted by, among other factors, the rebuilding of the pier from 1752; increased trade resulting from herring fishing; the success of the cotton spinning industry; and the establishment of a customs house.

This oblique view of St Ninian's Point captures a multi period landscape. Still occupied, the fishermen's cottages provide a focus to a group that includes nausts, a ruined kippering house (78647) and landing points along the shoreline. Just below and to the left, the remains of a small Early Christian chapel (40437) and circular enclosure still survive. DP062655

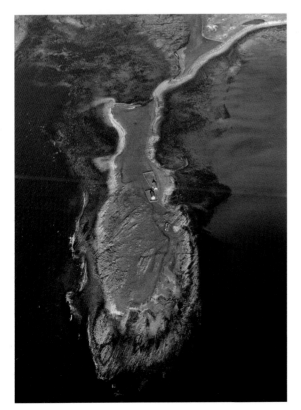

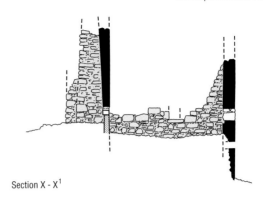

Section X - X^1

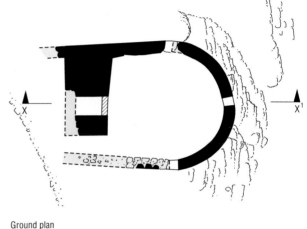

Ground plan

1:200

Plan and section of one of two salt pan houses (40721) at the south end of Ascog Bay. The date of the building of the pan houses is not recorded and there is some doubt as to whether they were actually ever put into production. They are very similar to those at the Cock of Arran (39803), which were in use between 1710 and 1735. GV004727

Maps of 18th and 19th century date graphically show that much of the almost continuous ribbon of settlement between the south end of Kames Bay and Ascog was under cultivation until the mid to late 19th century. The villas that now dominate this shoreline are testament to the changing fortunes of the island, particularly in the late 19th and early 20th century when it was a successful holiday resort. Nevertheless, elements of the earlier landscape may well still exist within the present urban sprawl.

Mount Stuart (40637) is a late 19th century mansion house with a private chapel, designed for the 3rd Marquess by Robert Rowan Anderson. The wings of the early 18th century house, depicted on John Foulis' map, were incorporated in this much larger building. DP066039

Bute, general (183832). Arbeg Point became a focus for development in the 19th century, although only a handful of farmsteads are recorded in this area on Roy's map. The tram depot and a new street layout was created by 1900, at least one significant burial cairn being removed during the process (40315). DP067193

Elsewhere, the settlement at Kilchattan Bay initially grew out of the need to house workers for the adjacent lime quarry and kiln (241523) and the more dispersed settlement at Kingarth owed much to the location of the parish church, mill and brick-and-tile works. The early 19th century village of Kerrycroy, notable for its design and layout, was built to house workers on the Mount Stuart estate. The settlement at Ettrick Bay (88712), which included a mill, smithies, a school (233610), an inn and a farmstead (88711), was almost completely removed in the early 19th century. The bay was to become one of the most popular destinations on Bute for tourists in the late 19th century.

Conclusion

The publication of this booklet marks the culmination of a very successful partnership project between RCAHMS and the DBLPS, a venture that saw a hitherto unprecedented involvement by members of the local community in the day-to-day work of the Commission's field teams. The legacy of the project is great and tangible. The RCAHMS database now contains over 900 archaeological records for Bute; 525 records, which represented the situation prior to the project, have been thoroughly revised and for the first time the location of each site and monument has been accurately recorded using GPS technology.

Those who have previously accessed Bute archaeological records through Canmore will be struck by the vast amount of new information that has recently been added. In addition to the revised site descriptions, approximately 1,600 digital images have been made available to public view through the internet, supplementing the 400 images that already existed. These new images include aerial and ground photography as well as scans of site-surveys, drawings of carved stones, illustrations from books, 19th century Ordnance Survey (OS) maps, OS records cards and RCAHMS Emergency Survey manuscripts. Never before has an RCAHMS archaeological survey placed so much emphasis on the enhancement of individual records through the use of digital imagery.

Looking beyond the enhancement of the record, a far less tangible, but no less important, outcome of the project was the work that the Commission's field staff undertook with the people of Bute. Individuals representing a broad spectrum of the local community played an active role in accompanying Commission staff during their weeks on the island. For those with little or no previous archaeological experience this provided a valuable insight into the character and diversity of their heritage; for those already active in recording aspects of their past, some of them for many years, this offered the opportunity to become more aware of different survey practices and methods of recording.

This is a legacy that will endure and provide a rich and abundant reward in years to come. This booklet has already hinted at possible topics of future research – from searching for prehistoric sites by fieldwalking through studying agricultural landscapes to recording aspects of Bute's extensive and varied industrial heritage. Whatever areas of study are pursued by the local community, the Commission is confident that, as a result of this partnership project, all involved will now be well equipped to better appreciate, understand and record their heritage.

Further Reading

Aitken, W G 1955
Excavation of a chapel at St Ninian's Point, Isle of Bute, *Trans Buteshire Natur Hist Soc* 14, 62–76

Aiton, W 1816
General View of the Agriculture of the County of Bute. Glasgow

Anderson, J 1900
Description of a collection of objects found in excavations at St. Blane's Church, Bute, exhibited by the Marquess of Bute, *Proc Soc Antiq Scot* 34 (1899–1900), 307–25

Ballin, T B, Barrowman, C & Faithful, J 2008
Blackpark Plantation East, Bute, *Trans Buteshire Natur Hist Soc* 27, 23–51

Bryce, T H 1904
On the cairns and tumuli of the Island of Bute. A record of explorations during the season of 1903, *Proc Soc Antiq Scot* 38 (1903–4), 17–81

Cormack, W F 1985
A note on mesolithic sites in Bute, *Trans Buteshire Natur Hist Soc* 22, 6

Ferrier, J 1966
Robert Thom's Water Cuts, *Trans Glasgow Archaeol Soc* 15 (3), 129–138

Fisher, I 2001
Early Medieval Sculpture in the West Highlands and Islands, Edinburgh: RCAHMS and the Society of Antiquaries of Scotland, Monograph Series 1

Foulis, J 1758–9
A Survey of the Isle of Bute. Bound volume of sheets and explanatory text held in Bute Archive, Mount Stuart, Bute. Copy held at the National Archives of Scotland (RHP 14107)

Gilmour, T 1955
Kilchattan Brick and Tile Works, *Trans Buteshire Natur Hist Soc* 14, 47–52

Harding, D W 2004
Dunagoil, Bute, re-instated, *Trans Buteshire Natur Hist Soc* 26, 1–19

Henshall, A S 1972
The Chambered Tombs of Scotland Vol 2. Edinburgh: Edinburgh University Press

Hewison, J K 1893
The Isle of Bute in the Olden Time Vol 1, Edinburgh & London: W Blackwood & Sons

Jay, M & Montgomery, J 2008
The Beaker People Project, *British Archaeology* 101, 26

Lowe, C (ed) 2008
Inchmarnock: An Early Historic Island Monastery and its archaeological landscape, Edinburgh: Society of Antiquaries of Scotland

MacKinlay, J 1862
Notice of two 'crannogs' or palisaded islands, Bute; with plans, *Proc Soc Antiq Scot* 3 (1857–60), 43–6

MacLagan, I 1996
Robert Thom's cuts on the Island of Bute, *Trans Buteshire Natur Hist Soc* 24, 3–19

MacLagan, I 1997
The Piers and Ferries of Bute, Rothesay: Buteshire Natural History Society

MacLagan, I & Spiers, A 2002
Bute: An Island History, Rothesay: Buteshire Natural History Society

MacFadzean, H 1985
A prehistoric chipping-floor of agates on the hills of south Bute, *Trans Buteshire Natur Hist Soc* 22, 33–4

Mann, L M 1915
Report on the relics discovered during excavations in 1913 at cave at Dunagoil, Bute, and in 1914 at the fort at Dunagoil, Bute (with suggestions as to the probable history and chronology of the site), *Trans Buteshire Natur Hist Soc* 8 (1914–15), 61–86

Mann, L M 1925
Note on the results of the exploration of the fort at Dunagoil, *Trans Buteshire Natur Hist Soc* 9, 54–60

Marshall, D N 1938
A survey of the caves of Bute and the Cumbraes, *Trans Buteshire Natur Hist Soc* 12, 113–18

Marshall, D N 1963
The Queen of the Inch, *Trans Buteshire Natur Hist Soc* 15, 5–16

Marshall, D N 1964
Report on excavations at Little Dunagoil, *Trans Buteshire Natur Hist Soc* 16, 1–61

Marshall, D N 1969
The long narrow 'house' at Glenvoidean, *Trans Buteshire Natur Hist Soc* 17, 45–8

Marshall, D N 1976
The excavation of Hilton Cairn, *Trans Buteshire Natur Hist Soc* 20, 8–26

Marshall, D N & Taylor, I D 1979
The excavation of a chambered cairn at Glenvoidean, Isle of Bute, *Proc Soc Antiq Scot* 108 (1976–7), 1–39

Marshall, D N 1985
A report on early artefacts found at St. Ninian's chapel, *Trans Buteshire Natur Hist Soc* 22, 27

Marshall, D N & Spiers, A 1992
History of Bute, Rothesay: Bute Museum

Marshall, J N 1915
Preliminary notes on some excavations at Dunagoil fort and cave, *Trans Buteshire Natur Hist Soc* 8 (1914–15), 42–9

Marshall, J N 1930
Archaeological notes, *Trans Buteshire Natur Hist Soc* 10, 50–4

Marshall, J N 1935
Old kiln at Kilwhinleck, *Trans Buteshire Natur Hist Soc* 11, 84–7

Maxwell, J H 1941
The vitrified fort on Eilean Buidhe, Kyles of Bute, *Trans Glasgow Arch Soc* 10, 60–70

May, A *et al* 1782–1827
Farm Inventory. An inventory and valuation of farmsteads owned by the Bute Estate between 1782 and 1827. Archive (Bute Estate Box 13, BE/6) held in the Bute Archive at Mount Stuart

May, P c1780–2
A series of estate maps held in the Bute Archive at Mount Stuart, Bute

Milligan, I D 1963
Corn kilns in Bute, *Trans Buteshire Natur Hist Soc* 15, 53–9

Mudie, G & Richardson, P 2006
Excavation of a possible Neolithic structure, lithic finds and later ditch features at Kingarth Quarry, Isle of Bute, *Scottish Archaeol J* 28 (2), 105–124

Munro, I S 1973
The History of Bute, Newton Abbot: David and Charles

Noble, G & Stevens, F 2008
An island of fluctuating perceptions: the landscape and archaeology of Bute, in Noble, G, Poller, T, Raven, J and Verrill, L (eds), *Scottish Odysseys, the Archaeology of Islands*, 37–60, Stroud: Tempus

Oram, R 2008
Medieval Inchmarnock to c1600, in Lowe (ed), 2008, 35–53

Ordnance Survey c1863–5
Original Object Name Books for parishes within the County of Bute, Nos. 4 (Kingarth), 5 (North Bute) and 7 (Rothesay). Held on microfilm at RCAHMS

Proudfoot, E 2000
A short cist from Ascog, Rothesay, Bute, *Trans Buteshire Natur Hist Soc* 25, 5–10

Proudfoot, E 2008
The excavation of a second short cist on Kildavanan farm, Bute, *Trans Buteshire Natur Hist Soc* 27, 5–22

Proudfoot, E & Hannah, A 2000
Deserted settlements on Bute, *Trans Buteshire Natur Hist Soc* 25, 25–56

Reid, J E 1864
History of the County of Bute, Edinburgh: Paton and Ritchie

RCAHMS 1943
Diary (MS 36/24/8), notebook (MS 124/3) and manuscript (MS 36) relating to Angus Graham's visit to Bute in 1943 to undertake fieldwork for the Emergency Survey. Held at RCAHMS

RCAHMS 1971
Argyll: an Inventory of the Monuments Volume 1, Kintyre, Edinburgh: HMSO

RCAHMS 1988
Argyll: an Inventory of the Monuments Volume 6, Mid Argyll & Cowal, Prehistoric & Early Historic Monuments, Edinburgh: HMSO

RCAHMS 2009
Commissioner's Field Meeting 2009 (unpublished guide), Edinburgh: RCAHMS

Ritchie, J N G (ed) 1992
The Archaeology of Argyll, Edinburgh: RCAHMS and Edinburgh University Press

Ross, J (ed) 1880
Blain's History of Bute, Rothesay: W C Harvey

Roy, W 1747–55
Military Survey of Scotland

Sandeman, J 2000
Kames Estate and Castle: Bannantynes and later owners, *Trans Buteshire Natur Hist Soc* 25, 14–24

Scott, J G 1968
A radiocarbon date for a west Scottish neolithic settlement, *Antiquity* 42, 296–7

Scott, J G 1985
Finds from the chapel site at St Ninian's Point, Isle of Bute, *Trans Buteshire Natur Hist Soc* 22, 28–30

Scott, J G 1992
Dorothy Marshall, *Proc Soc Antiq Scot* 122, 5–6

Sharp, R 1909
The cotton industry in Bute, *Trans Buteshire Natur Hist Soc* 2 (1908–9), 12–22

Sheridan, J A 2008
Radiocarbon dates arranged through the National Museums of Scotland during 2006/7, *Discovery Excavation Scot (2007)*, 220

Stat. Acct. 1791–9
The Statistical Account of Scotland, Sinclair, J (ed), Edinburgh

Index